Walking with Buddha

Pilgrimage on the Shikoku 88-Temple Trail

C.W. Lockhart

Labrador & Lockhart

a small press

Ocean Shores, Washington

Copyright ©

2020 by C.W. Lockhart

All Rights Reserved
Published in the United States by Labrador & Lockhart Press, LLC
Seabeck, Washington
LabradorandLockhart.com

Lockhart, C.W., 1967- author.
Walking with Buddha: Pilgrimage on the Shikoku 88-Temple Trail /
C.W. Lockhart

Trade Paperback ISBN-13: -10: 978-0-578-86426-6
(Labrador & Lockhart Press, LLC)

First Edition

CONTENTS

Map of
Shikoku Island

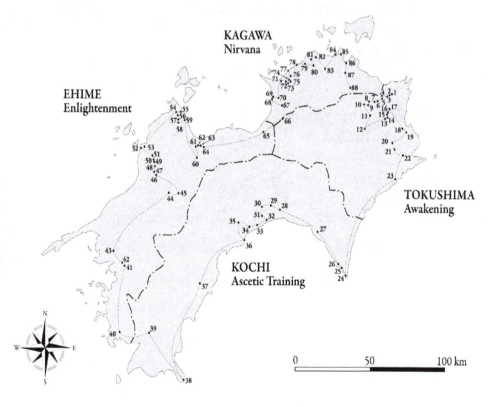

KAGAWA
Nirvana

EHIME
Enlightenment

TOKUSHIMA
Awakening

KOCHI
Ascetic Training

0   50   100 km

Part One
Awakening

Walking with Buddha:
Pilgrimage on the Shikoku 88-Temple Trail

The Awakening

We carry the weight of our fears. I have yet to meet a distance-hiker who would argue otherwise. We carry rain gear because we are afraid to get wet. We carry guidebooks, maps, and smartphones because we are afraid to lose our way. Practical, frivolous, ordinary, and extraordinary, each item carried alleviates one fear or another.

On my body, I wear khaki hiking-pants, a black tank top, a long-sleeve white blouse to protect me from the sun, a soft-yellow scarf, a pair of high-performance undies, toe socks, and comfy trail shoes.

My backpack holds a change of clothes, extra socks, a tent, sleeping bag, mat, and a smattering of toiletries. Slung across my torso, a messenger bag carries my money, passport, and other valuables I'm too afraid to store in my pack.

Currently, the weight of my fear is roughly 17 pounds or eight kilograms. For a woman of my sturdy-build, this fear is not much of a burden. This experience differs significantly from the past, as I've learned many lessons the hard way.

I am no stranger to peregrination or long-distance hiking. I first nurtured my pilgrim-heart in 2014, along the *Camino de Santiago*, a 500-mile journey across western Spain. I returned four more times to hit that life-altering, magical *reset* button that, thus far, only the Camino provides.

Not a day goes by that I don't pine for Spain or just one more day on the Camino de Santiago. However, my current professorship in Okinawa, Japan, proves too great a logistical challenge to overcome.

And now, north of 50 years old, I find myself in need, once again, of a magical reset button. I'm tired. And disenchanted. Dabbling in menopause. And bordering on burnout. I need a strategy and new tools to embrace this second-half of my life.

I know little of Buddhism, and my understanding of Japanese culture is immature, to say the least. Immersion is my favorite way to learn. However, I question if there will be enough room in my heart and head to house my Christian underpinnings and the *Buddha Nature*?

Takahara-san hands me a blank postcard with two stamps affixed to the upper-right hand corner. The long wooden dining table in the dimly lit kitchen is already set for tomorrow's breakfast. There is a place for me, one for Takahara-san and one for another pilgrim I've yet to meet.

I'm relieved to see a banana on each plate. I consider myself an adventurous foodie, but my eagerness to explore Japanese cuisine has yet to replace a western breakfast staple. The potassium-laced bananas are as good as gold.

Takahara-san and I don't share a common language, but this hardly matters. Intuitively, I pull a purple gel pen from my messenger bag and write my name and address on the postcard's front. Then, I flip the card over and admire a water-color print of *Ohenro-sans*.

I take a moment to scrutinize the image. The Ohenro, clad in white robes and conical thatched hats, gather around the Buddha in repose.

The depiction of Buddha is unfamiliar to me. My Buddha is fat and happy, like the one found in nail salons and Chinese restaurants – not a Buddha at all, but a bodhisattva named *Hotei*.

Henro or *Ohenro* are Japanese words for *pilgrim*. I am a self-proclaimed *peregrina*, the Spanish word for a pilgrim. Tomorrow, I will join the ranks of Ohenro-san circling the island of Shikoku.

I suppose pilgrims are pilgrims, regardless of cultural or religious values. I imagine we share similar goals. We seek the intangibles of wisdom, grace, and light.

On the backside of this card, I am supposed to write a wish. Tomorrow, Takahara-san will mail the card to my address in Okinawa. The card will serve as a fond memory of my meditations and physical efforts along the way.

My impromptu trip to Shikoku leaves me unprepared. Over the past few days, I scoured the internet and managed to obtain a guidebook hours before my departure. I have read about the wish-tradition but haven't given it much thought until now.

Coming up with a wish is more challenging than it should be. Despite a few first-world hiccups, life is ridiculously good. In front of me stretches 1,200 kilometers of trail, countless villages, 88 temples, shrines, mountain passes, waterfalls, rivers, streams, bamboo forests, highways, tunnels, cultural differences, language barriers, probably a snake or two, and other wild beasties standing or slithering between me and this wish. So, I've got to make it count. *What am I struggling to overcome?*

For starters, menopause is knocking at my door. Blessed with three sons and two stepsons, my angst is not about fertility. The parenthood box has been checked off the bucket list – several times over, but it is the *Big Change*. I'm mostly concerned about age-related decline. In short, I don't want to grow old.

I'm also less than thrilled with my job. After accepting a promotion, my time with students decreased. Administrative and management functions increased. Quite frankly, leading other professors is worse than herding cats. Frustrating. Stressful. Soul-crushing. I'm a butterfly ensnared in a web of bureaucratic bull-shit, and I can't find the way out.

And my marriage? Well, I am married – very married. I'm *all in*, but my husband is not. He splits his time between Okinawa and our home in Washington state. Of course, the decision to accept my post in Japan was mutually made, but he's unhappy and resentful, and his glowering moods dampen even the sunniest of Okinawan days. And for now, there is nothing I can do about it.

I furrow my brow and concentrate on the postcard. I feel Takahara-san's warm gaze shining down like a ray of sunlight. She likes me. I'm not exactly sure why, but she genuinely likes me. I felt her affection the moment she opened the door to her home and welcomed me in.

Takahara-san runs a *Henro House* near the first temple. Henro houses are an essential part of the logistical infrastructure along the Shikoku Pilgrimage, and luckily, reservations can be made online. This is a bonus, mainly because I lack Japanese language skills. The family-style homes dot the trail and provide unique and cozy alternatives to hotel stays.

My hope is to rely on henro houses, primitive henro huts, and temple lodgings, called *Shukubo*, whenever possible. If the need arises, I am also prepared to camp.

Hovering above, Takahara-san nods to cheer me on. She speaks to me in Japanese. I have no idea what she is saying. So, with a touch of hippy-dippy, I translate her words. "Use this time to manifest reality."

Silly. But it works. *I wish for the wisdom, courage, and grace to embrace the next chapter of my life.* It's a little watered-down – an umbrella to cover not only the biological changes but personal and professional upheavals too. As a working thesis statement, it'll do.

Takahara-san leans over, offering another nod of approval. Her hovering makes me nervous, but I'm happy to have her company. She is warm and grandmotherly and familiar, and I have spent the better part of the day feeling entirely foreign and alone.

Before arriving at Takahara's doorstep, I negotiated the heavy traffic of *Okinawa City*, found my way through the airport, survived a bumpy landing in Takamatsu, and narrowly caught a bus from the airport to the train station. Once at the station, I inadvertently jumped the turnstile and hopped a train to Bando without paying my fare. For nearly an hour, I fretted over the unintentional theft.

Certain I'd be humiliated and tossed off the train to make my way in the dark, I attempted a low-profile. But I was the only Caucasian on the train, and I was considerably taller than my fellow passengers. Keeping a low-profile was well beyond my reach.

Fortunately, when I was found out, the stoic conductor simply held out his hand for payment. Expressionless, he took the 2,000 yen note, handed back the change, and issued me a ticket. Whew!

The conductor's behavior was my first gift of grace. The second gift came after I hopped off the train in Bando and walked through the dark streets, hoping to chance upon the henro house. With my head down, studying the directions on my phone, I nearly ran into two ladies out for an evening stroll. They asked me something in Japanese, and I responded by putting my hands across my chest and saying, "Henro." That's all they needed. Without another word, the ladies escorted me to Takahara-san's door.

I am tired and ready for bed. I hoped after finishing my postcard, I might be excused for the evening. Instead, Takahara-san assigns another task. She pushes a stack of narrow, white paper slips in front of me.

Each slip contains the black and white image of *Kukai*, the monk posthumously known as *Kobo Daishi*. Kukai was born in 774. Credited with establishing hundreds of temples throughout Japan, he is the founder of *Shingon* Buddhism, also known as Japanese *Esoteric* Buddhism.

The paper slips carrying his image are called *osamefuda*. I am supposed to print my name, address, and wish on the slips and deposit them at temples along the way as a calling card of sorts. I'll also use them to show appreciation for random acts of kindness.

From what I have read, I am to expect random acts of kindness. Based on the tradition of *osettai*, villagers offer pilgrims gifts of food or money or perform acts of benevolence. Performing osettai honors Buddha and garners favor.

I'm uncomfortable receiving charity. I don't want to be fraudulent. I'm more of a tourist than a henro. Does it matter I'm not a Buddhist? Or that I have no plans to become one?

However, greater than the fear of fraud is fear of offending. I don't wish to buck cultural norms with misplaced pride. So, I vow to accept acts of kindness with grace and humility. This will be but one of many challenges I'll face going forward.

I switch pens, alternating from purple to turquoise. I want my osamefuda slips to be festive. I dig in my backpack, pull out a sheet of tiny floral decals, attach a glittering flower to a corner, and pass it to Takahara-san. This is my first osamefuda, my first act of appreciation.

Takahara squints. She tries to decode the loops and squiggles of my penmanship. It is as foreign to her as the alternating alphabets of *Hiragana*, *Katakana*, and *Kanji* I failed to decipher during my travels to her home.

Takahara-san retrieves a small, black device from the sleeve of her lavender *yukata* robe. She holds it up, smiles, and speaks in English, "Pocket talky-box."

Next, she speaks Japanese into the talky-box, and the device translates, "Good job, Christine-san! Keep writing."

She counts off the slips on her fingers, ensuring the stack contains enough osamefudas for my first day on the trail. I plan to visit the first six temples tomorrow, and if I understand correctly, I will drop at least two slips per temple – one at the main hall and one more at the *Daishi* hall.

I type the word *osame* into my translator app and read *a payment*. I add the *fuda,* and the app serves up *rice balls.* Obviously, something is lost in translation. While kind of fun, this distraction isn't going to get me off the hook, so I press on and complete the stack osame-fuda.

Hoping to be excused for the night, I follow the sleeve of Takahara's yukata up to meet her kind eyes. However, she meets mine with a look of shock. Shock melts into horror, and horror stiffens into disapproval.

Standing on the threshold is the human-embodiment of a half-starved, stray cat. The Cat-lady's long, white hair hangs in wet ringlets, and her bare-feet press against the cold tiles. Dressed only in silky, black long-underwear, her skeleton quakes with a chill.

Inventorying her from bunions up, I stop at the sag of her tea-bag boobies. I don't mean to stop here. But elongated nipples poke from behind the immodest material and hold me hostage.

Speaking rapid-fire Japanese, Takahara-san breaks the silence. The sweetly feminine voice of the talky-box says, "It is cold. You must wear clothes." But the translation fails to convey the originator's tone and body language. With a stiff palm, Takahara makes a stop sign. The gesture is crystal clear – in any language.

But Cat-lady does not retreat. Instead, she opens her arms wide. Takahara-san shrinks, and Cat-lady moves in for the kill. The embrace is awkward, purely one-sided, and lasts far too long for comfort.

Oh my gosh! I hope she is not an American. I love my country and her people, and I love hugs. However, we Americans are poster children for dragging our western ways where these ways are not wanted. It is evident. Takahara-san clearly does not wish to be hugged.

Temple 1: Ryozenji

Walk as if you are kissing the Earth with your feet.
— Thich Nhat Hanh

In the morning, Takahara-san and Kassy pass the talky-box back and forth. They are debating the weight and contents of Kassy's backpack. The argument is not new. It's a continuation from last night, and the frustration is showing on Takahara-san's gentle face.

Apparently, Kassy arrived yesterday afternoon with an even heavier pack. Heeding Takahara's advice, Kassy went to the post office and shipped several items home. Now, Takahara is urging her to do it again.

Kassy is a frail-looking woman in her seventies. Her backpack hulks in the corner. Out of curiosity, I heft it from the floor. It's got to be at least 25 pounds. A good rule of long-distance hiking is to carry not more than ten percent of one's body weight. This pack is meant for a pilgrim at least twice Kassy's size. Soaking wet, I doubt she tips the scales at a hundred pounds.

Kassy is no stranger to long-distance hiking. In her younger years, she summited *Mount Rainier* in Washington state three times. This is a significant accomplishment. Like me, she is a peregrina. She's trekked across the French Pyrenees all the way to Santiago de Compostela. However, like many peregrinos, she used a backpack forwarding service – a leg-saving wonder not yet established along the Shikoku 88-temple trail.

I have no dog in this fight. I sit down to breakfast and mind my own business. To accompany the banana, Takahara-san has added a boiled egg, cold broccoli florets, and a fat slice of toast topped with pretend cheese. The cheese is of the single-wrapped variety some folks call *easy-cheese*.

My kids call the wrapped slices *sleazy-cheese*. While I'm not a picky eater, I don't prefer processed cheese. I'm not above eating it, but my children won't touch the stuff.

Sleazy-cheese was never on my grocery list, but my husband grew up eating it. Several years ago, while running a grocery errand, he brought home a brick. In a silly power struggle, the kids refused to eat a slice. Asserting his tenuous step-parent authority, Jim announced that there would be no more cheese until the brick was consumed.

We were a cheese-less household for months. Not wanting to undermine authority, I hoped the cheese would rot. Of course, it would not.

I tried feeding two slices a day to the dog, but after a week, even she turned up her nose. Desperate to end the great cheese-famine, I took to dumping a piece in the trash every day, and 72 slices later, we were set free.

Like a fly on the wall, I listen to the backpack debate and eat my sleazy toast, banana, egg, and broccoli. I've never considered broccoli as a breakfast food, but I enjoy it immensely.

The argument fizzles. Kassy refuses to ship anything more. In an odd twist, Takahara-san agrees to drive the backpack to the sixth temple, where Kassy and I will spend the night.

Takahara lifts my pack from the floor. I'm nervous, but she nods and sets the bag down. I've passed the test.

Considering my current relationship with *plantar fasciitis*, I scrutinized and weighed each item. I even purchased a Japanese-brand pack for this trip. My trusty Camino backpack, *Little Agnus*, weighs six pounds empty. The svelte Japanese number, *Little Miho*, checks in at a wispy three pounds. While I do feel like a traitor, the difference between the two is remarkable.

Fully loaded and ready to roll, Little Miho is like holding an average sack of groceries. Strapped on my back, I hardly notice her at all. Had I the courage to ditch the tent and sleeping bag, I could have gotten her under ten pounds.

The camping gear may be unnecessary, but I fret. What if I get lost? Or can't find lodging? And I worry about my health. My history with chronic vertigo and migraines may force a retreat into an emergency trail-side refuge. Again, we carry the weight of our fears.

Just a short jaunt from her doorstep, Takahara-san leads us to the temple. I tilt my head to the side. I try to fight it, but I can't help but feel deflated. Esthetically, at least from the outside, *Ryozenji* is not quite as imagined.

I expected something serene – high on a hill or tucked in a grove of pine. Instead, Ryozenji sits on a busy street, flanked by a large parking lot and vending machines. I blame urban sprawl.

Gyoki, a Buddhist priest born in 668, founded Ryozenji. The *honzon* or main deity of Ryozenji is *Shakyamuni*. Shakyamuni was a monk, philosopher, and sage. In Japan, he is respectfully known as *Shaka Nyorai*. Nyorai is the transliteration of *Buddha*.

Takahara-san guides us into a small shop to buy our gear. Kassy has already dressed the part. The only thing she is missing is a *Kongozue* or a walking staff. The staff is a henro's most sacred piece of equipment because it represents Kobo Daishi. When a henro uses a kongozue, he or she is said to walk side-by-side with Kukai.

I don't want to offend, but I won't be purchasing the cedar-personification of the great master. Instead, I rely on aluminum. Vexed by near-constant vertigo, my balance is crap. For safety's sake, I require two trekking poles to traverse rough terrain.

Typically, I rely on *Jasper*, my service dog. His four paws and gentle demeanor make up for all I lack. Unfortunately, Japan's disability laws differ from American laws. Jasper cannot travel freely with me like he can in Europe and North America. This general lack of access makes my life in Okinawa challenging.

Measuring me up, Takahara-san a sleeveless *hakui* of white cotton. It's comfy and looks like a top one might wear when practicing martial arts. Printed on the back are Japanese characters. I point to the inscription, and Takahara says, *"Namu Daishi Henjo Kongo."* This is a shout-out to the great master, Kobo Daishi.

Takahara-san grabs a wicker basket and tosses in a brick of osamefuda slips. The supply should last the whole trek. She loads the basket with incense, a box of tiny white candles, a lighter, and a hard-plastic bandoleer to protect the incense and candles from wet weather.

Next, she holds up a royal purple collar with gold lettering called a *wagesa*. I nod, and she puts it in the basket. How did she guess my favorite color?

We scan a shelf of bells. The bell fastens to the Kukai stick, which I am not buying, but to be a good sport, I pick the tiniest gold bell. If nothing else, it will make a nice souvenir.

The basket grows heavy, but Takahara-san is not done with me yet. We look at prayer beads called *juzu*, and I forget all about the weight. A strand of picture-stone jasper with amethyst accents and royal purple tassels catches my eye.

I don't even know how to use the beads, but the tassels match my collar. More importantly, the stone reminds me of my own Jasper waiting patiently for my return to Okinawa. I don't leave him often, and when I do, it is not without considerable loneliness.

With variegated beads of amber and brown, the juzu is heavy and cold in my hand. Jasper the Labrador is black. It's silly, but holding the strand connects me with him.

The shopkeeper places a conical-shaped, thatched hat, called a *Sugegasa*, on my head. It is heavier than it looks and not at all comfortable. I squat, making myself shorter, as the sales lady checks the fit. She attaches a strip of gauze, securing the ends in a bow beneath my chin.

Next, Takahara-san leads me to a table of stamp books. Like on the Camino, I'll need to collect stamps along the way to prove the completion of my pilgrimage.

On the Camino, I collected two stamps per day. On Shikoku, I must earn a stamp from each of the 88 temples. But unlike the Camino, each stamp will run 300 Japanese yen. That's roughly $2.75 each or $245 for the entire route. Once completed, this will be the most expensive book on my shelf.

The Shikoku stamp books are heavy. I find the smallest one, an accordion of folded pages between a hardcover wrapped in teal and gold brocade. The book contains a page for each of the 88 temples, plus one more to close the loop at temple one and another to collect a stamp at the burial place of Kobo Daishi on *Mount Koyasan.*

Takahara flips to the back of the book, which is technically the front in Japan, to show me the first temple's pre-stamped image. I examine the hand-scribed, inky-black calligraphy accented with three intricate vermillion stamps. This is the mark of Ryozenji. With luck, I'll return in a couple of months to collect another.

Takahara-san and I exit the shop, and Kassy follows. After handling no less than a dozen walking sticks, Kassy leaves the shop empty-handed. She shrugs and says, "I'm super spiritual, and none spoke to me."

I bite my lip to keep from smiling. I have no place to judge. After all, I picked the heaviest set of prayer beads because the strand makes me think of my dog.

Standing before the temple gate, Kassy and I admire a foreboding statue of a musclebound guardian. He looks positively fierce at nearly ten-feet tall like an angry genie prematurely disturbed from his lamp. Takahara-san points to the guardian and says, "O-nio-sama." Like schoolchildren, Kassy and I repeat, "O-nio-sama."

Takahara-san drops a coin into a metal box and bows. Digging in her apron, she pulls out another gold-colored coin with a square hole in the center – the equivalent of a US nickel. The talky-box says, "You do not need so much that your children go hungry."

Takahara-san puts both palms together in a reverent bow before passing through the gate. Like two ugly ducklings, Kassy and I repeat the action and follow her over the threshold. Once inside, all aesthetic disappointment dissolves, and awe takes over.

Kassy veers off toward a tranquil koi pond to snap photos. I resist primal touristic-urges and stay close to my mama duck. I follow Takahara-san to a stone trough of water fed by the mouth of a dragon's head.

Takahara-san selects one of several tin ladles resting on a bamboo rack above the water. She dips the ladle with her right hand and pours a small amount over her left palm, allowing the water to splash on the gravel below. Then, she switches hands and pours water into her right palm. She changes hands again and pours into the cup of her palm. Next, she sips the water from her palm and spits it out in the gravel below. Finally, she tips the ladle up, so the remaining water runs down the handle, purifying it for the next user.

Nervous, I step up to the trough and draw my weapon. Dipping out the cool water, I wash my left palm. Takahara-san crosses her index fingers and taps them in a *no, no, no!* The water from my palm splashed back into the trough. Damn! I have single-handedly contaminated the purification pool.

I bow apologetically and beg for pardon, "Sumimasen, Takahara-san. Sumimasen."

Embarrassed, I restart the ritual. This time, I make sure the spent water lands in the gravel and not back in the trough. I vow to never make this mistake again.

Kassy lopes up alongside and grabs a ladle. Before I can warn her, she draws a big mouthful straight from the cup and spits directly into the trough. Well, shit. The Americans have arrived.

With a stern face, our mentor turns on a heel and leads us toward the steps of a belfry. I have read about the bell ritual in my guidebook. A henro rings it once to announce his or her arrival to the deity enshrined in the main hall. Ringing the bell on the way out is bad luck and said to erase any wisdom gained while visiting the temple. At this point, I cannot afford to lose any precious nuggets of wisdom.

An intricate bell covered in green patina hangs in the center of the belfry, and a rope attached to a ramming log hangs down within my grasp. I heave the line toward the beautiful bell, but it takes me three swings to gain enough momentum to hit the mark. A resounding gong reverberates in my chest. How satisfying. Kassy follows. We have successfully negotiated this ritual without further cultural insult.

Crossing an idyllic bridge over the koi pond, I spy five golden babies praying. Each one kneels on a lily pad, and each has his own bottle. The lily pads are strewn with coins tossed from the bridge, like some sort of carnival game. I touch Takahara-san's sleeve.

"Jizo," she says. I've yet to learn about these Jizo babies, but I am smitten.

To our left, a rustic, two-story pagoda catches my eye. We lose Kassy again. Dutiful, I stay on Takahara-san's heels and follow her to the main hall. She pulls out a candle and three sticks of incense from her bandoleer. I do the same. The talky-box tells me the three sticks represent the past, present, and future. I love this idea.

Takahara-san lights her candle and uses it to ignite the incense, and then skewers the tiny taper on a spike in a glass-enclosure housing dozens of candles from henro before us. I light my candle and the incense and place the taper next to hers. When Kassy returns, she burns incense and a candle. Apparently, the walking stick isn't the only item that hasn't spoken to her.

In front of the main hall, we place our incense sticks in a ginormous bowl heaped with the ash of collective pasts, presents, and futures. My sticks smell like an old wardrobe – musty with undertones of cedar. I catch wafts of rose, and pine, and clove, and patchouli. Mingled together, the smoke is intoxicating.

Incense Bowl
- Temple 1

My mentor rings another small bell. She drops a crimson-brocaded slip in a box to the left, deposits a coin in the offertory, and bows. I follow, pausing to look down into the box at her osamefuda. It sparkles red and gold in the warm glow of paper lanterns. My white slips, adorned with glittery stickers and two colors of print, pale in comparison.

The plain white slips are for the new henro, like me. More experienced henro purchase levels of green, red, silver, gold, and brocade. Gold signifies at least 50 pilgrimages. Takahara-san's brocade slip means she has completed the loop at least a hundred times. I had no idea my mentor was an Ohenro rockstar!

Ready to chant, Takahara-san flips through my guidebook and finds the *Heart Sutra*. I fumble along, trying my best to keep up. My voice, along with my confidence, fades in and out. "...Kanji zai bosatsu, gyo jin hannya hara mitta ji..." Takahara-san traces a finger beneath each line, but only a few syllables escape my lips.

The sutra goes on and on. When it's complete, we move on to another sutra and then another. I find my voice in the familiar phrase, "Namu Daishi Henjo Kongo" – the words written on the back of my hakui. Finally, we bow and say, "Arigato gozaimasu" – a reverent thank you.

We repeat the whole process, from candle to thank you, at the Daishi hall. Just think, I have 87 more temples to go. On the bright side, I have loads of opportunities to practice my Japanese.

Our leader heads toward the gate. She stops, turns to face the main hall, and bows. And again, like obedient ducklings, Kassy and I do the same. Temple one is nailed.

Back on the busy street, Takahara-san points to a post adorned with a white sticker. A cartoon henro indicates the path, and an arrow in red points toward temple two. I'm so used to following the yellow arrows and scallop shells marking the Camino. The new symbol and color scheme will take some adjustment.

Before parting ways with Takahara-san, she gives us each a brocade osamefuda. I hold it close to my heart like a treasure. The talky-box tells us she has completed the loop 144 times. We are astounded. I make a walking gesture with two fingers, but she shakes her head. The box says, "No walking. Only driving." Kassy and I nod. I'm still impressed.

I bow and say goodbye to Takahara-san. Of course, Kassy wraps the poor woman up in another awkward embrace. Side-by-side, whether I like it or not, I'm off to temple two with the Cat-lady.

Temple 2: Gokurakuji

Japanese vending machines thrill me. A couple of blocks from the first temple, I stop at a machine next to a fruit stand and introduce Kassy to the magic of hot and cold beverages available from the same machine. She has her eye on a hot can of green tea with honey and ginger, and my heart is set on an icy-cold *Aquarius*, a brand of sports drink I thought I'd never see after leaving the Camino.

I fish around in my pockets for change, but before I find any, a man with white hair and wire-framed glasses yells to me from the window of a small truck loaded with oranges. He hops from the truck, waving a fist in the air. Intuitively, I grab Kassy's arm and step back off the sidewalk. What does he want?

"Osettai, Osettai!" He yells, shaking his fist.

I try to back up another step, but we are pinned against a display of bananas. The old man reaches for my hand. Dulled by confusion, I allow him to take it. I feel the transfer of a cool, heavy coin from his hand to mine.

Oh, now I get it. The man has given me *osettai*, a gift of money. I know to expect kindness, but I wasn't expecting it so soon.

I bow and thank him, profusely, "Arigato gozaimasu, arigato gozaimasu!" He hops back in his truck and sputters away.

I plunk the 500-yen coin into the drink machine and treat Kassy. The coin is a generous gift. I can buy a second round with the remainder.

Kassy and I walk, sipping our drinks and beaming with good fortune. We are contemplative for several moments until Kassy breaks the silence. "I had no idea what was going on back there," she says. "At first, I thought he was some crazy man. All that waving of his fist…"

"I know! It totally caught me off guard."

"Well, you recovered quite gracefully."

"Thanks, except I forgot to give him my osamefuda. It all happened so fast."

"Don't worry," she says. "I have a feeling you will receive many osettai from old men in trucks."

I laugh because I know Kassy is probably right.

The second temple is a short walk from the first, less than two kilometers. The way markers are inconsistent; nonetheless, we trek through a residential area and arrive at a two-story, orange gate. Wooden guardians flank each side of the entrance. They are as muscular and ominous as the guardian of temple one.

Like the first temple, Gokurakuji was founded by Gyoki. However, Kukai carved the main deity, *Amida Nyorai,* the Buddha of limitless light. This depiction of Buddha is said to have superpowers. He is everywhere, shining down on all beings. In the afterlife, followers are invited to his land of pure and everlasting light.

In ancient times, after Kukai carved the deity of light, fishermen complained because the illumination reached all the way to the sea, spoiling their catch. Solution-oriented monks built a hill between the statue and the sea, restoring the fishing trade.

Kassy and I wait our turn at the purification station. The fountain is sheltered beneath a stone pagoda-roof held up by four columns layered in overlapping dragons. It's a lot to take in. The adornment makes me need to whisper like I do when entering a cathedral. While this isn't my holy place, it certainly is for others. I can feel Kassy, next to me, radiating with awe.

"Super spiritual," she says. "Women come here to pray for easy childbirth."

I nod, trying to preserve the hushed tranquility of the temple grounds.

Kassy continues, "I'm a retired nurse. I've helped bring hundreds of babies into the world."

"That's so cool," I whisper.

"And my daughter grew up to be a midwife."

Kassy is about to burst with pride. I smile and squeeze her arm.

Like temple one, small ladles rest on a bamboo rack above the purification water, but this time, the water is caught in a bowl carved into a massive stump of petrified wood. I've never seen anything quite like it. Above, a delicately fierce, patinaed dragon spits water into the bowl. I gently remind Kassy to allow the wastewater to fall on the concrete pavers below. Dragons may spit into the pool, but we shall not.

Without a fumble, we head toward a large bell and announce our arrivals. On our way to the main hall, we stop and admire a gentle-faced statue of a monk holding a baby. Perhaps it's another version of Jizo, like the babies in the koi pond at temple one.

I lend Kassy supplies, and we light candles and plant incense sticks in another great bowl of ash. In front of the main hall, we pathetically bumble through the sutras. Our voices lower to whispers whenever other henros draw near.

We repeat the whole routine at the Daishi hall before searching for the *nokyosho* or stamp office. Since my book was pre-stamped when purchased, this will be my first experience.

My scant research warned of long lines and delays at stamp offices. Thankfully, this is not the case. I step up to the counter and pay my 300 yen.

A calligraphist moves three rubber stamps from a red pad of ink and presses each on the page. Next, she dips a brush into black ink to compose the characters representing Gokurakuji. Watching the methodical process is gratifying.

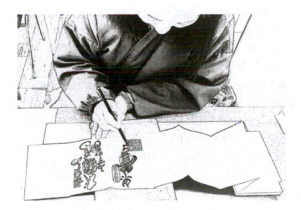

Temple 3: Konsenji

On the way to *Konsenji*, Kassy and I continue to get to know each other. We talk about the usual things in the usual order: dogs, kids, grandchildren, travel, and men. She lives in my home state of Washington, a couple hours north of my house.

Although I've lived abroad for the past five years, we have yet to sell the property. It's nice to have a home base. Currently, my husband is there, and I am here. Thousands of miles, the Pacific Ocean, a plot of real estate, and pride drive a firm wedge between the two of us. We are at an impasse.

Kassy is full of surprises. Not only is she a retired nurse, but she also plays the drums. While I find her life interesting and her stories entertaining, I was hoping to carve out a little quiet-time. I do my best to keep up my end of the conversation, but my perseverance is waning. I don't want to talk, and I don't want to be talked at.

Silence is a precious commodity. I can't meditate without it, and walking is my brand of meditation. Rarely have I found a hiking companion who understands this need for peace. I've tested a plethora of diplomatic ways to say, "Shut-the-hell-up," but I've yet to perfect a tried and true, inoffensive formula.

Kassy talks, and like a bobble-head doll, I nod. I'm testing the *firehose-formula*. The idea here is to remove as much of myself from the equation, allowing my companion to blast me with a flood of stories, fun facts, observations, opinions, and non-sequiturs. Happily, Kassy babbles on, flowing from topic to topic.

The hypothesis behind this formula is simple. Eventually, Kassy's well will run dry, and her firehose will grow limp. Unfortunately, there is a major flaw — data recycling.

The flow is interrupted by a young Japanese man yelling from an embankment above. "Ohenro-san! Ohenro-san!"

He runs down the hill toward us. A large camera beats against his chest, and a messenger bag swings about his waist. Lacking a thatched hat and white clothing, I doubt he is a henro.

"I am Hirosho," he says. "I am a Shikoku researcher." Kassy and I nod, and he continues. "May I ask honorable Ohenro-san some question?"

Hirosho is darn adorable, and his English pronunciation is excellent. Gone is my want of silence as I embrace the opportunity to chat with a local. He pulls a pad and a fine pen from his messenger bag.

First, he wants to know why we are walking the Shikoku pilgrimage.

"Because it's here!" says Kassy.

I chime in, "To experience Japanese culture!"

For me, it's not enough to live and work in Okinawa, primarily because I teach mostly Americans on a US military base. I live off-base in Okinawa City, but most of my neighbors are Americans. The island's military presence is so thick that Okinawa feels like an Asian-infused version of little America. The food is fabulous, and crime is almost non-existent. I've yet to meet kinder humans than Okinawans. I like it there, but it doesn't feel very *Japanese*.

Hirosho asks how we plan to complete the pilgrimage. He explains that walking clockwise and visiting temples in sequential order like we are doing now is to walk *Jun-chi*. To walk jun-chi is to experience the four dojos in order. Dojos are the training periods of *Awakening, Ascetic Training, Enlightenment*, and *Nirvana*.

Kassy is walking *too-shi-u-chi*. This means she plans to complete the pilgrimage all at once. Working people, like me, often walk *ku-gi-ri-u-chi*. This means dividing the expedition up into more manageable sections.

Sadly, I don't have 50 to 60 days of available vacation. However, I do have about ten days between class sessions, a couple long weekends, and spring break on the horizon. I will fly back and forth from Okinawa until I've completed the loop.

Kassy hopes to complete the entire loop on foot. I'm keeping my options open. I am gun-shy about public transportation. However, if an old farmer in a truck laden with oranges offers me an osettai lift, I'm not going to hesitate.

It is not necessary to walk the Shikoku 88. In fact, very few henro are walkers. Of the hundreds of thousands of people who annually visit Shikoku's 88 temples, less than ten-percent are walking-henros. Most pilgrims arrive by the busload. Others make the loop in hired vans, taxis, and private cars.

It does not matter how one arrives at each temple. Instead, it matters what one does at each temple. This resonates with me.

Hirosho wants to escort us to Konsenji, and we are thrilled with his company. Wayfinding has been a tedious task all morning. The white and red henro stickers are few and far between, and my eyes are not yet trained to spot them.

Kassy suffers from glaucoma and cannot see a marker until she is within a couple of paces. This bothers her little, as she seems content to leave the navigating up to me. For now, I happily surrender the task and allow Hirosho to take the lead.

Kassy tries to explain to Hirosho about her former life as an obstetrics nurse, but he doesn't understand. Persistent, Kassy tries again, but she cannot convey the connection. Finally, Kassy jogs ahead a few paces and turns around to face us. She spreads her legs wide, bends down, and puts her hands between her legs. She looks like she is about to granny-style a basketball. Instead, she plunges deeper into a squat and pantomimes a baby emerging from her crotch.

"Baaay-beee," she says.

With both hands, she makes a sweeping downward gesture of the babe leaving her birth canal.

"Baaaaay-beee!"

I burst out laughing but sober when I see Hirosho grimace. In a rebound, he pulls out his phone and holds up a picture of his two-month-old daughter. Like grandmothers-without-borders, Kassy and I huddle around his smartphone to coo at the hairy little baby smiling back at us.

Mutually refreshed by the baby-break, we walk on. In a role-reversal, Hirosho becomes the interviewee. I point to bundles of brown stalks hanging from A-frame racks in a field of stubble.

"What is this?" I ask.

"Rice," he says.

"And how about way over there?" I ask.

"More rice."

"And what are those tiny green shoots down here?"

"Oh, that is more rice."

Apparently bored by agriculture, Kassy commandeers the interview.

"So, what do you think of Donald Trump?" she asks.

It's a rhetorical question, and she continues before Hirosho formulates a polite response.

"How does it make you feel that there are only his finger and the red button between total world destruction?"

Hirosho stammers.

Undaunted, she carries on. "Don't you think it's weird we come here as tourists after we bombed you guys in Hiroshima?"

He's lost for words and clearly uncomfortable. I move in for the save, but I can't get my words out either.

And so, Kassy continues, "It's really odd the Japanese government allows us into your country. Americans are killers!"

"Okay, okay," I intervene. "Let's shift gears, shall we?"

I shoot Kassy a glare. She shakes it off and changes the subject. "Do you sing karaoke?" She asks Hirosho.

He nods and sings a few lovely lines in Japanese. His voice is smooth and surprisingly deep.

"I'm a singer too," she says. "And I play the drums!" She beats on a pair of invisible bongos and picks up her pace.

I fall behind as she teaches Hirosho the words to the *Row, Row, Row Your Boat*. There isn't room on the narrow lane to stride three-abreast. I don't care to sing along.

I'm happy to leave the awkward topics of Trump, warfare, and childbirth behind. But after the eighth iteration of *Row-Row-Row-Your Boat*, I know I must find a way to tactfully ditch Kassy.

Outside the gate of Konsenji, Kassy and Hirosho exchange contact information. I use the distraction to slip inside and enjoy the serenity of the temple grounds. A scarlet-red, two-story pagoda catches my eye.

Historically Chinese, the pagoda is derived from the Indian *stupa* and used to store relics. Pagodas come in all sizes and are usually made of stone or wood. However, the stone pagodas are typically ornamental.

After completing my rounds, a tall young woman catches my eye. While it's not nice to profile, I'm confident she is American. I stroll across a courtyard to greet her.

Rochelle is not only American, but she also lives in Washington state, near the Canadian border. Her home is about three hours from mine and less than an hour from Kassy's. So far, Kassy and Rochelle are the only other non-Japanese henro I have seen today. We all share the same home state. What are the odds?

Two years ago, Rochelle lived on Shikoku, taking part in a program offered by her university. She taught English in *Tokushima* for nearly a year. Rochelle has returned after graduation to reunite with friends and walk her pilgrimage. Like me, she is contemplating change and the next chapter of her life.

Rochelle and I visit a reflecting pool said to predict longevity. The idea is to gaze into the pool to see one's reflection. If a henro sees her reflection, she can expect to live beyond her 92nd year. If a henro does not see her reflection, she should prepare to die within three years.

Without hesitation, Rochelle saunters poolside and glances down. She smiles and gives me two thumbs-up and motions me over, but I shake my head. She rejoins without question, and we make our way to the stamp office.

I didn't peer into the well because I have an unhealthy preoccupation with death. It's not a new thing brought on by menopause or anything like that. I've been this way since childhood.

I was seven when my big brother, Irv, died. He was only thirteen. I was ten when my cousin, Holly, died. She was also ten.

The loss of my brother, followed by Holly, was more than a little girl should endure. At such a tender age, loss and my own mortality had reached up and punched me right in the face. I wasn't prepared for that level of grief.

I hate feeling unprepared, and so did the little-girl-me. To manage future grief, I developed a morbid game of *make-believe-funeral.* I imagined the death of each grandparent, each sibling, each cousin, my parents, my friends, and myself.

I'd conjure up the cause of death, some more creative or grisly than others, and then I'd pick out caskets and flowers and lovely words to include in a eulogy. Death would not catch me by surprise ever again. But, of course, it has.

I know the reflection pool cannot determine my fate. If Rochelle saw her reflection, there is no scientific reason I should not see mine. But why risk it? If I'm going to die in three years, I'm not ready to know right now. That kind of knowledge would be a total buzzkill on this otherwise sunny and utterly delightful day.

Temple 4: Dainichiji

Rochelle and I exit the temple and make our way to *Dainichiji*. I wave to Kassy and Hirosho, who are still engaged in conversation. I should probably supply Kassy with more incense and another candle, but maybe she is ready to purchase her own.

Rochelle strides quietly beside me. I appreciate her calm companionship, but I know it will not last. She is a leggy girl in her early twenties. Little by little, she picks up the pace. I know better than try to keep up.

After years of hiking with miserable blisters, I learned my lesson. I am a student of hard-knocks. Eventually, I gave up the race and slowed down.

Overextending my gait increases friction. Friction leads to hotspots, and hotspots turn into blisters. I've tried every pair of magical socks, padding, tape, insoles, and miracle salve. For me, the one thing that consistently works is stride-control.

Proper footwear is crucial. It's essential to choose the right shoe for the job. Heavy boots are not required on the Shikoku. Unfortunately, 80-percent of the path is hardscaped. While there are a few rough patches, I'm sure a pair of trail-runners with good traction will suffice.

I wear motion-control gel cross-trainers made by ASICS. The shoe is stable and supportive. It's perfect for flatfooted walkers, and the gel offers relief from plantar fasciitis.

We pass a rusted *Kirin* beer vending machine displaying cans and bottles and growlers. I haven't walked far enough to want a beer, but I cross the street to take a closer look. It's non-operational, but the prices listed are convenience-store comparable. It probably hasn't been derelict for long.

Rochelle pulls ahead, and I let her go. About 100 meters up the road, she looks back to make sure I see the trail cutting to the left. Finally! I'm going to get off this blacktop. I pump my fist in the air and yell to Rochelle, "Gan-bat-te!" Japanese for, *Go for it*.

Just before the cutoff, I stop to admire a vegetable garden. Fat bodies of greenish-white tubers poke up from the earth. It looks as if the daikon radishes are trying to wiggle themselves free.

I love daikon. I buy an obscenely long tuber in Okinawa once a week from a farm stand near my apartment. Basically, daikon is an elongated turnip-radish fusion with a peppery bite. I chop it into fat matchsticks and douse it with rice wine vinegar.

A little old woman wearing a straw hat and gingham-print apron gazes up from her squat to nod at me. She is as old and dark as the soil beneath her trowel. It would be no surprise to learn she is a centenarian.

Meeting a centenarian is not uncommon in Okinawa. Okinawa is a blue zone, an island historically known for longevity. Okinawan women live longer than any women on the planet. Life, diet, and longevity in rural Shikoku are probably quite similar.

The way marker leaving the road looks nothing like the smattering of white stickers I have followed thus far. Instead, a hand with a pointing index finger, carved in relief on the face of a large stone, indicates the proper path. Beneath the pointing finger, green and white snowflakes of lichen camouflage the columns of Japanese characters. The lichen makes the characters nearly impossible to read – even if I could.

My feet rejoice as I turn off the road and onto a path no wider than two-sneaker widths. I bob and weave beneath bows of citrus trees. All-day, I have coveted the offertory fruits left at the feet of stone deities without digestive systems. Now, here are hundreds all within an arm's reach. I know better than to pillage a farmer's crop, but I do long to taste a homegrown orange.

I've only hiked about seven kilometers, but the blacktop has been unforgiving. I stop to sit on a rock, hydrate, and rest my feet. In front of me, I spy a flash of orange through the tall, lush grass. Wary of vipers, I use my hiking-poles to part the blades. There, waiting for me like an Easter egg is the most perfectly-orange globe I have ever laid eyes on. I inch it close with a pole and stuff it in my pack for later. It will be an ideal post-hike reward.

I follow the path through two raised fields. I assume these are rice paddies, and the grass-like seedlings are baby rice. The sprouts look like the oats, wheat, and alfalfa growing in the fields of my childhood. A little dog barks at me from a farmhouse porch, and I think of Jasper and home.

I bow reverently and enter the Dainichiji compound. Kukai founded this temple. He also carved the *Dainichi Nyorai*, the supreme deity in Esoteric Buddhism.

The temple grounds are packed with people. Caught up in a white wave of elderly bus-henro, I float through the rituals. The wave gushes down a walkway lined by 33 *Kannon* statues. Kannon Bosatsu is the bodhisattva of mercy and compassion. I want to stop and admire the depictions, but the wave of geriatrics pushes me onward.

Despite the crowd, I'm excited to see only three people in line outside the stamp office. My heart sinks when the man in front dumps out a duffle bag of books on the desk. Evidently, he is the tour bus driver. Fortunately, my disappointment is short-lived, as the thoughtful driver motions me to go ahead.

The monk behind the desk creates an inky-black dot centered at the top of my page. He follows with a smaller dot below. He works slowly, making each stroke and curl of the brush an accomplishment.

He wears two rings, a smooth silver band on his right hand and gold on his left. Slivers of little white moons crest each nail bed. The monk's hands are beautiful, and I must peel my eyes away as he hands me back my book.

Temple 5: Jizoji

I exit the gates of Konsenji and make my way toward *Jizoji*, the fifth temple. After Jizoji, I'll walk on to the sixth and stop for the night. I'm tired, and I'm ready to hang up my hakui and thatched hat. I need a hot bath and a good meal.

So far, walking from temple to temple has been the easy part of my day. Going through the rituals at each temple is stressful. It shouldn't be, but it is. It's all so new to me, and I don't want to make any more mistakes. It's an awful lot of chanting too. My tongue is tired, and my jaws are sore. Who knew my mouth would get such a workout?

The energy from Takahara-san's thoughtful breakfast fizzled after the second temple. Vending machines dot the route, but so far, none that vend food. My blood sugar is tanking, and when it tanks, I get these annoying little sparkles in front of my face. The sparkles are a type of migraine aura, an early warning sign I'm about to crash.

I seek refuge in the shade of a rustic, four-post shelter furnished with two wooden benches. I pull out my water bottle, find my migraine medicine, and dig around in my pack for the orange that was supposed to be tonight's treat. Hydration and food should work wonders.

At first, I thought this shelter was a bus stop, but now I realize it is a henro-hut. This is the first one on the loop. Henro-huts, like henro-houses, are a vital part of the logistical support available to walking-henros. Some huts are for day use, while others may be used for primitive camping. This hut is wide open, but it would be an ideal spot to pitch a tent.

The migraine medicine works immediately. However, the homegrown orange is a major disappointment. It's not sweet and juicy. Instead, it's dry and fibrous and bitter. It's still edible, and it will supply enough energy to finish the day's walk, but it is not a treat. No longer will I covet the offertory fruit left at the temples. The stone deities without digestive systems aren't missing a thing.

The walk to Jizoji is two-kilometers, but I'm procrastinating. It feels good to sit. I fish out my phone and look up information about *Jizo*, the next temple's main deity.

Along with the babies on lily pads back at temple one, I've admired several statues I think could be depictions of or related to Jizo. Jizo is not a *Nyorai*, the Japanese word for an enlightened being who crosses over into Buddha-hood. Instead, he is a bodhisattva. He remains this side of *Nirvana* as the guardian of children, and he vows to work until all those trapped in hell are freed. Appropriately, his name means *Earth Womb*.

Parents and grandparents of deceased children, along with mothers who suffer miscarriages, dress the statues in knit hats and baby bibs. The bibs and hats vary from brilliant vermillion to soft pink. The differing shades always fall within the red spectrum. Red clothing is thought to ward off evil spirits and protect the lost little souls. Earlier today, I noted statues dressed in bibs and hats. I also saw toys, trinkets, and candy left at Jizo's feet. But up until now, I failed to realize the significance.

The story of Jizo makes me sad. I think about my brother and little cousin—thirteen and ten, how utterly unfair. With five healthy and happy sons of my own, I cannot fathom the kind of hell my parents and aunt must have endured.

I wish I had known about Jizo. I'd like to leave an offering in the names of Irv and Holly, but a bib doesn't resonate. They were not babies. I'll pick up something more suitable to carry on my next trip.

A handmade broom stands in the corner of the shelter. I grab it and give it a go. A whirl of pink snow scatters with each swing. the more I sweep, the more the wind blows the cherry-blossom petals back into the shelter.

It's early March and a bit premature for cherry-blossoms, but a few blushing trees are kicking off the season. I am lucky to begin this journey just as the trees start to bloom. Perhaps the serendipity is symbolic of the beautiful things to come. I do hope so.

I'm lost in thought when a silver sedan pulls up to the hut. An old man in a bucket hat reaches across the cab and pops open the passenger door. Without a word, he motions me in, and I obey.

Cradling Little Miho in my lap, I inventory the contents of his cab. The floor is littered with white osamefuda. The visors hold strips of gold, green, and red. Pinned to the dash are several brocade-slips from super-henro like Takahara-san. The top of the dashboard is burnt and pocked by crushed-out cigarette butts. Nooks and crannies are jammed with small silver and copper coins. Obviously, this generous man makes a habit of gifting henro with osettai via transportation.

It's unnerving to travel at such speeds. We are going under 40-kilometers-per-hour, but after a slow day of walking, these fleeting moments feel death-defying. Fortunately, he delivers me to the temple unscathed. I bow and present an osamefuda to express my gratitude. He nods and tosses my strip behind him to join the collection on the floorboard. Without a word exchanged between us, I enter the gate of Jizoji.

I rest Little Miho at the base of an 800-year-old Ginkgo tree and prepare to make my rounds. I try to slow down and complete each task as methodically as Takahara-san demonstrated. I patiently move through the sutras, chanting above a whisper. I offer coins to Jizo and wish comfort to the parents of lost babies, and then I say a prayer, to my god, for Irv and Holly.

I exit Jizoji feeling heavy. Unlike Kassy, I would never describe myself as *super-spiritual*. However, something feels peculiar. Perhaps it's the thought of so many lost, little souls weighing me down. Or maybe, I am merely tired. Either way, I'm not looking forward to the final five-kilometer slog to my stopping place for the night.

An old man stands on the corner, smoking the stub of a crinkled cigarette. His yellowed fingers quake as he pulls a drag. A grubby length of frayed twine replaces a belt to hoist his threadbare woolen pants. A brown flannel, two sizes too large, drapes his stooped frame.

I almost don't recognize him, but he nods, and I follow him to the car. It's my driver. I can't believe it. He has been out here for nearly an hour, waiting to chauffeur me to the next temple.

I fight a pang of rising guilt. I don't want to take advantage of the old guy or use up his fuel. If he is driving me, he can't offer osettai to another. Who am I kidding? I am in no mood to walk. I lean into his act of kindness and climb into the front seat. He never speaks, and I don't talk to him, but I love our relationship.

Temple 6: Anrakuji

In the parking lot of Anrakuji, I break the silence. "Koko de neru." I hope I am saying *I sleep here*. It's cavewoman-ish, for sure. Sometimes less is best. Unfortunately, my driver stares straight ahead.

Reluctantly, I grab the door handle, bear-hug Little Miho, and execute an ungraceful departure. I bow before entering the temple gates. When I pop up from the bow, I'm surprised to see the old man standing beside me. Damn! He's quiet – and super quick!

Feeling a tad uncomfortable, I head toward the temple lodge before completing my rounds and collecting a stamp. The old man follows me to the lodge entrance, but a monk holds out his palm to stop my chauffeur. I'm not sure what to do, so I dig in my messenger bag and pull out another osamefuda. I also hand him a 500-yen coin to replace the fuel I used.

From the check-in desk, I see the old man waiting. His head is low, and his shoulders sag. He holds out the coin I gave to him in the palm of his hand. I realize my fumble, and I feel terrible. I have treated him like a bellhop or a taxi-driver.

The young monk handling my check-in understands more English than he speaks. I explain the situation, and he steps outside to talk to my driver. Expressionless, the old man turns and shuffles away.

I follow the monk down a long hall. He stops, slides open a partition, bows, and heads back toward the lobby. Albeit spartan, my little cell is charming. Woven grass tatami mats trimmed in turquoise line the floor. Along the back wall, a rice-paper shade diffuses light from a large window. The room is furnished with a squat, wooden table and an equally short entertainment stand. In such traditional lodging, like this temple, I had not expected to see a television. I take off my hakui and drape it over the set. In the closet, I find my bedding and set to work creating a sleeping pallet.

I need to make the temple rounds and collect my stamp. However, I'm nervous about leaving my belongings unattended. There is no lock on the sliding door leading into my room. There is no way to secure the sliding partitions that create two sides of my room. I peak through each wall and see empty cells. Perhaps I will be without neighbors.

Japan has a low crime rate. It's even lower in rural Shikoku. I'm sure leaving items unsecured in a temple cell is common. However, I'm not quite ready to trust the process. I pack up my messenger bag and sling Little Miho on my back.

I meet Kassy in the lobby. She missed the turnoff after the third temple and ended up retracing her steps. Undaunted, she is bubbling over with the magic of the day. This woman is a hiking machine!

The temple grounds are stunning. I walk a narrow rock path dividing two koi ponds. Yellow and white speckled fish follow alongside with gaping mouths begging for food. I have nothing to offer.

Yakushi Nyorai is the main deity of Anrakuji. He is the Buddha of healing and holds an apothecary jar in his left hand. In the past, people traveled from afar to soak in a healing hot spring and pray for cures. The spring now feeds the communal baths inside the temple lodge. I plan a long soak tonight to soothe my tired legs and feet.

I've never had the pleasure of a Japanese bath. Traditionally, the communal bath is enjoyed after dinner, but I'm in a bit of a pickle because I am tattooed. From what I have read, tattoos are not only frowned upon but often forbidden in *onsens* or bathhouses. I don't want to be a rule-breaker, but after walking all day, I need a bath or a shower.

Bathhouses are segregated by gender, and in this male-dominated temple, I doubt anyone scans ladies for tattoos. The real obstacle is other women. To avoid detection and offense, I'll slip in early.

My bathhouse strategy pays off in spades. Not only do I enjoy a trouble-free experience, but I also have the whole place to myself. The tranquility satiates my hunger for peace. I relax, feeling the tension leave each muscle.

I've visited several European spas, but this is my first Japanese onsen. The bathhouse is a work of art. A shallow pool serves as the centerpiece, and a burbling fountain delivers piping hot mineral-water from a natural spring. Rustic granite paves the floor, and a gnarled tree trunk supports the ceiling.

Several shower stations line one wall. Each station is fitted with a bench, bucket, shower hose, body wash, shampoo, and conditioner. I am in heaven!

After scrubbing head to toe, I tiptoe toward the pool. The water is near scalding. I find a tap, adding just enough cool water to keep from boiling alive. Scrunching down, the water barely covers my body, but it doesn't matter. The relief is instant, and I drift off to sleep.

I enjoy a semi-conscious state, aware of my surroundings but too heavy to move. I hear the bubbling fountain, feel the rough stone against my backside, and smell an ever-so-slight sulfur tang.

I move in and out of a pleasantly lucid dream. I can do this sometimes, control my dreams, but only when deeply relaxed. I am home, somewhere, but not in my house, and not in my flat in Okinawa. But it is *my* home.

I'm playing a trivia game with my husband and kids, and I'm killing them with one correct answer after another. They all laugh, astounded by my brilliance. They have no idea I am cheating – that I'm in control of all the questions asked. A couple of times, just to show off, I shout out the answer before the card is read.

It's a wonderful joke. My trickery makes me laugh aloud, and the laugh shakes me from my dream. I wake and find myself homesick for a home that does not yet exist.

Back in my cell, I work on a little craft project a monk gave me when I checked in. It's for the *Goma*, or fire ceremony. Most of his explanation was likely lost in translation, but I think it is a ceremony to honor our ancestors.

The kit includes a pink paper tag with a wire attached, a narrow slab of cedar plank, and a camphor tree branch. He instructed me to prepare a special osamefuda with a wish for myself. Next, write a wish for someone else on the slab of cedar. Then, on the pink paper, write the names and death dates of ancestors who are on your mind and attach the pink paper to the camphor branch. It's a complicated process, but I think I got the gist.

My paternal grandparents live on in vibrant, loving memories. My grandpa died over 30 years ago, but I hear his voice and see his features and gestures in my oldest son. I feel his warmth and steady simplicity in my youngest boy. This is the wonder of the ancestors. We may behold them again in our children.

My grandmother passed away quite recently. She was 97. She never seemed to struggle or worry or want or envy. She lived with such grace. The wound of her loss is still a tender bruise.

On the cedar slab, I write a wish for my sons. The job calls for a felt-marker, but I have a ballpoint. Nonetheless, it's legible – to me, at least.

A gong calls me to dinner. Like one of Pavlov's dogs, I'm suddenly starving. I dress in haste, run fingers through my wild mop, and slip out for supper.

I'm excited and a bit nervous about my first Japanese dinner in a temple. I've eaten in plenty of Japanese restaurants at home and in Okinawa. But I'm wondering how the cuisine transfers to the asceticism of esoteric Buddhist culture.

Finding the dining hall through a maze of paper walls is challenging, but I make it with five minutes to spare. Even though I am early, the dining room is packed. Crammed elbow to elbow, there are several tables of Japanese pilgrims. The room hums with the buzz of friendly conversation and laughter. I see beer, and my heart leaps with joy.

A monk shows me to my table. I sit next to a woman who looks about my age. She speaks no Japanese, and her English is limited to introductions. Her name is Bianca, and she is from Naples, Italy.

Bianca and I try speaking in Spanish together, but we don't get far. Instead, we surrender to the awkward stillness of our table, but I'm not worried. I see Kassy's name on a place-marker across from me. There will be plenty of talking once she arrives.

I had hoped for the chance to mingle with Japanese henro. But we've been divided by east and west. With only three non-Japanese henro, there's a whole lot of available real estate in the western front.

I catch the eye of a young monk serving drinks. "Biru, kudasai," I say.

He grunts and nods.

I stifle a cry of joy as the monk returns with a giant bottle of Sapporo, complete with a frosty glass. I'm a one-beer-wonder, and this is a beer and a half. I offer to share with Bianca, but she flatly declines.

A monk leads the evening chant. I read along from the slip of paper left at my place setting. Of course, the prayer is written using Japanese characters, but it is also written in my alphabet, so I can read the sounds. Even better, it is translated into English. How thoughtful.

The monk's voice is low and deep, "Hito-tsu-bu no ko-me ni-mo..." *Even one drop of rice is made from efforts by thousands and millions of people.*

Kassy bursts through the sliding door looking positively feral. She's doing the whole stray-cat thing again. The monk stops chanting, and the room quiets, waiting for Kassy to sit. I send her a frantic wave, but she doesn't understand. She saunters over, completely oblivious.

The monk continues, "Ten-chi no me-gu-mi ga..." *Even a drop of water is a blessing from heaven and earth. I will have these with thankfulness.*

Despite Kassy's untimely entrance, the blessing is perfect. I fold up the paper and tuck it into my messenger bag. I'd like to teach my grandchildren to recite it before a Thanksgiving dinner.

Kassy is shivering. She's just come from the bath, and her white hair hangs in wet braids down the front of her impossibly thin, long-underwear top. The dining hall is cold, and the front of her shirt tells the temperature. I take off my fleece. She tries to refuse, but I insist.

I hold up my bottle and gesture to Kassy. "Beer?"

"Oh, no. I've never been a beer drinker," she says.

"Just as well." I resign and commit to down the entire bottle all by myself. I got this.

Kassy is a foodie. One by one, little bowls and plates appear in front of us. She is as excited and curious as I am, and we are hungry from the day's walk. We wait to begin until the last bowl arrives, a tiny glass dish holding a gelatinous, fleshy-pink blob.

I recognize most of the food. There is rice, miso soup, and a shallow dish with yellow shreds of pickled daikon. I see a basket of tempura vegetables with a dollop of radish paste held in a tiny boat made from a leaf. There is a clear amber sauce to dip the tempura, a box of steamed shrimp sprinkled in black sesame seeds, and a bowl of what looks like tofu topped with two steamed pea-pods and a carrot slice stamped into the shape of a cherry-blossom. The final plate holds opaque slabs flanked by cherry-tomato halves and garnished with shreds of carrot and broccoli stems. I'm guessing the white slabs are raw squid.

Except for the occasional whisper, the only sound in the dining hall is the tap-tap-tapping and scraping of chopsticks. I move through each mini-course, starting with the tempura. The steamed shrimp and raw squid are lovely, but I mourn the empty basket that once held expertly fried veggies.

Slyly, I peer across the table. Kassy is kind of a health nut. Maybe she doesn't eat fried food.

But I'm too late. Kassy has plowed through everything but the pink blob and her bowl of rice. She may look half-starved, but the lady can throw down the food!

With cheeks full of rice, she gives me a guilty grin. I shoot her a wink and take a chug of beer. The exchange speaks a thousand words. We have died and gone to epicurean heaven.

The miso soup goes down quickly and warms to the toes. I eat the tender pea pods and the carrot flower and give the tofu a poke. I tolerate tofu, but it's far from a favorite. This stuff is spongy and watery and tastes like nothing.

The pink blob is a mystery. I assume it is *mochi*, a starchy, rubbery rice-flour treat filled with something squishy. I haven't yet learned to love Japanese desserts. I pick up the ball with my chopsticks and give it a good squeeze, but it doesn't squish like typical mochi.

I hold it up for Bianca to inspect. "So, what do you think?" But Bianca just shakes her head.

"Mochi," Kassy says with a mouthful. "Reminds me of eating a hunk of skin."

I run my tongue along the inside of my cheek. Yes. The mochi I have sampled in Okinawa was fleshy and flattened and circular, like my cheek. I shudder at the comparison, but the image doesn't squelch my curiosity.

I bite the ball in half and examine the starchy, muddy-red filling surrounded by pink flesh. It's sweetened red beans! It's like the worst piece of Valentine candy in the box. If hell served chocolate truffles, they would all be filled with red-bean paste. Beans are not for dessert! I swallow and drop the remaining half back in the bowl.

"Are you going to eat that?" Kassy asks.

I push the bowl toward her. She plucks the half-orb up with her chopsticks and pops it into her mouth. I smile, admiring her gusto and zest for life.

Temple 7: Jurakuji

In the morning, I meet Kassy in the lobby. It's pouring down rain, but I'm looking forward to the day's walk. Kassy is all smiles. We are Washington girls, after all. What's a little downpour?

She slides into a rain jacket and says, "No bad weather. Just bad gear."

We plan to walk the 22-kilometer stretch to temple eleven today. Unfortunately, there are no temple lodgings between here and eleven. However, there is a henro house inconveniently located off the route. After nailing temple eleven, we must backtrack four kilometers to find our beds. There are no other options unless I want to camp – and I do not.

To make life easier, Takahara-san planned our first few days. She booked last night's stay and tonight's beds. Even though my guidebook says there are no overnight facilities at *Shosanji*, the twelfth temple, she managed to find our space.

For walking-henros, temple lodging is scarce. The rooms are reserved months in advance by tour companies and filled by the busload. It is early in the season, and Takahara-san may have called in a favor.

As a henro-tourist and non-Buddhist, I realize how fortunate I am to enjoy this intimate window into Japanese Buddhist culture. It can't get any more authentic than eating, sleeping, bathing, and participating in a temple's rituals. Last night's fire ceremony blew me away. It will take me some time to unpack the experience in my head.

I'm putting on my shoes when Kassy snatches up Little Miho. She carries my backpack to the front desk and hands it over to a monk. She returns empty-handed and quite satisfied with herself.

"Hey, what's that all about?" I ask.

"Well," she says proudly, "I worked out a deal with the young man. He's going to deliver our packs to the henro house."

"Really? Why?"

"I told him my pack was too heavy, and I needed help."

"Did you pay him?"

"No. He wants to do it. That's how they are here."

"They?" But she doesn't get my meaning.

I am annoyed, and I don't do a good job hiding it. I don't think Kassy is purposefully taking advantage of this kid. The young monk is just a kid. Refusing Kassy's request is probably akin to denying his grandmother or another elder. It feels skeezy to me.

Unlike the Camino, the Shikoku 88 lacks the logistical support to transfer luggage for walking-henros not involved in a tour. Along the Camino, several companies vie to transfer backpacks. The process is simple, but it is not free. Luggage transfer runs from five to seven euros per day, a real bargain when suffering an injury or facing a steep climb.

I do not need my Little Miho transferred. In fact, I enjoy carrying her. She is light and lovely and packed for success. Had Kassy listened to Takahara-san, she too could manage her own load.

I slip off my shoes and tiptoe to the front desk, but the young monk is adamant. Since he must deliver Kassy's pack, he will manage mine as well. I reach in my pocket and grab the day's vending-machine allowance. Although hesitant, I follow my gut and offer him the money. He bows and gratefully accepts. The exchange feels right and different from yesterday's fumble with the old man. This kid did not offer his services as an osettai; therefore, it seems only fitting to compensate.

The walk to temple seven is short, a tad more than one kilometer. I'm so irritated, but Kassy is unfazed. She talks the entire way. I set my jaw and grit my teeth.

Gritting my teeth is a bad habit. The vice is left over from my military days and leads to migraines and admonishments from my dentist. When things did not go my way, as was often the case, I'd clamp my mouth shut to keep my disrespectful words from traveling up the chain-of-command. Now I'm doing it to spare Kassy, my elder.

Honoring one's elders is admirable and an attribute firmly enforced by my parents – but perhaps, too firmly. For me, the practice hasn't always paid off. When befriending women closer to my mother's age, I fail to set proper boundaries. Typically, the friendships end up one-sided, and I find myself contributing more than intended. It's exhausting and unfulfilling.

This has happened with my neighbor back home, a woman 15 years my senior. She lives alone and has a plethora of needs in the gardening and home repair departments. Weekly, she sequesters my husband to fix a leaky faucet, clean the gutters, or replace this or that. Her honey-do list for my man is longer than the ones I write for him. While he worked through her list, I mowed her grass, weeded her garden, and pruned shrubs and trees. But it was never enough.

I'm not saying my neighbor lady is the same as Kassy. In fact, the two women are complete opposites. My neighbor knows what she is doing. She has pushed and pushed, and I always caved. Kassy, on the other hand, seems utterly oblivious. Giving my backpack to the monk was intended to be an act of kindness and talking my ear off all morning is supposed to be an act of camaraderie. She isn't trying to piss me off – but damn, she's doing a fine job of it.

Side-by-side, Kassy and I bow before entering Jurakuji. Once inside, I am disarmed. Irritation drips off me like the rain sheeting down the plastic cover of my thatched hat.

I admire a spindly cherry-blossom tree responsible for my sudden mood-swing. Bursting in showy-pink, the little tree defies the storm. I realize I ought to get over myself.

Kukai built this temple to obtain the ten pleasures, or *juraku*, of Buddhist paradise. Within the gated campus, there is also a Jizo statue said to heal maladies of the eyes. Maybe Jizo can help Kassy with glaucoma.

I drag Kassy over to the statue and introduce her. I also firmly but kindly explain I need alone time for the rest of the day. She says she totally understands, but I detect a hint of panic welling up in her eyes. To ease my guilt, I supply her with ten candles, my spare lighter, and a bundle of incense to get her through the day.

I stumble through the sutras at both halls, just as fast as my tongue will carry me. I collect my stamp and make a hasty exit. I hate to rush, but Kassy is a speed-walker. If I hope to enjoy a moment's peace, I must get a head start.

Temple 8: Kumadaniji

Despite the rain above and the hard blacktop below, I am enjoying the four-kilometer walk to the next temple. Tension leaves my body, and only a dull ache in my jaw remains. I admire the gnarled branches of magnolia, patiently waiting for her turn to bloom.

I step off the road to walk a muddy trail flanking the side of an old barn. The falling rain on the tin roof sounds like the rush of penny-nails dropping into an old coffee can. The reverberations make me think of my grandfather and his barn, and I smile.

Breaking through the gray morning, a swath of sunny daffodils reaches out to greet me, as they always have. As a kid, I scanned the field between my grandparents' house and barn, looking for the first bloom. The early daffodil reassured me that winter's depressive grip would loosen, and spring would usher in another year. I was born the day after the March equinox of 1967 and reborn every year after spring's first blossom.

I'm a scant kilometer from *Kumadaniji* when nature calls. I was in such a stinking hurry to get away from Kassy, I forgot to use the potty at temple seven. And now? Now I am paying the price. It totally serves me right.

For such emergencies, I carry a discrete apparatus. When accessed through an opened zipper, the oval-shaped pink funnel allows me to stand up and pee like a man. After a little practice, it served me well on my last four Caminos. But Shikoku is not the Camino. I'm learning this the hard way. Even in this mildly rural area, there isn't a suitable place to relieve oneself.

Is public peeing legal in Japan? I wouldn't think so. In Okinawa, I've seen many an old man with his back to traffic taking care of business. But I've never seen a younger man, nor a woman.

The constant trickle of rain falling from my thatched hat does not help matters. Biological need trumps social order. I must act swiftly.

Road traffic is slow but steady. I cannot fathom whipping out my little pink-wonder in public, not even with my back turned. So, I find another barn and tuck in behind it.

I'm about to release when I hear a little cough behind me. I nearly leap out of my rain jacket, which is thankfully covering the device and my lady parts. Keeping my back to the cough, I look over my shoulder.

A small lady in red galoshes holds out an opened umbrella of clear vinyl. "Osettai," she says.

I don't need an umbrella, but I take it and thank her kindly. I want to give her an osamefuda, but my other hand is tucked beneath my rain jacket and currently engaged. I know she knows. She covers her mouth with her hand to conceal a smile. We exchange bows, and she leaves me to my exploding bladder.

Back on the trail and accident-free, I take a narrow path leading to the temple gate. The idyllic approach to Kumadaniji takes my breath away. This is the isolated serenity I had hoped to find back at temple one.

Mossy stone walls rise to frame the lane, and the twisted branches of dormant fruit trees arch in a lonely tunnel. Crumbles of worn asphalt, pocked from the wash of floodwater, slides beneath my feet.

I am alone. All alone. No dog. No kids. No students. No husband. No Kassy. Only me. A comforting blanket of solitude falls around my shoulders. I gather it up and wrap it snuggly around me – separating myself from the world.

At the purification fountain, a solitary henro nods to me and shuffles off toward the main hall. He doesn't ring the bell to announce his presence, and neither do I. In unspoken agreement, I hang back to give him space.

I climb the steps of a two-story, wooden pagoda, silvered by the progressing seasons. The wrap-around lanai is planked in old-growth cedar, or maybe cypress. Each plank is wider than both of my feet set heel-to-toe. My maternal ancestors were loggers, but I've never seen such timber. I squat and quench my urge to trace the wood-grain patterns smoothed by the footfalls of time.

Kukai founded this temple by carving a large statue of *Senju Kannon*. The deity has one-thousand arms. In the palm of each hand is an eye to see all the suffering and pain in the world. Her visions assist her mission of mercy and salvation for all beings.

In my temporary vow of silence, I move through the rituals without a sound. Syllable by syllable, the sutras flow freely in my head, and the inner-chant gains momentum.

I complete my tasks in front of the second hall and find my way to the stamp office. An old woman, half-asleep, extends her hand to collect my book. I slide the coins across the leather desk pad. The soft thud of three red stamps is followed by the whisper of her calligraphy brush against parchment. She places a square of newspaper over her mark before closing the book and handing it back to me.

She stands and reaches into the pocket of her apron. She holds out three wrapped pieces of candy and offers me a gapped grin. Without a word, I return her smile, bow, and accept her gift.

Temple 9: Horinji

The short walk to the next temple is a bit over two kilometers. The route shoulders the road, flanking rice paddies, fields of kale, garden plots, greenhouses, dilapidated sheds, and old barns. Still relishing the hush of Kumadaniji, I settle into my stride and enjoy the rural countryside.

I grew up on a farm in Oregon. The property was settled by my great-grandfather, and my grandfather lived on the farm his entire life. My father built our home on the other side of the acreage. As a kid, I literally went *over the fields and through the woods* to my grandmother's house. Now, my oldest son and two grandkids live on the original farmstead, with my parents still on the other side.

My family raised cows, pigs, sheep, horses, goats, chickens, rabbits… You name it. In the spring, we planted an enormous vegetable garden. In the winter, I dabbled in a small greenhouse. I lived my first 18 years on the farm but spent the final five desperate to escape. I wanted the hell out of there and joined the Army to make my getaway.

Enlisting wasn't the best strategy, but I stuck it out for 24 years. Now, I can't help but laugh at my overly-dramatic younger self. No matter where the military sent me in the world, I sought out the familiar comforts of forest and farm. Except for my troubled-teens, I've always found peace in wide-open pastures and tall timbers.

And that's how I'm feeling today – content and perfectly at home in my surroundings. If not for my conical hat and white henro gear, I could almost forget I am on a small island in Japan. For me, agriculture makes the world feel small.

Up ahead, amongst the rice paddies, I see a walled compound. This must be temple nine. I'm nearly there. Despite the rain, my pace is strong and consistent. I have another 18 or 19 kilometers before I'm done for the day, and the generous temple-breakfast is already spent. I haven't seen a café or convenience store all morning, and my feet ache — but only a little bit.

The barefoot evening at temple six, along with the morning's walk on blacktop, has taken a toll on my heels. Battling plantar fasciitis is all about arch-support and cushion. Normally, I wear orthotic flip-flops instead of going barefoot. Takahara-san allowed me to wear them in her house, but I knew better than to even ask at temple six.

At the weathered temple gate, I notice several hand-made straw sandals lashed to the wooden rails housing the larger-than-life temple guardians. As it turns out, I'm in luck! *Horinji* temple is regularly visited by folks wishing to cure ailments of feet and legs. I'll be sure to say a prayer for my barking dogs. A little divine intervention may do wonders because sometimes, good gear is not enough.

I'm also pleased to find a small shop adjacent to the temple. It's ten in the morning, but I need lunch. My stomach rumbles, but the pickings are slim. The shop is more of a farm stand, and the farm stand is more of a bake sale with bananas and a vending machine. A woman stands behind a single table of plastic-wrapped mochi and other sweets I bet are stuffed with red bean paste. I stave off my hunger, at least for now, and cross the street to the temple gate.

I bow, enter the compound, and find the purification fountain. While this is only my ninth temple, I'm sensing a strong dragon theme. I saw this same little guy spitting fiercely into a few other troughs along the way. The temples are already starting to run together, and I have another 79 to go!

Like most temples on the Shikoku loop, Kukai carved the main deity, but this temple is unique. Kukai depicted *Shaka Nyorai* in a rare, reclining position. Typically, the deity is standing or sitting in the lotus position. Horinji enshrines the only reclining Shaka Nyorai on the island. Unfortunately, I don't get to meet him because the statue is on display once every five years, and this is not the year.

According to legend, Kukai founded this temple after hearing stories of an enormous, white snake living in the forest. The snake was known to protect Buddhists from harm. On my walk here, I passed several posted signs warning of pit-vipers, and I am not a fan. Perhaps, I could be charmed by a Buddha-loving serpent.

I exit the temple and return to the bake sale. I buy a banana, a bottle of Aquarius, and a plastic tray holding three half-moons wrapped in a fuzzy green leaf. The food makes me think of tacos. I don't want to deal with trash on the way to temple ten, so I stand next to the drink machine and eat my Japanese tacos.

I don't know if I'm supposed to eat the leaf, so I take a cautious nibble. It's hairy on my tongue but also quite tasty. Not sweet but not savory either. I peel away a larger piece and try again. It's refreshing and familiar, but I'm sure I've not eaten this leaf before. I would remember. It tastes a tad like lemon balm and probably belongs to the mint family. I bite into the mini-taco – the leaf pairs nicely with the vinegar-seasoned rice and salty bonito-flake filling. Bonito-flakes are slivers of dried fish. I eat them, but like tofu, I never crave them. However, I'll pick bonito over the starchy-sweet of red bean paste, any day.

The tacos are gone before my hunger. I wolf down the banana and buy another for the trail. Mildly satiated, I set off, hoping to find more food down the road.

Temple 10: Kirihataji

Following the quick pitstop for lunch, I reenter the reassurance of wide-open space. I feel my shoulders relax, and my legs grow loose and springy. Rice paddies and greenhouses stretch as far as the eye can see. Everything is as it should be.

The daffodils, and old barns, and the rain intertwine and repaint my childhood home. Disembodied, I hover above and see the family farm with new eyes. It's far from the imagined hell-hole I was once desperate to escape, but it doesn't call me to return, not at all. I also don't want to return to my house in Washington, either. I've been abroad for five years, going on six. I can't stay away forever. Or can I?

I'm adrift – a dandelion-seed carried by the wind. Homeless. Not homeless in a physical way. And not in a financial way. I'm homeless in a social and familial way. And, of course, by choice. I've loved it, but I'm weary. The need to replant is heavy in my bones.

Steeping in memory and contemplating the meaning of home, I make my way to *Kirihataji*, the tenth temple. My grandma and grandpa feel closer than ever. Last night's fire ceremony must have conjured my ancestors to walk with me today.

The fire ceremony was a foreign experience in a foreign language, but I didn't feel left out. In some ways, it was like attending a Catholic mass along the Camino. My Spanish is oodles better than my Japanese, but I cannot keep up with the clip of normal Spanish conversation nor the speed of a sermon. I'm not Catholic. I don't take communion, but I do feel included, involved, and affected. This is how I left the ceremony last night. Included. Involved. And deeply moved.

Before the ceremony, I met with Kassy to help her prepare. Like me, she received a craft kit containing a camphor branch, a pink tag to list an ancestor and date of death, a blank osamefuda to make a wish for herself, and a cedar plank to write a wish for another. But she had not understood the young monk's instructions. I wasn't exactly sure I knew what I was doing, but I rested in the comfort of being wrong together.

We were in her sleeping cell when the special gong sounded, calling us to report. Dressed in our henro-whites, we worked our way through the paper-walled maze to the main temple. We were most certainly on time, but everyone was seated and settled in. A few were already deep in prayer. Arriving on time by American standards must mean arriving late by Japanese standards. It won't happen again.

In the dim candlelight, we moved to the back of the room and found seats conveniently located next to a kerosene heater. The air, heavy with incense and oily kerosene fumes, lined my nostrils and mouth in a sticky rose and sandalwood perfume.

It was an intimate affair, about a dozen of us. Gone were the elbow-to-elbow henro from the dining room. Bianca, our dinner companion, was not in attendance. Could it have been by invitation only? And if so, how did Kassy and I score the invites. My guess is our guardian angel, Takahara-san, pulled a few strings.

The young monk from the front desk led us through the *Heart sutra*. Like big dummies, Kassy and I didn't bring our guidebooks with the sutras printed in a recognizable alphabet. Even after chanting all day long, only a few lines imprinted to memory. Instead, we moved our lips, chiming in whenever we could. "Han-nya ha-ra mitta..." We moved in and out like the tide, "mu shiki mu ju so gyo shiki mu..." It was far from perfect, but at least we were able to participate.

After a few rounds of chant, the young monk introduced an elderly priest. I didn't understand a word the priest uttered, but I didn't need to. The tender intonation of his words and thoughtful gestures communicated the blessing. Despite the chilly temple air, I grew quite warm. It wasn't just from the kerosene heater. I glanced at Kassy. Her eyes were shut, and tears streamed down her face. She felt it too, whatever it was, and was deeply moved.

After the priest's blessing, another monk sat with his back toward us, creating warm tones on a set of brass bowls. The ethereal reverberations tickled my ears and sent a tingle up my spine. I closed my eyes and invited the pleasant sensation to flood my body.

The old priest shepherded us behind the altar. We followed him down a passageway connecting to a cave. In the cave, a small fire crackled, sending great leaps of light up the dark walls. The smell of smoke reminded me of a thousand campfires of my youth.

A smattering of candles illuminated a stream bending around large rocks and small islands of sediment. The stream was silty, like that of a glacier. And the water was an opaque powder-blue.

A monk handed me a small, wooden boat with a candle attached. I observed another henro roll his osamefuda like a cigarette, wedge the paper into a groove on the bow, light the candle, and set his boat afloat. I rolled my wish, repeated his process, and watched the swift water carry away my heart's desire.

I followed the parade of henro downstream, shuffling in the dark for secure footing. The group halted alongside a peninsula jutting out into the stream. One by one, each henro walked the narrow path out to the end of the peninsula and back.

I anxiously awaited my turn. In the dark, my balance is terrible. In the daylight, vertigo is manageable because I find a focal point to keep me stable. I rely way too much on my eyes. I didn't want a wet foot, and I really didn't want to fall in and contaminate the sacred stream.

When it was finally my turn, I hesitated. A heavy hand pressed on my shoulder, and I turned to meet the kind eyes of the old priest. He nodded and sent me on my way with a gentle push. A few steps in, I could still feel his hand. Teetering my way to the end, I squatted amongst the camphor branches adorned with pink-paper tags from henro before me. In the dim glow, I read the names and death dates of my grandparents. I sent up a quick prayer, planted my branch in the sand, and headed back across the peninsula. Steady as I've ever been.

Kassy was the last to plant her camphor. Her tag held the name and death date of her late husband. Mike and Kassy lived together for years, but he asked her to marry after receiving a terminal diagnosis of throat cancer. They lived in matrimony for one month before he died.

Kassy married and raised children with her first husband. She confessed that in her lifetime, she has loved many. However, Mike was her one true love – her soulmate. She has a boyfriend now. He was Mike's best friend. While they mourn the loss together, nothing fills the void left by her true love's passing.

When Kassy returned to the shore, the crowd shuffled off toward the flames. I hung back, but only for a moment. Neither of us wanted to be left in the dark.

When it was my turn at the fire pit, I tossed in the cedar plank, carrying the purple-inked wish for my sons. The fire crackled and popped. Flames licked and devoured the wood, and the prayer for my sons went up in smoke.

My daydream about last night has taken me off course. I haven't seen a henro marker for quite some time. I whip out my phone and punch in *Kirihataji*. As a rule, I try not to way-find via phone because the directions stick me to known roads. I prefer to follow the henro way that sometimes cuts atop narrow berms separating rice paddies or meanders canal-side or through orchards and beside garden plots. I cannot wander all day. So, I'm thankful for a back-up plan.

Fortunately, I haven't wandered far. I cross a busy intersection to a quiet lane. Within a few hundred paces, I'm at the temple gate.

Kirihataji is famous for a legend about a beautiful young woman. When Kukai was in the area, completing a seven-day regimen of ascetic training, he found himself needing to replace his threadbare clothing. He asked a young weaver for some old cloth to wrap about his body. Instead, she gifted him with a beautiful, new kimono.

In return for her kindness, Kukai granted the girl's wish to be ordained as a Buddhist nun. Newly ordained, the young weaver set out on her mission of compassion and mercy. Miraculously, she was transformed into the deity *Kannon*, devoting all eternity to saving souls.

Temple 11: Fujiidera

The nine-and-a-half-kilometer jaunt along the rural but busy road to Fujiidera is boring. I amuse myself by trying to interpret several hand-painted signs around ditches and creeks. The cartoonish images include Japanese characters, but the writing is illegible for my translator app. So, I'm on my own. My best guess is these signs are meant to warn parents about the dangers of allowing children to fish or play near culverts or other water-related hazards.

A little less amusing is the multiple signs warning of the *Mamushi*. The Japanese Mamushi is a pit viper. Along with the Okinawan *Habu*, these vipers are the deadliest snakes in Japan. The advice in online forums encouraged me not to be overly concerned, but my own research has made me wary. Annually, three-thousand people in Japan suffer bites. Victims usually require a week of hospitalization, followed by a month of outpatient care. Severe bites require intensive care. The viper claims about ten lives per year, but common side-effects of the venom, even with treatment, include kidney failure, loss of vision, and paralysis. No thanks!

The Mamushi prefers a diet of rodents, making farmland the preferred real-estate. The vipers hunt from the camouflage cover of fallen leaves, striking out at hapless prey unfortunate enough to scamper near the hiding spot. The plan is to circumvent tall grasses and debris. My hiking-poles double as weapons, but this is where the longer Kukai-staff would come in handy.

Like many road signs in Japan, the snake warning is ridiculously cute – or *kawaii*. In the orange grove near temple four, I studied a couple of equally adorable warnings regarding bees. Smiling cartoon wasps with long stingers suggested I tread lightly. What is so cute about wasps? Or vipers, for that matter?

Unlike the wasp warnings, the viper signs are partially in English. On a white backdrop in red lettering is the word *CAUTION*. Below the red lettering, Japanese characters translate to *Mamushi Viper*. To the right of the characters is an adorable caricature of an innocent-looking, big-eyed snake with polka-dots. It's hard to take the warning seriously, but I most certainly do.

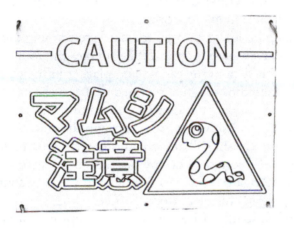

The wind and the sideways rain render my conical hat utterly useless. The wind blows beneath the brim and picks the hat off my head. The gauze string tied beneath my chin strangles me with each gust. The osettai umbrella of clear vinyl is now my most treasured item. I use it as a shield to battle my way through the sideways rain.

My feet slosh inside my shoes, and the rain penetrates the water-resistant fabric of my hiking-pants. I'm suddenly thankful Kassy arranged a backpack transfer. Dry clothes sound lovely. Looks like I'll be eating crow for supper, a dish I've eaten many times before.

Temple eleven is tucked at the base of a steep mountain-pass leading to the twelfth temple. The pass is heavily forested and promises to be soft underfoot. After walking the roadside all day, I'm looking forward to the change of scenery.

I'm cold and wet and approach the purification fountain with trepidation. I don't want to pour cold water over my already wrinkled palms. With pruned-fingers, I clutch the ladle and get to work.

Long puddles of standing water are framing each side of the walkway to the main hall. It takes me four tries, but I finally light my candle and place it in the glass enclosure. I attempt to ignite my incense from the candle flame, but my candle goes out. I try again but with no luck. I give up and shiver my way through the sutras.

At the Daishi hall, my chattering teeth won't allow me to shape the sounds. I do my best and offer a stiff-body bow. "Arigato gozaimasu." I head toward the stamp office, hoping my meager efforts suffice.

In the stamp office, an old man sleeps in front of the flames of a kerosene heater. I clear my throat, but the sound does not rouse him. I don't want to frighten him, so I whisper, "Konichiwa. Konichiwa." One eye opens, and then the other. He shakes his head to free himself from the grips of the z-monster.

The old man stamps my book, then dips his brush, and makes a single stroke on the page. He pauses. Dips. And makes another stroke. His movements are so slow, I fear he will fall back to sleep before the final flourish of his brush. Thankfully, he doesn't.

He looks out his window at the downpour and then examines the drowned rat I have become. "Taxi?" he suggests.

I thought he'd never ask! Folding my hands in prayer, I reply, "Hai. Taxi. Hai."

It's around three in the afternoon when the cab driver dumps me in front of the henro-house. Unlike Takahara's home, this place looks like a hostel. Also, unlike Takahara's house, the hostel is closed. A note in Japanese and English informs me I have a full hour to kill. I am miserably cold, but I perk right up when I see a 7-Eleven on the other side of the busy street.

When I was a kid, my parents invested in a 7-Eleven franchise store. In my teens, I spent weekends and many summers working behind the cash register. The store became somewhat of a second home. I'm comfortable in the convenience of a convenience store.

I've never seen a 7-Eleven on Okinawa. Instead, Lawsons or Family Marts dot every corner. I find it peculiar that so many business names on Okinawa are written in English. This speaks volumes about the saturation of US troops on the island.

Inside the store, I wrap my cold hands around a can of hot green tea. I have time to kill. I wander up and down the aisles, pleased as punch to be out of the rain.

Tonight's lodging does not include dinner. While I loved the experience of the communal temple-supper, I'm looking forward to a more casual affair. I hunt for a snack to hold me over.

Later, after Kassy arrives, I'll introduce her to the wonders of a Japanese convenience store. All the little snacks and tidy packages of wrapped sushi and sashimi and rice balls are exhilarating to new eyes.

I find a display of *Onigiri*. These are triangles of rice wrapped in crisp seaweed. The packaging is brilliant. The entire triangle is wrapped in cellophane. Another layer of film separates the rice from the seaweed. This layer keeps the seaweed wrapper crisp. If opened correctly, the inner layer magically slips away with the outer. It took me about three months to figure out how to open one correctly, but the effort was life-changing.

Rice triangles are my go-to snacks to get me through long evenings of lecturing. I like the ones filled with smoked salmon, tuna, or shrimp and mayonnaise. I usually eat one during the first break but then must brush my teeth before returning to the classroom. Nobody wants a professor with fish-breath or seaweed stuck between her teeth.

My bank card won't work in convenience stores in Okinawa, but I read in an online forum to use 7-elevens and post offices along the Shikoku loop. I am not yet in need of yen, but I'm curious. I give it a go. To my delight, the transaction may be conducted in English. Success!

I am carrying way more money than usual. Since I wasn't sure about bank card success, I withdrew the equivalent of six-hundred American, hoping the amount would get me through this first section. I never carry much cash in Europe or the United States, but here in Japan, I'm not at all worried about muggers or pick-pocketers. I'm chilled out, and I feel safe. It's uplifting to trust human-kind again.

By comparison, mainland Japan's crime rate is refreshingly low and almost nonexistent on the island of Shikoku. Okinawa is similar, but whenever there is trouble, it almost always involves an American GI.

Driving through the military gates to work, I often witness the peaceful protests of Okinawan citizens. They quietly hold signs in English, so we are sure to get the message. The protest signs read, *No Marines, No murder,* and *No Soldiers, No rape.*

Having served as an Army soldier for 19 years and an officer in the Coast Guard for another five, the Okinawan conflicts make me feel ashamed. I'm not embarrassed about my country nor my service. Instead, I am mortified by how we often behave, and I feel sorry because the signs speak the truth.

I huddle in the doorway of Henro-house *Channel-Kahn* until a lovely, young woman pulls up in a baby-blue Volkswagen beetle and unlocks the door. She invites me inside and makes me a cup of tea. I'm pleased to see Little Miho perched high and dry on a chair beneath the stairwell. The idea of dry socks thrills me.

The young lady gives me a tour of the hostel and shows me to my bunk upstairs. There are two four-person dorms, one for women and one for men, and one other room meant for a couple. The bathrooms are across the hall, but the shower is outside on the fire-escape platform – which is a touch bizarre.

My bunk is much more than a bed. It is a luxury sleeping pod complete with privacy curtains, reading light, electrical outlets, and a USB port to charge my phone. It's like a little fort! I can't wait to climb in and try it out, but first, I must hit the shower.

I'm downstairs enjoying a cup of tea when Kassy emerges from a cab. She is soaked to the bone. Evidently, even her "good gear" failed to overcome this bad weather. I meet her at the door and help her out of her wet parka. She is shivering too hard to manage zippers and shoelaces.

After another cup of tea, Kassy and I tuck into her sleeping pod to warm up and share the day's adventure. There is plenty of room for both of us to sit upright and chat. It's a lot of fun and makes me feel like a little girl away at camp.

Kassy seems in need of company, and after my day of solitude, I'm ready to engage. Besides, I was a bit of a jerk to her this morning, and for that, I am truly sorry.

I'm trying to teach Kassy to use her new iPhone. A month before flying to Japan, she owned an old flip-phone. Like many older adults, she has slipped into the great chasm of the digital divide. She holds power in her hand, but she has no idea how to wield it.

She jokes about the impatience and impertinence of her grandchildren. "You need to give that phone back, Nan," said her granddaughter. "You don't deserve an iPhone." Kassy laughs it off, but I don't. I don't find this kind of disrespectful bullshit funny at all. Her grandkids should have helped her.

First, I show her how to create a friend request on Facebook. Kassy has a Facebook profile and a handful of friends her daughter arranged, but she never learned the process herself. Next, I post a couple of photos I snapped of her, along with a selfie of Takahara-san back at the first temple. I tag her in the post, and in mere moments, her friends and family start commenting. Her phone pings multiple times, carrying the responses of loved ones who are terribly thankful to learn she is alive and well.

Kassy's eyes brim with tears, but she shakes it off and says, "How is this all possible?"

"Technology, Baby. Technology." I show her a few more tricks before hunger gets the best of us. We take a training break and head out to find some grub.

Temple 12: Shosanji

Last night, a Japanese henro joined us in our dorm. Her name is Haruka, and she is about the cutest thing I've ever seen. The urge to hug her was overwhelming. Like Kassy, I'm a huggee-person, but I've learned to exercise restraint while in Japan.

Haruka is 23, the same age as my youngest son and the same age as Rochelle, the young woman I met earlier at temple three. Like Rochelle, Haruka recently graduated from university. She spent her last year abroad in Michigan, but she's home now, living near Tokyo. She misses her American boyfriend and her college pals. Like me, and like Rochelle, Haruka is trying to figure out where she belongs.

She shrugged and said, "Where is my home? America or Japan? I am somewhere between."

I sighed. "Trust me, kid. I know the feeling." She moved in for a hug, and I did not hesitate.

In the morning, a shuttle drops Kassy and me at temple eleven. Haruka must return to temple nine. Yesterday was her first day on the trail. The same old man who picked me up the day before offered her a ride outside the first temple. Less than a kilometer into her pilgrimage, the man chauffeured her all day. However, when arriving at temple nine, the stamp office was closed. Kassy and I had wondered how the lucky girl arrived so fresh-faced and dry when we were drowned rats.

Today's stretch up and over a mountain pass to temple twelve will surely take me all day. The first elevation gain is 600 meters. The trail dips 100 meters and climbs back up to 800. Then it drops back down 400 meters before ending back up at 700. It's going to be a roller-coaster of a day, but I'm looking forward to the thrill.

We are off to an early start. We left the hostel before seven, but not without another debacle over backpacks. Again, without my approval, Kassy arranged for our bags to be transported. This time, the bags were to be shipped via a local carrier.

I was the last downstairs. Kassy and the shuttle driver were waiting in the van out front. When I checked out, the lovely young woman reminded me I still owed for the bag delivery. With my pack strapped on my back, I was rightfully confused.

"Four-thousand yen," She announced, writing the amount on a scrap of paper to make sure I understood.

"What? Wait! No," I tapped my crossed index fingers together. "No, I carry my pack."

She paused for a moment, trying to formulate a response. She punched the keys on her phone and handed it over to read: *Reservation cannot be canceled. Channel-Khan has paid for pickup.*

"But I don't have a reservation."

Pointing to Kassy's blue pack by the door, the woman said, "Your mama make a reservation."

I apologized for the misunderstanding and passed her the money and my pack. What else could I do? The current exchange rate is about a hundred and ten yen per U.S. dollar. To estimate, I dropped two zeros. So, basically, I blew 40 bucks.

Rain or shine, flat road, or mountain pass, $40 is too much. I could have caught a cab to temple twelve for the same price and tossed my bag in the trunk. I don't consider myself a cheapskate, but I am sensible. Spending that kind of cash makes no sense to me.

I wanted to strangle Kassy, but I did not. Instead, I climbed inside the shuttle and kept my mouth shut, gritting my teeth all the way. I'll talk to her tonight after the day's hike up Burning Mountain has burned away all my fire. There is no sense ruining the day. After all, it is only money.

Kassy and I walk through the temple grounds, negotiating puddles of brown water. She didn't make it here yesterday. Instead, she grabbed a cab at temple ten and headed straight to the hostel.

Temple eleven is unique and worth a second look. It is one of three Zen Buddhist temples along the route. In 815, Kukai carved *Yakushi Nyorai* and founded the temple. Yakushi Nyorai is the Buddha of healing, and he holds an apothecary jar in his hand.

Fire, neglect, and war have destroyed much of Shikoku's history. Like most temples along the route, this one has been replaced a few times. The current buildings were constructed in 1860.

It's no longer raining, but the grounds are flooded. I stop in front of the glass enclosure at the main hall and find a lone candle. It's exactly where I left it yesterday. Could I have been the day's sole visitor? That would explain the sleeping old man in the stamp office.

In yesterday's downpour, I did a shoddy job. So, I dab the wick dry, light it, and then light the incense sticks. Kassy bums a candle but shows off her new box of incense she picked up yesterday. She also bought a Kukai-staff. So, the walking-stick and incense spoke to her, but the candles kept quiet? She's an odd lady.

We hit the trail together. The incline is steep and immediate. So much for a warmup! Within 15 minutes, I'm stripping off layers and panting like a dog. Kassy is unfazed. She is a little nanny-goat springing up the trail and leaving me to eat her dust.

How does she do it? Kassy is 20 years my senior! Well, I'll be damned. I dig deep and try to catch her. I'm not going to be outpaced by a woman as old as my mother.

She's waiting for me as I round the bend of the umpteenth switchback. I try to control my breathing by stopping and pretending to be overly interested in the bark of a large cedar tree. To buy time, I pull out my phone and snap a few photos.

I point out a beautiful camellia bush. Native to Japan, the red flowers and glossy, dark foliage grow leggy and wild beneath the canopy of trees. My maternal grandmother kept a hedge of camellias, wrapping a privacy-screen around the front of her house. The showy pink and red flowers reminded me of roses. The blossoms drew me near but always left me disappointed. How could flowers so lovely lack a fragrance?

The cool forest air is damp and soothes my burning lungs. I feel ridiculous. Apparently, I'm not as fit as I thought. It's true. I don't get out and walk as much as I used to. Island life on Okinawa has made me lazy. It's humid and hot all year long, and I'm not a fan of trudging down city sidewalks next to heavy traffic. I hit the beach and swim a few times per week, but this obviously has done nothing to bolster uphill endurance.

Kassy and I leapfrog up the trail all morning long. She stops and waits at a bend or a fork. When I catch up, she takes off again. Clearly, I cannot keep up. Pride aside, I don't really want to keep up.

I like being in the forest alone. I love the bird song, and the trickle of little streams, and the rush of bamboo. There are so many beautiful sounds – sounds I would miss if walking alongside Kassy.

I stop at a small, concrete shrine housing a stone Jizo. The tiny statue is dressed in a soft-pink, knit hat and a floral bib with dark pink trim. I touch the cool cheek of Jizo and wish I had a piece of candy or a trinket to offer.

Switchback after never-ending switchback, I make my way up the first elevation gain. Two hours have passed, and the trail offers peek-a-boo vistas of the valley below. My body stops fighting, and the going gets easier.

Atop the first summit, Kassy waits in a trailside henro-hut. She looks amazing. A pink flush of exertion gives her a dewy glow, taking a full ten years off her face. I snap her photo – a vision of vitality and contentment.

I'm impressed, and I can't hide my envy. "Damn, girl. You're a monster!" She just smiles.

For the next kilometer, I enjoy a narrow trail cutting across the ridgeline. The wide-open valley below makes me feel like Godzilla. I am on top of the world.

The path widens as it descends. Kassy and I walk side-by-side, chit-chatting about our families. We talk about motherhood, a topic we know well. We talk about our own mothers. My relationship with my mother is complicated, and I don't feel like sharing. So, Kassy tells me about her mother, Florence.

Before she died, Florence suffered a cocktail of Alzheimer's and dementia. She hadn't uttered a sound in over two years. "It's like she had forgotten all of the words," says Kassy.

Florence lived with Kassy's older sister. Kassy assisted whenever possible. "She required constant care. Feeding, bathing, you name it…" says Kassy.

"I was never close with my mother," She admits. "I could never talk to her." Kassy slows her pace to a relaxing stroll.

"During my divorce, I was desperate to talk to someone." She continues, "Since mom couldn't speak, I poured my heart out, thinking she could just listen."

Kassy had finished spoon-feeding her mom a bowl of oatmeal, and her mother was still slumped over the dirty dish. "Mom," Kassy started. "Mom, I have a big problem."

To Kassy's surprise, Florence lifted her head. "Problem?" Florence grunted. "We all got problems."

It was the first time in two years Florence had spoken. It was also her last. "I sat there, contemplating the size of my problems," says Kassy. "And then I compared them with the problems in my mother's world."

Kassy raises her arms in the air. "Here was this woman – a woman who could no longer feed herself or handle daily hygiene. A woman dependent on the kindness of her daughters…"

Kassy stops walking and pauses for effect. "Well, I decided right then and there that divorce really was not much of a problem at all."

We grow quiet. I assume Kassy is thinking about Florence because I certainly am. I can't imagine submitting to that brand of helplessness and vulnerability.

In our stillness, I ponder my own aging process. I don't like how my skin is losing elasticity. There is another crease forming above my top lip. My joints are stiffer than they used to be. Arthritis made a home in my hips and knees, and I'm fighting a battle with the bathroom scale, and every now and again, I must pluck a stray eyebrow sprouting randomly from my chin.

But honestly, I have nothing to complain about. Kassy's mom summed it up best. "Problem? We all got problems." Damn straight, Florence. Damn straight.

We pick our way down a rocky trail to a clearing in the forest. Hopping rock to rock, we cross a shallow creek and come to a small, abandoned temple. I jangle the bell in case the deity is still in-house. I'm a little more than surprised when an elderly gentleman in hiking clothes appears around the corner.

"Konichiwa," I smile and wave.

The man draws near and places both hands upon his chest. He bows slightly and says, "Yoshimado."

I bow and tell him my name, and Kassy follows. She asks him a question about the old temple, but he doesn't seem to understand.

Yoshimado-san shows us a length of bamboo pipe. Water trickles into a smooth bowl worn into a boulder. From the bowl, the water overflows into another length of bamboo, followed by yet another bowl. This pattern continues downstream to a henro-hut in the clearing.

I nod my head, "How clever!"

Yoshimado-san says, "Good water."

I take up a ladle. I'm hesitant, and I have giardia on the brain, but I suppose a small sip can't hurt. I catch the water from the bamboo pipe, pour it from the ladle into my palm, and wet my mouth. It's icy-cold and minty. Perhaps, the spring burbles beneath a patch of wild mint before making its way to the forest floor.

I hand the ladle to Kassy. She dips from the bowl, drinks directly from the tin ladle, and nods her head in appreciation before taking another gulp. This time, she swishes the water around and spits right back into the bowl. Yoshimado shakes his head, and my cheeks redden.

To redirect, I point to the logo on his khaki cap, a well-known brand of Japanese hiking gear. "Montebell," I say and follow with a thumbs-up.

He touches the logo and says, "Montebell," and gives me a double-thumbs-up. It's not much, but I'm satisfied with the exchange.

Apparently, Yoshimado is a caretaker of the trail. He carries a clear garbage bag of trail-trash. Amongst the day's pickings, I recognize a Snickers wrapper and the iconic red and white of a Coca-Cola can.

He leads us to the henro-hut and invites us to stay the night. We shake our heads. Kassy shouts, "We are going to temple twelve!" Swinging her arms and lifting her legs, she pantomimes marching uphill. Yoshimado nods in understanding. Kassy seems pleased with yet another successful exchange.

The man reaches out and gently clutches one of my braids. My creepo-meter arcs into the red. There is no reason he should feel compelled to touch me. I've done nothing to encourage his familiarity. From my limited experience with Japanese culture, his behavior is highly unusual. I don't want to make a scene, so I smile and take a step backward, freeing my hair from his hand.

Kassy doesn't pick up my vibe. Instead, she engages him in a game of 20-trail-questions he clearly cannot understand. For some reason, she is suddenly acting all freaked out about getting lost.

I don't understand Kassy's newfound concern. We've had no trouble. None. The trail is worn and well-marked. Maybe it's a pride thing, and quite possibly my imagination, but it burns me how some women shift into helpless mode once in the company of men.

Meanwhile, I'm giving her the signal to move out. Gesticulating wildly behind our new pal's back, I cut a knife-hand across my own throat. Daffy-Kassy totally misinterprets my signals and offers me a friendly wave. What a little dork!

Yoshimado turns around and grins. He pulls out his phone and a pair of reading glasses. It takes him a while to get the translation, but then he says, "Your face is a peach. Your tooth is a pearl."

I take a step back and scowl. Ho-l-y shit. This old dude is hitting on me. And what's with the pick-up lines? *My tooth is a pearl?* Which tooth?

In a different setting, I'd probably burst out laughing. But I am not amused. Without a word, I turn and head up the trail. Kassy had better catch a clue or be stuck alone in the forest with Uncle Pervy.

Of course, I don't get far before the little nanny-goat lopes up alongside me. And she's brought a friend. Terrific.

The trail crosses a mountain road where a silver van is parked. This must be his vehicle. Yoshimado says something, but I keep walking. I hear the van door open and close, and I wait for the engine to crank.

The trail inclines steeply, and the nanny-goat springs ahead. I try not to look back toward the van. After the safety of a couple of switchbacks, curiosity gets the better of me.

I turn around on the narrow trail, and Yoshimado runs smack into me. I yelp and lose my balance. He grabs my arm to brace me, but my thatched-hat tumbles down the trail. While I'm grateful he saved me from a fall, I'm also highly annoyed.

Like a faithful Labrador, he hustles down the hill to fetch my hat. I wasn't about to go back down after it. The thing has been more trouble than it's worth.

Polite but not inviting, I render a curt, "arigato gozaimasu." I extend a hand to receive my hat, but he clutches it to his chest. Apparently, he's going to carry it for me. But for how long? It's at least another three hours to temple twelve.

Trail chivalry aside, I'm stuck walking with Uncle Pervy. Kassy is nowhere in sight. A prickle of fear tries to settle in my gut, but I fight it off. I will not be afraid of this old fart. I used to be frightened all the time, but that was pre-Camino. After walking the Camino de Santiago, I buried my bogeymen – at least for the most part.

I lengthen my stride, but it does not help. Why can I not move any faster? Faithfully, Yoshimado follows behind. My pace is slow enough for him to punch into his phone and ask questions.

"Married?" he says.

"Hai! Very Married." I don't turn around.

"Children?"

"Hai! So many children."

"Do you enjoy Japan?"

"Hai! I enjoy Japan."

"Do you like me?"

I say nothing and keep walking.

Yoshimado tries again. "Do you like me?"

I don't know the Japanese word for *no*. While I know the hand gesture, I am not turning around or letting go of my hiking-poles. I say nothing, and he seems to get the picture. We continue in awkward silence.

Ahead, I see blue bits of sky indicating another summit. I work my way through a few more switchbacks and find Kassy standing at the base of a flight of stairs. Yoshimado follows us up the stairs to a statue of Kukai set before a mighty oak.

I take advantage of the photo-op to gain custody of my hat. Instead of handing it to me, Yoshimado puts it on my head and pats my cheek. I step back, and I don't thank him. He is really getting under my skin.

Kassy snaps my picture, and I take one of her. Without permission, I covertly snap one of Yoshimado. I am not afraid of him, but I am wary. Something in my mother-bones wants to warn Haruka and Rochelle. I exchanged contact information with the two girls, hoping to meet up again on the trail. I'll send each a message and include his photo. While I don't know Rochelle's whereabouts, Haruka will pass this way tomorrow. I don't want either of them caught off guard.

Kassy plops on a bench beneath a covered pavilion. She peels an orange and offers me half. I sit next to her and hold up two seaweed-wrapped rice triangles. "Take your pick!" She grabs the tuna, and I am happily left with salmon.

Our lunch break should be Yoshimado's exit cue. But that's wishful thinking. Instead, he sits beside me and fishes a small banana from the pocket of his hiking vest.

After eating the last bite of banana, Yoshimado stands and points down the trail. Finally! This *is* going to end well, after all. He opens his garbage bag and offers to haul away our trash. I appreciate the gesture, toss a wrapper in the bag, but avoid eye-contact.

Kassy envelops him in a long embrace, cooing how he is her trail angel. Earlier today, she told me a hug must last at least ten seconds to transfer energy. I don't know what in the hell this means, but she clings to him for what feels like an awkward 30 seconds.

He turns to me and opens his arms. I could throttle Kassy. I don't want a hug, but I also don't want to be rude. I deliver a *teacher-hug*. It's a modified, half-hug, half-pat-on-the-back gesture I sometimes offer students on the last day of class.

But obviously, Yoshimado has taken a lesson from Kassy. He pulls me in and goes for a kiss on the lips. I turn and offer my cheek. A rising pressure sweeps back and forth against my leg, and I know he doesn't have another banana in his pocket. Disgusted, I give him a shove.

Undaunted, he rebounds and comes in with an open-mouth kiss.

"No!" I shove him again and hold out my palm.

My adrenaline spikes. It's *fight or flight*. And heaven knows I am not fast enough for flight.

If I must, I am more than prepared to kick this old man's ass. Thankfully, I don't have to. He shrugs and walks away. I storm off in the other direction.

Kassy catches up and tries to laugh off the situation. "Well, on the bright side," she says. "He finds you attractive even at your worst."

I don't reply. Yoshimado's behavior was not a compliment. Besides, who says this is my worst? I think I look great. I like me sans teacher-clothes, no makeup, and with my hair in braids.

Kassy tries again. "Just think. You could have enjoyed the company of a trail lover."

"Gross," I say. "Please don't talk to me right now."

Two hours pass beneath my feet before arriving at our destination, *Shosanji*. Despite golden stands of bamboo, sunny orange groves, towering cedars, and tranquil mountain streams, I am still pissed-off. I'm angry at Kassy, and I'm furious at Yoshimado for acting like a cocker-spaniel humping the postman. I'm mad at myself. When he first touched my hair, I should have slapped away his hand. That may have ended it right then and there. My creepo-meter does not lie, but I often fail to take heed.

At the temple gate, I am too irritated to execute the ritual tasks. Instead, I ditch Kassy and set out to find my lodging. On the plus side, a cardboard box bearing Kassy's name waits in the lobby. Our backpacks have arrived safely.

A shy, young woman shows me to my room. She slides open the door, motions me inside, and bows. I return the bow, and she moves down the hallway without a sound.

I strip off my clothes and slide into a freshly pressed yukata robe and tie the sash. The stiff cotton feels lovely against my skin. But I desperately need a hot bath.

The room is cold and damp and sparsely furnished with a folded sleeping pallet, squat table, and kerosene heater. I fiddle with the heater, trying to figure out how to light it. I locate a push-button ignitor. It takes a few tries, but on the third strike, a blue flame licks up the sides.

The heater seems awfully dangerous, especially in a room lined with woven-straw mats. I'm concerned about carbon monoxide poisoning. I slide open the rice-paper shade and crack my window to be on the safe side.

I hear Kassy's voice in the hallway as she is shown to the cell next to me. A sliding partition, once separating our rooms, opens. She pokes her head in and says, "Oh, there you are!"

"Yup. You've found me." I carry her backpack into her room, light her furnace, and sit down to talk about the pack situation.

"Look, I know you were trying to be helpful – but please do NOT do this again. This is not the Camino. I want to carry my own pack, and you need to carry yours."

"But I can't. It's too heavy."

"Then, get rid of some things."

Kassy shrugs and gives me a lost look. I don't know what else to say. I don't want to hurt her feelings, but I need to be crystal clear.

I sleep with my legs beneath the short table to take full advantage of an infrared light some cleverly thoughtful soul has installed. Quilted skirts fasten around the table's edge and trap in the heat. I am as warm as toast.

Shosanji is nick-named *Burning Mountain Temple*, and now I know why. All night, my thigh and calf muscles cramp and burn. Despite the burn, I prefer going uphill instead of down. Tomorrow's hike promises a 22-kilometer, knee-jarring drop in elevation by 700 meters. My poor legs are not looking forward to that.

In the morning, I take my time making the temple rounds. I breathe it all in, trying to get my fill. Shosanji, set high above rolling green hills and guarded by great-granddaddy-cedars, is majestic in the morning dew.

I grew up amidst the Oregon timber trade. There were at least 100-acres of trees on our family farm, but I've never seen trees like these. They are magical.

I'm a bit of a tree hugger, and the urge to hug each one is powerful. I wrap my arms around a massive trunk. I would need at least five or six friends to complete the circle.

I hug several more cedars before visiting the main hall. I know it sounds silly, but the tree-hugging energizes me, reconnecting me to the art of peregrination. Outside of Spain, this is a new sensation. For the past 50 kilometers, I've been a foreigner exploring a foreign way of life, but here, atop *Burning Mountain*, I am home. And the great-granddaddy-cedars are my ancestors.

I stop at the temple office to collect a stamp and inquire about tonight's lodging. I'm hoping for another temple stay at *Dainichiji,* the thirteenth temple. Making reservations along the Shikoku is often a telephone affair, and I'm terrible on the phone. Even if I recite my reservation request accurately, there's no way I can be sure if I have a room or not. I can speak the words, but I cannot interpret the responses.

I wait my turn in line as Kassy tries her hand at swindling a lift for her pack down the mountain. Obviously, my gentle lecture fell on deaf ears. The monk working the desk explains that no one is driving down the mountain today. He also explains last-moment shipping via courier is not possible. Kassy won't hear of it and pulls out her wallet and offers money. The monk shakes his head, but Kassy won't give up the fight.

To my horror, the temple priest intervenes. He is a burly man with a stern countenance. His English is perfect, but not even he can convey the message.

Kassy is either passive-aggressive or totally clueless. I can't decide. With a bowed head and Bambi eyes, Kassy looks up at the priest and argues in that persuasively demure way that is meant to bolster a man's ego. I could positively throw-up.

Kassy's *Bambi* eyes don't seem to be working. Perhaps, they did in her younger years. Or maybe, the strategy is best not used on a Buddhist priest.

The old priest and Kassy go back and forth, while the younger monk stamps my book and makes a reservation for me at the next temple. The monk whispers an apology, "I'm sorry, but your mother doesn't understand."

Embarrassed by the scene, I don't correct the monk. Instead, I pack up my book, apologize, and leave with a bow. I need to put a lot of space between me and my trail-mother.

Temple 13: Dainichiji

Before leaving the grounds of temple twelve, I drop my pack, strip off my collar, hat, and hakui, and duck into the public restroom. I read somewhere that one or more of these henro items are not to be taken into unclean places, like the public toilet. It's probably just the collar, but there is no sense risking it.

Typically, I open each stall until I find the *western toilet*. Western toilets in Japan are not at all like toilets in Europe or the Americas. Instead, these porcelain thrones are infused with Japanese technology. I'm talking about heated seats, privacy music, automatic lifting lids with backup lighting, and an ever-so-refreshing warm-water bidet.

But the facility is dated, offering only the Japanese squat toilet. A squat toilet is, as the name implies. Theoretically, I have nothing against a squat toilet and use them all the time in Okinawa; however, my knees do protest. So, whenever possible, I opt for western comfort.

Typically, the trough is placed lengthwise, front to back, and aligns with the door. Like western toilets, I face toward the door. However, this setup is sideways, and I must examine the trench to find my bearings. A grip rail attached to one wall gives me a clue, and I get down to business.

Midstream, an epiphany strikes. The built-in porcelain splash guard is toward my front parts. And here, I had always assumed the guard was for the back-blast area. I've been doing it wrong for months!

I don't know if it's the lack of sleep or the carbon monoxide fumes from the kerosene heater, but I burst out in uncontrollable laughter. I can barely hold myself above the trough. I exit the bathroom, laughing and dabbing tears. To make matters even funnier, an elderly monk emerges from the men's room and asks if I am okay.

I laugh all the way out the temple gate and to the trailhead. The toilet situation isn't the only thing I find funny. Moments before entering the bathroom, I was stewing in frustration over the ongoing backpack saga. And now? I'm free. I went from mad to glad in mere moments. This is the magic of laughter. There is no better medicine or full-body workout than a good belly-laugh, especially when laughing in a squatting-position.

I hiccup down the trail, releasing the occasional giggle until I come to a steep drop outfitted with two ropes. Seriously? I'm immediately sober. Like the squat toilet situation, it takes me a moment to orient direction.

At first, I thought I should head straight down the hill, clutching a rope for support. After contemplating the moss-covered boulders and playing out the whole scenario in my head, I now think it's wiser to go backward and hang on to both ropes.

I toss my poles down the hill and grab the ropes. Drawing in a deep breath, I gather my courage. My bodyweight keeps the lines taut as I ease myself down.

Once I reach the bottom and look up the hill, a tingle of satisfaction courses through my limbs. This is one of the joys of walking alone. It's my job to negotiate obstacles and test solutions. I am solely responsible for my success or failure. Failure is humbling, and success is empowering. Both are useful.

The slippery trail down *Burning Mountain* is treacherous. Small rocks, disturbed by my passing, slide beneath my feet, tumbling along the path in front of me. But I take my time and stop to marvel and snap photos of waterfalls and mountain streams.

The forest-curtains part, and I am treated to a stunning vista of a valley tucked between a cascade of rolling mountains. Below, I see a two-story, wooden barn set atop a staircase of terraced rice paddies. The scene is watercolor-painting-perfect. I snap a photo, knowing the shot will never capture the beauty of right now.

The soft trail dumps me on a gently-sloping country road. Although paved, the road provides a welcome break to my shaking knees and ankles. I can relax now and focus on my surroundings instead of watching for loose or moss-covered stones. The road parallels an irrigation line. For the sake of amusement, I try to figure out how the innovative apparatus delivers mountain water to farms below.

I lengthen my stride and settle into a swift but easy clip. My tummy rumbles. Eating at temple twelve was a vegan affair. Last night's dinner included a vat of rice and a bowl of miso soup accompanied by several bowls of vegetables and a small side of cold and bloated brown beans. Breakfast was almost the same but with fewer veggies. While I don't need meat for supper, I sure miss my morning eggs.

On the valley floor, a henro sign directs me back into the forest. At first, the going is easy, but I know it won't last. Ahead, another 500-meter peak stands between me and the 12 remaining kilometers to the next temple.

I pass through a stand of dense bamboo. The wind ripping across the valley has scattered the poles like giant pick-up-sticks. These stalks are not golden, like the ones I admired yesterday. Instead, they are a silvery olive-green with black rings marking each joint, and the foliage is the color of spring grass. I've seen many types of bamboo, but I never tire.

I follow the path out of the forest and onto a graveled lane. The lane is flanked by an orange grove on one side and an open pasture on the other. In the distance, layers of heavily-forested peaks disappear into a blue haze. Indeed, this must be heaven on earth.

The leisurely path takes a nasty turn up a rock scramble. If I weren't staring at a trail marker, I'd swear this couldn't possibly be the correct path. The scramble is wet and mossy. I can't risk an injury. So, I drop down on all fours and bear-crawl up the rocks.

I reach the summit and take a break on the stone steps of a henro-hut. This hut is adorable. The building itself is a little rough, but the blue tin roof and the concrete pad look new. Inside, tatami mats and a couple of futons are available for campers.

The trail pops me out on a narrow tractor road cutting above another grove. I scan acres of glossy green leaves and sunny orange globes rolling down into the valley below. Above, jagged blue mountains fade into the cloud cover. This is even more spectacular than the Japan of my imagination.

I move off the road to allow a white pickup to pass. I wave at the driver. An old farmer in blue coveralls slows down to greet me. Unrolling his window, he offers me a beautiful orange. I accept it with a bow and present him with an osamefuda.

I continue down the lane and pass another white pickup. This time, the truck is parked in the ditch while the driver eats a rice triangle. The old driver wears blue overalls, like the old man in the truck before him. I'm sensing a theme here. I offer a friendly wave, and the darling old man raises his rice triangle to greet me.

I'm several paces beyond the truck when I hear the honking of a horn. I turn around, and the man is waiving a bottle of *Pocari Sweat*. Pocari Sweat is the stunt double to my beloved Aquarius. The two brands of sports drink taste almost the same, but I never purchase Pocari Sweat, mostly because I do not like the name.

With my water supply nearly depleted and another eight kilometers ahead, I cannot afford to be fussy about brand names. I hustle back to the truck and graciously accept the old man's gift. Truck-side, I take the first icy gulp and let out a satisfied, "aww." The driver nods and offers a tobacco-stained grin.

This old dude totally gets me right now. I hand him my osamefuda, pat the coverall-clad arm perched out the truck window, and skip back down the road. My faith in humanity, and old men, is renewed.

Before the narrow farm road dips into the village below, I stop at a roadside henro-hut. The triangular cedar shelter, cantilevered over a bluff, is an architectural wonder. I sit a moment, enjoying a panoramic view. Before moving on, I sign the guest book and help myself to a tin of assorted chocolates, thoughtfully left for a lucky henro like me.

Entering a small hamlet, I can't find a henro placard anywhere. I have no idea which way to turn, so I take a guess and head down the main street. I see a family sitting outside on a bench. It looks like a grandma and grandpa with two grandkids. Perfect! I cross the street to ask for directions. As I move closer, I realize these folks will never speak to me because they are a family of life-sized stuffed dolls. They are a wee bit creepy.

Dressed in ordinary clothes, the plush-people appear to be waiting on the bus. I sidle up close, take a seat on the bench, and visit awhile. The conversation is one-sided, but I don't let that stop me.

I peel an orange and scan the quiet neighborhood. Two children hold a ladder about a block ahead and across the street, while Dad hangs ropes of peppers over an awning beam. I watch, but Dad and the kids do not move. More dolls! Such a curious little town. Where are all the real people? Maybe the dolls killed them!

I keep the puffy grandparents and grandkids in my peripheral view. I don't want to stare. But I also don't want to turn my back on them either.

My orange is sweet and juicy and nothing like the orange-of-disappointment from my first day. It goes down easy. So, I start in on another. I have several more. It was a good day for osettai oranges.

On my way out of town, I see a western man with fair hair leaning on a lamp post in front of me. His white hakui and thatched-hat tells me he is a henro. This is the first henro I've seen all day. His presence surely indicates I made the right choice back at the intersection. As I draw near, I realize I've been duped again. He is also a doll – an unsightly Caucasian male with one frayed eyebrow and a rather phallic-shaped nose.

I hear the ping of a car's engine coming up behind me. I move to the side of the road and wave. An older woman wearing a see-through rain bonnet leans out the car window. I catch a familiar waft of chemicals and know she's visited the hairdresser.

"Kawaii," I say and tug a strand of my hair.

She touches her bonnet and smiles. Of course, we both know there is nothing cute about a fresh perm, but *kawaii* is my one Japanese adjective, so everything in my world is *cute*.

"Dainichiji?" I point up the road.

"Hai, Dainichiji!" she says.

Before driving away, the woman reaches into a white paper sack and hands me a steamed bun wrapped in waxed paper. It's still warm! I bow, thank her, and offer an osamefuda.

In Japan, eating while walking is impolite, even when one is on pilgrimage. I tuck the bun in my shirt to keep it warm and continue up the road. For now, the mystery over what's inside the bun is satisfying enough.

Up ahead, three little kids stand along the road's edge next to a henro placard. The sign seems legit, but the kids are not. They are stuffed. In a garden patch next to the placard, a stuffed granny tends to her flowers.

By far, Granny gardener is my favorite. Dressed in purple, from crocheted hat to winter boots, she squats before a row of budding daffodils. She is too busy tilling up the dirt to notice me. And so, I walk on.

I leave the valley of the dolls and come to a river crossing. A long, narrow strip of elevated sidewalk rests on five concrete pillars spanning the water. I look up and downstream, hoping to find a proper bridge with railings, but find nothing.

The river is calm and does not appear deep. A fall would be a major inconvenience but not catastrophic. As a precaution, I tuck my phone in the plastic freezer bag carrying my stamp book. If I do go in, my pack will be fine if I can keep it upright.

The bridge is too narrow to use hiking-poles, so I hold them out for balance and get on with it. In the middle, I stop to take in the view. The flowing water beneath the bridge makes me feel wobbly, and I must keep moving.

I'm almost to the end when the wind shifts. A horrible stench wraps around me, and I know it immediately. It's chicken poop! The birds cluck and coo as I make my way up the gravel path alongside the barns.

At a vacant bus stop alongside a highway, I sit and eat my steamed bun. I don't know what I expected, but the sweet red-bean filling is a major letdown. However, I need the energy and genuinely appreciate the osettai.

The highway crosses a mountain stream. From the bridge, I catch a glimpse of flesh. It takes a moment to register. I stop, backtrack, and look up the creek. Below the tumbling water, a very naked woman with huge boobies floats in a pool. Dead body? Nudist colony? No – It's another doll, but this one seems to be of the blow-up variety. What in the heck? It's been an odd afternoon.

I reach the gate of Dainichiji shortly after three o'clock. A dark-green patinaed dragon greets me at the purification fountain. I wash my hands and face and swish the last bits of red bean paste from my mouth.

After visiting the main and Daishi halls, I head to the temple office, collect my stamp, and inquire about my reservation. A tiny woman about my age leads me through a corridor. She's so fast I nearly jog to keep up. She scoops up a large, blue backpack and tries to hand it to me. "Mama's pack," says the woman.

Oh, my goodness. This is Kassy's pack. I can't believe she convinced the old priest to arrange delivery. "No," I shake my head. "Not my Mama."

With so few Americans on the Shikoku, I see how Kassy might be mistaken as my mother. The age difference is spot on. Despite my best efforts, it does seem like we are traveling together.

Thankfully, the woman understands and puts the pack back down before leading me into an ornately decorated room lined with kelly-green tatami mats. In the center of the room sits a long wooden table with stubby legs. On the table awaits a porcelain teapot and one tiny cup. How perfect!

I'm dozing off when I hear rustling next door. I brace for the inevitable. The partitions slide apart, and Kassy's head pops in.

"Ding-dong," Kassy sings out, "Avon lady calling!"

My grandmother once sold lipstick door-to-door for the Avon company. So, I decide to view the invasion as charming. What else can I do?

Temple 14: Jorakuji

Last night's temple dinner at Dainichiji was a carb-lovers affair. There was rice, udon-noodle soup, starchy vegetables, and only a couple slices of white-fish sashimi. My body cries out for protein, and breakfast answers the call.

This morning, breakfast is presented on red lacquer trays loaded with eight matching little cups, bowls, and saucers. Of course, there is rice and miso soup, but this time the soup is packed with tofu chunks. While tofu may not be a favorite, I do appreciate the punch of morning protein.

I can't decide which item excites me most, the boiled egg, the salmon slab, or the half-banana. These are all such good things. I am a hungry, wild animal. But I still look up and down the table to make sure no one is watching before picking up the strip of salmon with my fingers.

The coast is clear. Kassy and three other lady-henros are bent over their bowls, slurping soup and shoveling rice at rather unladylike speeds. I love the company of hungry women. It is so judgment-free!

The first bite of salmon hits my taste buds, and I try to suppress a moan of satisfaction, but a little *oh* leaks out. Kassy looks up and smiles. Then we both start laughing. At the end of the table, the three Korean ladies cover their mouths and join us in trills of giggles. The food is really that good.

The salmon is buttery and crisp on the outside and slightly translucent on the inside. It's fried and seasoned to perfection! I devour the fish, skin and all, and then move on to the egg.

As I stuff the last bite of boiled egg in my mouth, the Korean ladies spring to attention. The cook rushes out of the kitchen and stands with her hands behind her back. Kassy and I exchange a questioning look and slowly rise to our feet.

The dining room is silent except for the sudden swoosh of taffeta. And then she speaks. Her melodic voice rises and falls with expressive intonation, and I know in an instant, she is not Japanese. Draped in a long white robe and wrapped in a kimono of gold and royal purple, she stands in the stairwell with her arms outstretched, like an angel offering a morning blessing.

The Korean henros respond, and Kassy and I are at a loss for words. I barely speak Japanese, let alone Korean.

"Good morning," I offer.

"Yes, good morning," Kassy follows.

"Oh! You are Americans? Yes?"

Kassy and I nod. I don't know if it's the richly-colored kimono or her perfect hair and makeup, but something about this woman is truly majestic. I find myself in awe and tongue-tied like I've met a movie star.

The woman motions us to sit, and we do. She glides down the staircase, kneels next to Kassy, and takes a seat across from me. "Please, please," she says. "Eat your breakfast. You'll need energy today."

Kassy and I hesitate, but hunger wins the battle. We resume our meals, but this time our backs are straight, chopsticks are in hand, and we display our finest manners. Who is this elegant being? The Korean ladies seem to know her because they freely converse back and forth, but I notice the ladies no longer slump over their trays or shovel in the rice. Grace has entered the building.

After a little small talk about the Shikoku pilgrimage, the stunning woman gives me a business card. Business cards are a big deal in Japan, so I receive her card like a precious gift. I glance down and see her name is Kim.

Kim and I talk about our sons and their accomplishments. Her kid seems way more on the ball than any of mine, or at least she has more to say. Maybe this is how it is when you have one instead of many. She pulls a small album from her kimono sleeve and shares photo of her boy. He's a monk. It's hard to tell with his shaved head and all, but he looks about 19.

I scroll through my phone, looking for something to share, but I have no pictures of my kids. This is terrible, but I do share a couple shots of the grandkids. I'm embarrassed because most of the photos are of Jasper, my dog. I am not going to win mother-of-the-year, that's for sure.

Kassy comes to the rescue with several pictures of her family, and I ease my way out of the conversation. This is a good thing because I was hogging all the airtime with Kim. This also gives me a moment to examine the business card.

Thoughtfully, Kim handed me a card printed in English. Pilgrims from all over the world visit Shikoku. So, I wonder how many other languages she has up her kimono sleeves.

According to the card, Kim bears the title *Zen Master Priest*. I have no poker face. When I look up from the card, Kim smiles brightly and nods her head.

No wonder everyone stood! And now it is all clear. It is Kim's image on the vase in my room. She's the priest of temple thirteen, and she is the reason this temple's atmosphere is so unique. The Kim-Kannon combo wraps this temple in a graceful shroud of the feminine.

I am terribly impressed. Kim is the first Korean priest along the Shikoku, and she is also the only *woman* priest. If this isn't enough, she is a world-class, traditional Korean dancer. Throughout my short stay, I have admired several gorgeous portraits of a silk-clad dancing woman, and I now realize the same magnificent woman is sitting across from me.

Starstruck and trying not to gawk, I shift focus back to my breakfast. I stare down at a small dish of white squiggly-somethings, and to my surprise, the squiggles stare back up at me. I dig out my glasses for a closer look. I'm met by a hundred sets of little black eyes. Maggots? Worms? Super tiny eels? Whatever they are, they are not going in my mouth.

Kim reaches across the table and pats my arm. "Mix them with the daikon paste," she suggests. "They taste better that way."

"Good idea!" I reply.

Well, hell. Now I'm stuck. I push a dollop of the daikon paste into the mound of eyeballs and mix it up. I pinch a generous glob of the slippery little suckers between my chopsticks and shove them into my mouth. It takes two swallows to get the worms down, but I do it without hitting the gag-reflex. Whew! I smile and nod my head in faked appreciation.

After the worms, or whatever they are, I am sick to my stomach. I know it's all in my head. I'm sure everyone else at the table chowed down without a second thought. Kassy's dishes are licked clean. I wrap my half-banana in a napkin and tuck it in my bag. I'll be ready for it once the pale little bodies with big, black eyes are out of my mind.

The two and a half kilometers to Jorakuji disappear beneath my feet. Kassy and I chatter the entire route, and I almost miss a silvery heron bathing in the morning sun. I stop lakeside to admire the bird, and Kassy makes her way up the temple steps.

I snap a couple photos and head toward the gate, but Kassy is long gone. We are about the same height, but her stride is longer and faster than mine. She's moving a bit slower than usual because she couldn't ditch her backpack. The women in the Dainichiji office flatly refused to assist. So, at least for today, she's stuck with it.

Kassy and Zen Master Kim have me contemplating my own physical health. Kim is a decade older, and Kassy is two decades older. Both women own such physical freedom and grace. I need to take better care of myself.

It's nearly nine o'clock, and *Jorakuji* is flooded with bus henro. The line to ring the bell is ridiculously long, so I skip it. Enough people are ringing to inform the deity, *Miroku Bosatsu,* of our collective presence. Instead, I head to the main hall and start the sutras.

Jorakuji is the only temple of the 88 housing *Miroku Bosatsu* as the main deity. Miroku Bosatsu is the future Buddha and will make his grand appearance in 5-billion, 670-million years after the death of *Shakyamuni.*

Shakyamuni died around 500 BCE. I try to run the numbers in my head, but I'm operating without coffee, and let's just say math has never been my thing.

In front of the main hall, I look around for a yew tree. According to legend, if a pilgrim afflicted with diabetes visits this temple, prays, and drinks a tea made from the leaves of this tree, he or she will be cured. Unfortunately, I don't know what a yew tree looks like; but fortunately, I am not a diabetic.

It is fun chanting along with the crowd. I'm still shy about my pronunciation, but I like how my voice comingles with native speakers. I suppose it's like singing in a choir. The more powerful and confident voices bolster the weaker voices, like mine.

Temple 15: Kokubunji

I look around for Kassy before leaving temple fourteen. I'm trying not to ditch her. She's either lost in the crowd, or she headed out before me. My guess is the latter, even though she asked me to stay with her today.

Yesterday morning, after leaving temple twelve, Kassy took a wrong turn and walked about ten kilometers in the opposite direction. She wandered into a sleepy hamlet and heard an American's voice. She followed the voice down an alley behind a strip of shops where a Japanese woman and her American husband own a café. Kassy had no idea she was lost until the couple told her so. Fortunately, the kind woman drove her all the way to temple thirteen.

Last night, I helped Kassy figure out a mapping app on her smartphone. Cell signal is dicey in the mountains, but the app can help determine direction. Even if turn-by-turn guidance isn't available, she'll at least know when she is ten kilometers off-trail. This afternoon, I plan to show her how to use the translator app to read signs. These two skills should really help.

The walk to *Kokubunji* takes me less than 15 minutes. The sun is shining, and the sidewalk is crowded. Like the first six temples, thirteen through seventeen are close together and easy to visit within a day. This makes the area popular for tourists wanting to experience the life of a walking-henro, but only for a day or two.

Kokubunji, the fifteenth temple, is the government temple for Tokushima. There are four Kokubunji temples along the Shikoku 88 loop, one in each prefecture. Initially founded by Gyoki, this Kokubunji was lost to war and burnt to the ground in the 16th century. The existing buildings were reconstructed in 1741. With the current collection of scaffolding and tarps, it looks like a hefty rehabilitation is underway.

The construction-site vibe lends a chaotic backdrop to the crowd of white-clad visitors. I'm usually overwhelmed by the masses. For some reason, I am not feeling any of the usual discomforts. I'm perfectly content.

The temple compound buzzes with energy, and the gonging bell and hum of communal chanting are invigorating. So, this time, instead of mumbling along, I read through my sutras with gusto. There's a strong sense of community, and I'm proud to be part of the collective noise.

Temple 16: Kannonji

Walking roadside, I admire impossibly long greenhouses stretching alongside a set of railroad tracks. I wonder what is growing. Tomatoes? Cucumbers? Or maybe zucchini? All three of these items are available year-round in Okinawa. I grow tomatoes and cucumbers on my balcony. I planted them before Christmas. It was a novelty to plan my container garden while everyone back home braced for winter. Once the heat and humidity of May roll in, my non-tropical plants will surely die.

The weather is much cooler on Shikoku, but I'm told late spring and summer can be miserable. The prime time to hike the loop begins in March and ends in early May. Quite by accident, I am lucky enough to have hit the sweet spot. I must fly home in a week, but I'll return as soon as I have another short break between classes.

The two-kilometer hike to *Kannonji* is all on blacktop, hard on the feet, and often uninspiring. I shift my focus from the road and enjoy the farm fields and distant mountains melting into the horizon. Up ahead, a farmer drives a blue tractor pulling a blue plow through earth the color of charcoal. I don't think I've ever seen soil so dark. I wonder what he will plant. Let me guess. More rice?

I haven't seen Kassy since temple fourteen. She is not my responsibility, but I did agree to walk with her. I've sent two messages, but she hasn't responded. She's proven to be resourceful, so I'm sure she is okay.

I bow at the gate of Kannonji and enter. The crowd is still thick but not as bad. Perhaps, I'm here between busloads. Like Dainichiji, the main deity is Kannon, but this Kannon is a slightly different version. She is *Senju Kannon Bosatsu*, the goddess of one-thousand arms with an eye in each palm. Senju Kannon sees all earthly suffering. At Dainichi, the Kannon is *Juichimen*, of eleven faces. I don't have a personal favorite, but I'm leaning toward the eleven faces. I appreciate a full range of emotions.

According to legend, there was once a woman henro camping near the area during the 18th century. Her hakui was wet from the rain. So, she stood by a fire to dry. Well, the cloth caught fire, burning her badly. She interpreted the unfortunate incident as punishment for her misdeeds. Apparently, she was known to strike her mother-in-law. The next morning, she reported to this temple to repent and atone for her behavior.

The fabric of my hakui is of a poly-cotton blend. It's probably flammable. I've had a couple of close calls when reaching across candles to place my own in the back row of the glass enclosures. Although I have never struck my mother-in-law, I have uttered a few course words. From now on, I'll be more careful when playing with fire.

Temple 17: Idoji

Outside of temple sixteen, my phone vibrates. It's probably someone from my work, so I try to ignore it. It vibrates again. Wait, what if it's Kassy? I dig around and retrieve it from my bag. It's not Kassy. It's Pete, the regional director of my university.

Pete is a great guy; however, he operates in a management-style that is almost always reactionary. By the time he reaches out for help, he is in full crisis-mode. I don't want crisis-mode. Not today.

My guess is he needs me to pick up a last-minute class. Usually, I don't mind, but this happens before each term. I don't physically need to be in the classroom until next Thursday. Bailing out Pete will most likely require me to cut my trip short.

The three-kilometer stretch of lonely road is pleasant but not overly stimulating. The asphalt is hard underfoot, but I enjoy the solitude. A henro sticker affixed to a guardrail reassures me. I'm on the right path, but where have all the crowds gone? And where is Kassy?

I bow at the gate of *Idoji* and enter. The first thing that catches my eye is an enormous pink, blown-glass vase set atop a water feature. This is the famous well I've read about.

One night, Kukai dug a well on this site using only his staff. It is believed if one makes a wish on a specific day, the wish will come true. So, here I am. I have a desire, and here is the well, but I have no idea which specific date I am to make a wish. But there is no time like the present.

I wish for health and happiness for my five sons. To seal the deal, I write the wish on two osamefudas. I will chant my sutras and deposit one wish at the main hall and the other at the Daishi hall.

After finishing the rituals, I head toward the stamp office. On my way, I'm pleased to find a statue of Jizo sitting on a lotus blossom. In one palm, he holds a chubby little baby. At his feet, three more chunky toddlers reach up to him.

Strewn about the statue's base are juice boxes, bottles of water, small toys, gold coins, and slips of paper. These are the gifts, prayers, and wishes of other parents. I smile at the serendipity, offer a coin, and tuck my osamefuda beneath a juice box.

Temple 18: Onzanji

On the steps outside of temple seventeen, I study my guidebook and wait for Kassy. If she were ahead, I think she would have slowed down for me to catch up. It's still before noon, but I'm feeling pressed for time. The walk to temple eighteen is nearly 19 kilometers. The route is flat, but I am slow. It will surely take me all afternoon, and I can't afford breaks if I want to meet my goal before the stamp office closes.

As I'm about to give up, a white sedan pulls up and out pops Kassy. "Got lost again!" she laughs and throws her arms in the air. Getting lost is part of her daily ritual, and she takes it in stride.

Bounding up the steps, she executes a quick bow and dashes into the courtyard. Kassy practices *sutra-light,* uttering a few lines before collecting a stamp. I'm not hard and fast on rules, and I'm not a Buddhist. Therefore, I pass no judgment. Besides, I might need to adopt her abbreviated routine. I've chanted eight times already, and my jaws need a break.

While I wait on the stoop for Kassy, work-related guilt gets the best of me. I dig out my phone to return Pete's call. It is exactly as I assumed. Pete forgot to assign a professor for a business writing class starting this Monday. To make matters worse, there are 25 students enrolled. I have two choices: I can cut my trip short and return to Okinawa or turn my back on the students. Neither option is appealing. I hesitate only a moment before agreeing to the bailout. It's all about priorities, I suppose. The walk can wait, but the students cannot.

Kassy is in and out of the temple gate in less than ten minutes. Back on the road, I share my employment woes. She listens and nods but offers no advice or consolation. Her silent understanding is what I need – to vent, to talk out the logistics, and to hatch a new plan.

I had hoped to walk the entire *Awakening* phase during this trip, but I'm not sure it will be possible. Initially, I gave myself 12 days to hike the 165-kilometer route and visit the first 23 temples. Now, I have seven days. To meet my goal, I'm going to have to pick up the pace or integrate public transportation. I have no qualms about jumping a bus or a train, but I'm terrible at it.

At an intersection, I see a convenience store, and my stomach rumbles. I try to ignore it, but I can't stop thinking about those clever rice triangles. My breakfast is long gone. I probably should have eaten the last bit of bug-eyed worms swimming in daikon radish paste.

"Hey, you hungry?" I ask Kassy.

"Ravenous!"

"Rice triangles?"

Kassy claps her hands in anticipation. "Oh, yes, please! That sounds delicious!"

You wouldn't know by looking at her, but Kassy loves food as much as I do – probably more. Over the past five days, she has cleared her plate and devoured any scraps left on mine. Kassy is a rail of a thing. How does she eat so much yet stay so skinny? I genuinely envy her metabolism.

We hustle inside the store and grab our lunch. Kassy completes her purchase and heads to the parking lot. I watch in amusement from the check-out counter as Kassy speaks to a woman in a small van. Kassy's arms flail about like a puppet. Whatever she is saying, she is doing it with gusto.

I exit the store to find Kassy loading her backpack into the back of the van. The driver is busy tossing toys over the backseat to make room for us. What is Kassy up to now?

"We're in luck!" Kassy says. "This wonderful lady is driving us to the Tokushima bus station!"

The driver looks at me and dips a slight bow. I return the bow with an apologetic smile. The poor lady looks as confused as I feel.

"O-kay, Kassy," I say. "But why would she do such a thing? Tokushima must be at least ten kilometers."

"I know! Aren't we lucky? I told her you had a work emergency and need Wi-Fi."

The just lady nods and smiles.

"Gomennasai," I bow. "Gomennasai."

The lady waves away my apology. "E-mer-gen-cy," she says and motions me to climb aboard. Reluctantly, I scooch across the backseat.

I'm not annoyed with Kassy. As always, she is just trying to help. It's true. I told Kassy I needed reliable Wi-Fi *A-S-A-P* to prepare and upload my syllabus to the online classroom portal, but I never said it was an emergency! The task could have waited until tonight.

My best guess is our new chauffeur understood enough of Kassy's words and flailing body language to discern we are in trouble and must get to the bus station. It's not even a half-truth. A work emergency is not a real emergency.

Before starting my pilgrimage, I vowed to accept help and osettai with grace, but this feels different. It's like we are receiving support under false pretense. The situation is awkward, and I don't know how to set it right. I'm at a loss for words. So, I buckle up and let it ride.

The traffic into downtown Tokushima is thick. It takes the better part of 30 minutes to reach the bus station, and once we do, it isn't enough for our lady-driver to dump us curbside. No. She parks and escorts us to the information center. She stays by our side until we are all sorted out.

I thank our driver and hand her my osamefuda. It's not much, but it is an appropriate gesture to show my appreciation. Kassy, not one to be outdone, wraps the woman in a tight embrace. Regrettably, the hug is one of Kassy's ten-second specials. The woman's pleading eyes look over Kassy's shoulder. I bow and whisper another apology, "Gomennasai. Gomennasai."

We have a full two hours to kill before the next bus. We could have walked here! Kassy and I find a cozy bistro near the station. The Wi-Fi is reliable, and the beer is cold. Who could ask for anything more?

I use the time wisely to work on my syllabus and send out a letter of apology to my new students. I'm mid-syllabus when the table rumbles. My beer sloshes to-and-fro. At first, I think my vertigo is acting up again, but Kassy feels it too. She grips the sides of the table and holds on for dear life. Dishes clatter and fellow diners grow quiet. Even the waiter and busser stop moving.

The restaurant stops trembling, but no one speaks. The tension is palpable, and the only sound is an amplified ticking of a clock. I turn to Kassy and eke out a hoarse whisper, "Earthquake?"

"Good heavens," Kassy whispers. "What do we do?"

"I think we wait."

A table of women resume chatting, and a few diners reach for their phones. The busser refills my water glass, and the waiter delivers a plate of crisp, mochi-chicken. And just like that, life carries on.

Kassy and I board the bus for *Onzanji*. "Look," she says, pointing out several henros. "We aren't the only lazy ones."

I never assumed we would be the only *lazy* henros jumping a bus to Onzanji. However, I'm happy to see the others because it will make it easier to disembark. We'll simply follow the crowd.

The bus stops a half-kilometer from temple eighteen. Before hopping off, I try to wake a sleeping henro sitting in the backseat. The poor old guy has been snoring the whole ride.

"Konichiwa," I tap him gently.

One eye opens. "Onzanji?" he asks.

I nod, "Hai, Onzanji."

His other eye pops open, and then he leaps to his feet. I suppress a giggle. I had tried not to startle him, but I am a tad delighted with his reaction.

Like members of a chain gang, Kassy and I join the stream of pilgrims shuffling up the hill toward the temple. Several henro, including the sleeper, peel off to the left at what looks like an old office building. I read the only words I can on the small sign in front. *Mr. Chiba.* Hmm. Why are so many pilgrims stopping to visit this Mr. Chiba? Perhaps, he is a doctor.

It's a quarter after four as we reach the grand statue of Kukai set atop the hill of Onzanji. I bow reverently and thank him for guiding us safely. I repeat the gesture at the gate and enter the tranquil campus.

My old friend, Jizo, greets me. He holds one baby in his arms, and five others gather at his feet. There's something comforting about him. He speaks to the mother in me, and I never tire of his babies.

The temple grounds are in peaceful contrast to the busy square in Tokushima. I swing the battering ram ever so gently. It takes me four tries, but finally, the butt of the log kisses the bell. A low hum announces my arrival to *Yakushi Nyorai,* the deity housed inside the main hall.

Founded by Gyoki, Onzanji was historically off-limits to women. However, this was before Kukai's mother came calling. Kukai endured a grueling, 17-day esoteric rite to lift the restriction and get his mom through the front gate. While I don't understand the logic behind the global and historical exclusion of women, especially in places and positions of worship, I'm pleased to learn what a boy will do for his mother.

I'm tired of chanting, but I make a systematic effort at each station and move through the sutras with care. The pronunciations are still tricky. I tuck behind a small group and allow their voices to carry me.

I marvel at the old-growth timber decking of the main hall. The wood is rough cut and silvered, and I can't get over the massive planks. Cedar, perhaps? How old were the donor trees? Once again, I align my feet heel-to-toe, taking four steps to cross the breadth of a single board.

I regret my lack of language skills because Shikoku holds countless natural wonders. I have countless unanswered questions. And for now, most of these questions are about trees.

I meet up with Kassy at the stamp counter. She is trying to explain, rather loudly, we have a reservation for temple lodgings, but the two women behind the counter are positively confused. I give it a go, using my well-rehearsed Japanese phrase for, "Hello, my name is Christine. I have a reservation this evening." But it doesn't work. So, I repeat myself, only louder this time. It still doesn't work.

Luckily, the ladies are good at charades. With very few English words and lots of gestures, I learn there are no temple lodgings at Onzanji. But I swear, the woman working in the stamp office at temple thirteen made the reservation this morning.

Kassy offers, "Maybe you booked rooms at temple nineteen instead?"

"Oh, shit! I totally screwed up." My heart sinks. Temple nineteen is an hour away. We'll never make it on time.

"It's okay," Kassy hugs my arm. "We can do it."

I dig out a scrap of paper the woman at temple thirteen gave me this morning. I show the phone number to the ladies and ask if they will call. Before we run our guts out, I want to make sure we have a room at the next temple.

Compassion replaces confusion, and the ladies set out to solve the mystery. One of them makes the call, and I can tell by the head nodding and the occasional "Hai, hai," we do indeed have a place to sleep. We thank the ladies and rush off down a trail toward the next temple.

I feel a great sense of relief, coupled with the pressure of making it to the temple before it closes. It's going to be a close call. I hate to be late, but now that someone at temple nineteen knows we are on our way, I'm confident they will accommodate us.

We are jogging along a dirt road when Kassy suddenly stops. "My phone! Oh, my God, I've lost my phone!"

She pats herself down, and I pause long enough to tell her to check her cargo pockets. I know she has the damn thing, and I know in which pocket she will find it. Kassy has lost her phone no less than eight times in the past five days. It is always in her right cargo pocket.

I keep right on jogging. One of us needs to make it there on time and guarantee our rooms. I pass through a farm dotted with barns full of beef cattle. I'm startled by a chorus of barking dogs, upset by my speedy intrusion.

I continue my jog downhill and through a bamboo forest. As I exit the bamboo and hit a small road, I hear the dogs go berserk again. I know Kassy has found her phone and is closing the gap between us.

My mouth is dry as I take to the side of the road. My body moves in less of a jog and more of an airborne shuffle. I sing a little military cadence under my breath and fall into an old rhythm. "I can run to Tokyo just like this. All the way to Tokyo just like this. I can run to Okinawa just like this. All the way to Okinawa just like this…"

I glance down at my phone and realize I have less than a kilometer to go. I'll only be five minutes late. I still feel bad; however, five minutes is forgivable, considering our circumstances.

I hear a car coming up behind, and I pop out my thumb. The vehicle pulls to the side of the road. How easy! I hustle up to the passenger door, but to my surprise, Kassy is already seated. A lady from the stamp office is behind the wheel.

I climb in the back, deeply appreciating the rescue. But the lady flips a U-turn and heads back toward temple eighteen. I'm confused and agitated, but I don't distrust this lady. What am I missing here?

Before the gate to temple eighteen, our rescuing-lady pulls to the side of the road and points to the old office building. "Mr. Chiba," she says. "He waits."

It finally dawns on me. There are no lodgings at temples eighteen or nineteen. The phone number given to me this morning belongs to the mysterious Mr. Chiba. Evidently, he is not a doctor. He is an innkeeper.

We thank the lady profusely. I bow and give her my osamefuda. Of course, Kassy hugs her.

The old office building buzzes with henro-activity. We are greeted in the dining room by our host, Mr. Chiba. He smiles broadly, "Welcome, Americans!"

The dining room is packed, and I feel the eyes of many as I take my seat. But I don't care. I've had a tough evening.

Mrs. Chiba brings me a cold bottle of *Asahi* beer. I press it to my forehead and sigh. Yes, the Americans are late. Yes, we are sweaty and frazzled. Yet, I find myself too grateful and too sleepy to savor the taste of shame.

Temple 19: Tatsueji

I feel like I have apologized at least 20 times or more, but this morning, Kassy waxes on about my fumble with last night's lodging. While less than ideal, we would have been fine. I would have set up my tent, and we would have gone to bed without supper.

"Kassy, I – am – sorry. But it wasn't the end of the world."

"Well, thank goodness, you have a big body."

I stare at her blankly.

"You have plenty of fat to keep us both warm!"

Seriously? *Screw, you Kassy.* Crazy Cat-lady or not, she can start figuring things out on her own.

"How far are we going?" She asks.

I point to temple twenty-one on the map.

"How far?".

"Less than 30K." I could see the gears grinding in her head.

"How many miles?"

"About 18."

"That's too far with my pack!"

"Tough cookies." For a brief and bitchy moment, I allow myself the fantasy of ditching Kassy.

"Oh no, you don't!" Kassy chirps. "You're not getting rid of me that easy!"

"Don't I know it."

There is no out-walking, no out-bussing, no out-hitchhiking, and no outfoxing Kassy. I'm not sure what the universe is trying to teach me, but I know I am stuck with her. She is mine, and I am hers, at least for the next few days.

With the help of Mr. Chiba, Kassy makes our reservations at the *Pilgrimage Inn Ryugasou*, ideally located between temples twenty-one and twenty-two. Mr. Chiba shows us the flyer, and it looks like a nice place. Even better, the innkeeper offers to collect us at the top of temple twenty-one, saving us several knee-jarring kilometers down the mountain.

Reservations are locked down. But not for want nor money, will Mr. Chiba forward Kassy's pack. She has no choice but to carry it up and over two steep inclines of 500 meters each. It's going to be a tough day for both of us.

Our fellow henros pour out of Mr. Chiba's inn and follow the road toward temple nineteen. Kassy and I know better because of our accidental recon of the alternate route last night. From the rear of temple eighteen, we cut through the same farmyard with the barns full of mooing cows. A chorus of barking dogs greets us again, just as they had last night.

Kassy turns to me and says, "Déjà vu." I smile, and we continue in silence.

As we hit the bamboo forest, the morning sunshine melts away all my icy grumpiness. I don't know why, but I cannot stay irritated with Kassy. Her *big lady* comments hurt my feelings, but she didn't mean harm. I must toughen up and learn to be more patient.

Our walk to *Tatsueji* is much slower this morning than it was last night. It is also way less stressful. We bow at the gate and enter the temple grounds.

There is a legend about a woman who visited this temple in 1803. Her name was Okyo, and she was a murderess. After killing her betrothed, she set off on a pilgrimage with her lover. Murder and pilgrimage make strange bedfellows, but the couple used henro disguises to escape the authorities. When the pair reached this temple, Okyo rang the bell to announce her arrival. Suddenly, her hair stood on end and intertwined with the bell-rope. In a struggle to free herself, she ripped out her hair and much of her scalp. She was left with a monastic tonsure. She took this new hairstyle as a sign, repented, and devoted her life to Buddhism. Okyo lived the rest of her days as a nun in a nearby chapel. The boyfriend became a monk and labored in the temple gardens. Okyo's hair and scalp remain on display in a glass enclosure on the temple grounds.

If the hair and scalp display isn't bizarre enough, I'm surprised to find a vending machine next to the purification fountain. It seems woefully out of place, but I offer Kassy a hot tea anyway. She looks at me and sniffs with disapproval, "Seems rather inappropriate."

Of course, Kassy is entitled to her opinion. I'm not one to waste a coffee opportunity. I plunk in 100-yen and purchase an aluminum bottle of hot, black liquid-gold.

Tatsueji is considered a *spiritual checkpoint* temple. It's a place of reflection and, if necessary, a place to reset. I flew to Shikoku Island to meditate, relax, walk, delve into Japanese culture, and make peace with life's changes. I had also hoped to enjoy much-needed alone time. Except for the latter, I'd say the trip is a success, at least so far.

The daily routine of peregrination suspends me in the now, and I've had little time to contemplate my professional future. However, I can say that the idea of retirement sounds better and better.

While it wasn't that big of a deal, facing menopause feels trivial. Even my previous concerns regarding age-related decline now seem grossly dramatized. This is where Kassy has been a great mentor. She proves age is just a number, and she does this by walking me into the ground every damn day. Chronologically, Kassy's body is decades older than mine. Physically, she is years younger. Two nights ago, she was she was standing on her hands in my room as part of her yoga regimen. I haven't attempted a handstand since my teens. I wonder if I still can.

Kassy hasn't been my only *sage-on-age*. I marveled at the grace of Zen Master Kim. And who could ever forget the vigor of Takahara-san?

It's simple, really. If I want good health and longevity, I must get off my ass and move. I don't know why I had to come all the way to Shikoku to gather this nugget of conventional wisdom, but I think I've got it now.

Continuing my evaluation, the professor in me wants to assign a letter grade. At first blush, I'd say I'm a B+ henro. Of course, I am an easy grader. However, after examining the *Ten Precepts* in my henro guidebook, I'm not as confident. The guidelines are as follows:

1) *I will not harm life.*
2) *I will not steal.*
3) *I will not commit adultery.*
4) *I will not tell a lie.*
5) *I will not exaggerate.*
6) *I will not speak abusively.*
7) *I will not cause discord.*
8) *I will not be greedy.*
9) *I will not be hateful.*
10) *I will not lose sight of the Truth.*

I have nailed the first five, but my actions on the following five are sketchy. While my words have not been outright abusive, not all have been kind. My snarky inner-dialogue is another story altogether. The need and greed for personal space creates disharmony and has caused discord in my own heart and probably in Kassy's, as well. I haven't been hateful, but I haven't been loving either. I also don't think I've kept sight of the *truth* – the true *Buddha Nature* living within me. I know I can do better.

I write the last five precepts on the back of an osamefuda slip, making the mastery of these standards my new wish. I write out a second slip for the Daishi hall. Doubling down never hurts for a girl like me.

With the story of poor Okyo's hair fresh in my mind, I smooth my chocolate-cherry curls and skip the bell altogether. I don't need that kind of drama today. I light my candle and three sticks of incense, deposit my slips and coins, and then chant my way through the sutras. My reset is complete.

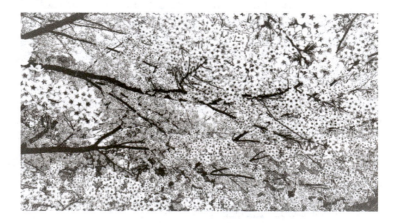

Temple 20: Kakurinji

So far, the morning's hike is primarily on asphalt.
I'm looking forward to the crazy elevation gains of
temples twenty and twenty-one if only to have a squishy
trail beneath my feet. Until now, I worried the road's hard
surface would wreak havoc on my plantar fasciitis, but it's
the outside of my lower-left leg calling out for attention.

Kassy thinks I have shin-splints. I'm not
convinced. I've known hikers and runners who have
suffered shin-splints, but I never have. The pain is intense
and throbbing, but it doesn't hurt directly along my shin.
Instead, a ligament or muscle, from knee to ankle on the
outside of my leg, feels strained. The inflamed tissue feels
like a cord tight enough to pluck like the string of a guitar.

I need to slow down, so I encourage Kassy to
walk on. She agrees to wait for me at the next temple. I
find a bench and administer a roadside massage. It hurts
to touch the afflicted area, so I massage my calf and ankle
instead.

A faint jingling grows nearer, and I know who is
approaching. It's *Jingle-Buns*! Aptly named for the large
bell clipped to his belt loop. Kassy and I walked behind
him this morning for as long as we both could stand it.
We watched the bell jangle with each swing of his tiny
hips. It's cute but also annoying.

Jingle-Buns eases himself down next to me, and
his bell is silenced between his backside and the bench.
"Everything okay?" he asks.

"Yes," I reply. "But my leg hurts." I draw a line
down the painful band.

"Shin-splints," he says with an apologetic smile.

"That's what my friend says too."

Jingle-Buns gets up to leave and grips my
shoulder. "Walk slowly," he offers. "And stay off the hard
road."

"Thanks. I'll try." Stay off the hard road? If only it were that easy.

Inside the gate of *Kakurinji,* a stone Jizo speckled with lichen greets me. He has his regular army of babies gathered around. For more than a moment, I forget about the throbbing of my shin.

Kukai founded Kakurinji before the year 800. When Kukai visited this area, he found a tiny statue of Jizo at the base of a grand cedar tree. Two white cranes sheltered the three-centimeter deity beneath their wings.

Kukai collected the inch-high idol, and just as he did at the last temple, he carved a bigger version and enshrined the tiny Jizo into the larger. Kukai's carving is 90-centimeters or about three-feet high. I'd love to see both, but these treasures are not available for viewing by the commonest of henro like me. I'll have to be satisfied communicating via chant on the steps of the main hall.

Temple 21: Tairyuji

As planned, Kassy and I reunite outside the stamp office at temple twenty-one. We flank a small river and are lulled by the gush of burbling water and the twitter of bird song. Everything sparkles in the mid-morning light. Kassy asks me the significance of an image she saw at the last temple, the one of *Fudo Myoo*.

I don't know anything about Fudo Myoo, except that he is a Buddhist guardian deity. He is fierce, with two tusks jutting from each side of his mouth. One tusk points up, and the other down. He stands in the backdrop of a great flame and holds an upright sword in his right hand and a rope in his left. One eye is open, and the other is closed. I make a mental note to do a little research on our friend once we find Wi-Fi.

The trek between temples is six kilometers, but it is a brutal six. The elevation diagram in my guidebook makes me laugh aloud. The trail begins at an elevation of 500 meters, drops to sea-level, flattens out for a short stroll through a valley, and then climbs back up another 500 meters. It looks crazy!

Fortunately, the steep trail down is soft and dry, and I have my hiking-poles to help keep me upright. For the first time, Kassy lags. When hiking uphill, she is a little mountain goat. But now, fearing a fall, she slowly picks her way down.

The wooded-path between peaks follows the *Naka River*. I wait beside a waterfall for Kassy and take in the freshness of the forest. The rushing sound of the water, mossy rocks, and towering cedars wrap me up in a bubble. I'm a tiny figure in a snow-globe without the snow.

I pluck a crimson blossom from the leggy foliage of a camellia bush and toss it in the water. The current carries the flower gently downstream, and I watch it bob about, pause against a log-jam of twigs, and continue out of sight. I think of my grandmother and pluck another.

My grandmother would have loved this spot. I close my eyes and imagine her. In my mind's eye, I see the spry grandmother of my teens and not the little bird who flew away two summers ago. I scooch over to make space on my mossy rock. Together again, bubbled in our Japanese snow-globe of cedar boughs and red camellia petals, Grandma and I sit shoulder-to-shoulder and just breathe.

The final few kilometers up the mountain trail are breathtaking – and I mean this in the literal sense. My lungs threaten to burst, and my heartbeat pounds in my temples. Switchback after switchback and false summit after false summit, I finally see the gate to *Tairyuji*. And, of course, the entrance is atop a long flight of stone steps.

Once through the gate, I know the near heart-attack climb was worth it. The sun shines brightly through the cedar trees overhead. Below, the plush forest canopy rolls out like a deep green carpet disappearing into the sea of a steel grey horizon.

Several times since starting my pilgrimage, I have caught myself saying, "This is the most beautiful place I have ever seen!" And each time I make such a proclamation, I shake my head in awe. How can one tiny island house so much beauty?

Shikoku makes me feel like a little girl again. I am experiencing the daily wonders of childhood – Of course, it's nothing like my own childhood, but that hardly seems to matter. The pure joy of discovery is the same.

Over the past week, so many things have delighted and surprised me. The temple grounds of Tairyuji add to the splendid collection of new encounters. Because the Shikoku pilgrimage is so far removed from my western culture, I am beholding with fresh eyes. And I'm surprised how often tears stream down my face for no apparent reason.

I move through my routine from purification fountain to bell and then to the main hall. In front of the building, I light my candle and incense sticks for the deity *Kokuzo,* the bodhisattva of wisdom and enlightenment.

Kukai visited this mountaintop when he was 19. He chanted the mantra for Kokuzo Bosatsu a million times. In exchange, Kukai earned superhuman powers of memory. Scholars visit this temple in search of wisdom, and students pray for academic success.

Before phoning the inn manager to pick us up, Kassy and I shift into tourist mode. A ropeway spans high above the lush forest. Constructed in 1992, the cable car runs from the summit to the village of Sanroku, serving as an alternate way to reach the temple. We aren't staying near Sanroku, but we purchase roundtrip tickets just to enjoy the ride.

Kassy and I sip delicious cups of complimentary mushroom tea while we wait for the cable car to make its way up from below. The taste of the hot tea reminds me of the smell of the forest. It is dank and a bit musty, but I can't get enough of it. In a failed attempt, I ask the shop owner for the brand. My question is lost in translation, but I do end up with a second complimentary cup.

The cable car is enormous. It could probably haul at least a hundred people. Besides the operator, Kassy and I have the place to ourselves. We move to the front and press our noses against the glass. Classical music, perfectly suited for an elevator, plays from the speakers above.

Soaring high above the canopy, we stand shoulder-to-shoulder. I tap Kassy's arm and point to a rocky crag below. A pack of bronze-sculpted wolves graces the rocks below. One sculpture is perched high on a boulder as if keeping watch, and another one howls to a hidden moon. Two wolves square off as if ready to fight. Partially hidden amongst the pine scrub, a lone wolf catches the scent of prey.

We are silent, but I imagine we share many of the same awe-inspired feelings. I drape an arm over Kassy's shoulder, and she wraps one around my waist. We stand there together, breathless and teary-eyed.

Temple 22: Byodoji

My evening at *Pilgrimage Inn Ryugasou* was fantastic. Before last night, I had only stayed in temples and henro-houses – nothing commercial. Therefore, I was a tad apprehensive, but most of that melted away when *Ishida-san*, the inn manager, collected us from temple twenty-one.

Ishida-san was tall, fit, and terribly good-looking. He spoke near-perfect English and has completed the Shikoku pilgrimage several times. I knew we were in good hands. He showed Kassy and me to our room, went over a few house rules, and gave us the schedule for bathing, dinner, and breakfast.

After the day's hike of endless switchbacks, I was thrilled to find a tub already full of near-scalding water. Out of habit, I carried my scrappy towel-of-disappointment with me. The microfiber letdown is a relic from my first Camino, and it's barely enough to cover one thigh. I hate using the thing, but I've yet to find a better substitute in terms of function and weight.

Fortunately, Mr. Ishida stocked the fluffiest towels I've had the pleasure of wrapping around my body. I tossed my old hiking towel atop a heap of discarded clothes, took a quick shower to remove the day's dirt and sweat, and climbed in the tub. Not ten minutes passed before the door swung wide open. It was Kassy.

Kassy isn't shy about the whole communal bathing thing, but I kind of wished she was. She showered off and looked at me with those pleading eyes. I scooted over, and she eased herself down.

I usually don't mind sharing. It's fun to sit and soak and chat about the day. While Mr. Ishida's tub was deep, it is only a tad longer than a standard American bathtub. With this big body of mine, two was a crowd!

According to Ishida's website, his inn is on the outskirts of the city of *Anan*. The term, *outskirts,* is an understatement. This place is in the middle of nowhere. Apart from a vending machine across the street, the only food and drink available were supplied by Mr. Ishida.

Temple life has spoiled me. Gone were the lacquered trays holding tiny sashimi dishes, tempura vegetables, pickled veggies, and hot miso soup. Instead, Ishida-san served a rustic bowl of curried soybeans over white rice.

Apart from miso soup and an occasional slab of tofu, I typically steer clear of soybean-anything. Naturally, I was skeptical. However, the humble and hearty meal was damn delicious and exactly what we needed.

After dinner, Ishida-san invited us outside to sit around a campfire and enjoy the stars. The crackling fire and heavy woodsmoke conjured memories of beach fires with my sons. Suddenly, I was homesick.

Five years abroad, I've relied heavily on technology to narrow the distance growing between my family and me. It helps. But it's not enough.

Work and travel are my grand distractions. It's hard to feel homesick when preoccupied with manufactured busyness. I'm always on the move. When I'm not traveling, I'm teaching. If not in the classroom, I'm grading papers, planning the next lecture, or putting out fires for the administration. I'm happy to be useful, but last night found me questioning my priorities.

The campfire ambiance cut deeper than I thought possible. I ached for baseball games, fishing trips, holiday meals, bike rides, and summers on the beach.

A quiet man in the shadows got up, picked his way to the woodpile, and gingerly bent down to add another log. I could tell by his movements he was suffering. In the firelight, I saw cuts and scrapes on his face and hands. He also had a fat lip. I was tempted to ask what had happened but thought better of it.

Once the man returned to his place in the shadows, Kassy piped up, "Did you hear about the prostitute and the dentist?" No one said a word. All I could do was hold my breath and hope she wouldn't continue. But that was wishful thinking.

"So, this prostitute asked a dentist if he'd like to have sex." I drew in a deep breath, and Kassy continued, "But the dentist was quite the mama's boy, and his mom warned him to stay away from vaginas – because vaginas were armed with dangerous teeth that could snap off a man's penis."

I let out a groan and put my head in my lap. Kassy soldiered-on. "Well, the dentist told the prostitute, 'No, I don't want anything to do with you. Heaven knows, you have teeth down there.' And of course, that made the prostitute laugh, but she also felt sorry for the silly fellow."

I lifted my head to see Mr. Ishida on the edge of his seat. His head was slightly cocked as he listened to Kassy's story unfold. The injured man in the shadows remained perfectly still.

Kassy continued, "Well, the prostitute finally convinced the dentist to come up to her apartment to take a look-see – for free! So, the dentist followed her upstairs, and the prostitute took off her clothes and sprawled across the bed with her legs wide open."

Kassy paused for a dramatic effect. Ishida-san scooted dangerously close to the fire to bridge the gap between his chair and the storyteller. I tipped my empty beer can and sucked out the last few drops.

Kassy continued. "The dentist moved in close to examine the prostitute's vagina. He pulled back in disgust and said, 'No wonder you don't have any teeth. Your gums look terrible!'"

A laugh exploded from my chest. I couldn't help it. In my defense, the circumstances couldn't have been more awkward or inappropriate. I laughed at the silly joke, and Kassy's indifference to cultural norms, and the tentative expression on Mr. Ishida's face, and the unmoved man sitting perfectly still in the shadows. Everything was utterly ridiculous, and I howled like a madwoman.

To make matters funnier, at the close of the punchline, Mr. Ishida simply nodded, got up, and fetched another two beers. He opened a beer and handed it to me. He opened another and sat back down, keeping the fire safely between Kassy and himself.

This morning, over a breakfast of rice gruel with black sesame sprinkles, Kassy and I plan our 26-kilometer day. Our goal is to visit temples twenty-two and twenty-three. The terrain is blessedly flat but almost entirely on the hardscape of a busy highway.

My lower leg, tucked beneath the squat dining table, throbs in painful anticipation. I get up to fetch more rice, not necessarily because I am hungry, but because I need to stretch. After hobbling to and from the rice pot, I gingerly squat back down to my cushion on the floor.

The quiet man from last night's campfire sits a long table away. Without rising to his feet, he scooches across the tatami mats to my table. He doesn't speak English, and he doesn't seem to speak Japanese. In fact, he doesn't utter a sound. He explains, through pantomime, he practices acupuncture, and he wants to massage my leg.

I try to control my body language, but it's no use. Repelled by the man's pulsating lip and bloody scrapes, my back arches, and I lean away. Ishida-san comes to the rescue.

"He's a different kind of doctor," Ishida-san says. "He knows powerful Chinese medicine. Let him help you."

I nod, and the Chinese doctor moves closer. He sets to work on the inflamed band running from the side of my knee down to my ankle. While he works, I examine the fresh scrapes and cuts on his bald head and face. He must have taken one hell of a tumble.

As he digs his fingers into my tender muscle, a deep red scrape along the back of his thumb lets loose. The wound oozes dark blood onto my neon-pink support socks. The round splotch looks like a cabernet stamp from the business end of a wine cork. Horrified, I remain still, and he seems not to notice.

Ishida-san offers the doctor a roll of stretchy sports tape to stabilize my injury. Wrapped and ready to go, I thank them both and struggle to my feet. I offer a hand to the sitting doctor, and he allows me to help him to his feet. I bow and divert my eyes from the new blotch of blood on my wrist.

The Chinese doctor's sorry shape, combined with my pitiful limp, compels Ishida-san to offer us a lift to temple twenty-two. None of us hesitate. We happily pile into his tiny car. His generosity shaves away six kilometers of road-walking.

Overhead, broad ribbons in yellow, red, white, green, and blue span from the temple gate, fluttering over the walkway and up a long flight of stairs to the main hall. It looks as if the grounds are decked out for a party.

Ishida-san accompanies me under the canopy of colors and up the stairs. In a low hum, he leads me through the morning sutras. The experience feels oddly intimate. At the stamp office, there's nothing left to do but bow our goodbyes. In an unexpected gesture, he reaches out to shake my hand, and I accept. Our handshake evolves into a little more than a half-hug. Heat rises to my face. Without another word, Mr. Ishida turns and heads back to his car. I blush a little more, realizing I have a tiny crush on my handsome innkeeper.

Temple 23: Kakuoji

The morning sun warms my shoulders, and a tender composition of birdsong lightens my heart. Kassy shuffles beside me, but she is unusually silent.

"You okay, kid?" I ask.

"Oh, I'm perfectly wonderful."

"Okay, just checking. You're kind of quiet."

"I'm feeling too blessed for words."

"Wow, that's good news."

Kassy nods, and like a little kid, she pretends to zip her lips shut. She's a touch nutty, but I can't help but adore her all the same. Over the past few days, I've fallen into a lovely friendship with Kassy. At first, she irritated the hell out of me with her never-ending chatter and backpack drama. I see her differently now.

Last night, I could have acted *the prude* and taken offense at her inappropriate joke. However, it was way more fun to laugh and to accept Kassy for all that she is. She ignited an unexpected emotional release, and I feel much lighter this morning.

Although the weather is perfect, the walk along the highway is boring me to death. I scan yards and gardens for sources of stimulation. I watch a stooped little man drag sacks of fertilizer from a stack near his house to the tailgate of his pickup truck. He tries to lift one up into the bed, but he cannot. As we near his driveway, I call out to him, "Ohayo Gozaimasu!" I smile and wave.

The old man nods solemnly before returning to his sacks. I cross the street and walk up next to his truck. "Sumimasen," I say. He looks up, and I engage in my best feed-sack-throwing-farm-girl pantomime. The old man nods in approval, and I load the sacks into the back of his truck.

After loading eight sacks, the old man waves me off. I'm guessing the man is on his way to his orange grove. The bags were heavy. But I feel stronger after turning a good deed.

When I return to the road, Kassy smiles at me in loving approval. She does not break her zipped-up vow of silence. We continue side-by side, watching our shadows stretch and fall in the morning light.

Off to the right, I see a wooden shrine tucked along a narrow path. I motion for Kassy to follow me. We are nowhere near temple twenty-three, but I'm in the mood for diversion. I drop an osamefuda and offer a silent prayer to whatever deity graces the tiny cedar structure with the dramatic pagoda roof. A squad of Jizo babies flanks the path, and I think about motherhood and how terribly lucky I am.

I lead Kassy along a wooded-trail that dumps us in a small field shy of the road. Hesitantly, we wade through tall grass and scrubby undergrowth. When we pop back out onto the blacktop, we both gasp at the hand-painted warning sign of a cartoon viper. Fortunately, we did not meet such a beastie.

Another narrow path takes us off the road again and up through a bamboo forest. The slender trunks shiver in the wind, and my feet fall blissfully on a soft pad of silvering leaves. I wish I could walk this path all the way around the island, but it doesn't last.

Once back out on the highway, traffic has really picked up. Kassy takes the lead, and I fall in behind. In a single-file, we prepare to enter the 301-meter *Kaneuchi Tunnel*.

Unfortunately, the narrow sidewalk is not on the side of oncoming traffic. I'd much rather see a vehicle coming, especially the large trucks. I wrap a scarf around my face before entering. This all feels terribly reckless, but protecting my lungs is the least I can do.

Once inside the tunnel, my vertigo tries to get the best of me. A low and narrow guardrail separates the sidewalk from the traffic lane. I work to correct my staggered-gait, focusing on a distant light and walking the straightest line I can muster. A gust of wind plasters me against the sooty tunnel wall. I freeze for a moment, fight back a lump of fear welling in the pit of my stomach, and continue.

Kassy waits for me at the tunnel's end. I imagine my eyes are as wide as hers. She breaks her silence for the first time since zipping her lips outside of temple twenty-two.

"Well, that fucking sucked!"

I laugh and give her a hug. Back home, in her *real* life, I don't think Kassy swears much. The contrived f-bomb left her lips with such force – like an indulgence meant to make me feel better. It worked. I have a major potty-mouth, and while I'm controlling it more than usual, I have slipped a few times.

Feeling beyond frazzled, I really want to rest for a moment against the safety of the concrete bulkhead, but something smells awful. I scan the side of the road for the source and find a flattened baby pig. Not much is left of the little guy, but I can tell he is a wild hog by his sharp teeth and tiny hooves.

"Aw, that's too bad." I point out the piglet to Kassy.

"Better him than us," she says. And we walk on, single-file, toward the next tunnel.

At 175 meters, the *Fukui Tunnel* is much shorter than our last. But it is every bit as dim, and there is no guardrail to separate the narrow sidewalk from the steady stream of traffic. However, this time, I keep my wits about me as cars and trucks blow on by.

Kassy drops behind to adjust her laces. Her feet are giving her problems today. I worry her pack's weight is taking a toll on her, but she won't hear of it. Yesterday, I suggested she send more stuff home, but I didn't push the issue. She is an accomplished hiker and a grown-ass woman. Who am I to tell her how much she should carry?

Up ahead, I see something in the middle of the road. Maybe it's a dog – like a super large dog? No, it doesn't move like a dog. It's slinkier. Oh, my gosh. What if it's a mountain lion. Do they have mountain lions in Japan?

I squint to make out the form. It looks so unusual to me. I cannot unwrap what it is I am seeing.

Suddenly, the animal leaps across the road in a single bound and scrambles into the forest. Holy shit! It's a monkey! I've never seen a monkey in the wild. I pull out my phone, hoping to catch a photo, but then I worry. Are wild monkeys dangerous? I wait for Kassy to catch up. There's always safety in numbers.

Unfortunately, or maybe, fortunately, we don't get another glimpse of the monkey. While I have read about the monkeys on Shikoku, I hadn't prepared myself to see one. I love animals, especially monkeys, but I'm not sure I'm ready to meet one face-to-face.

Kassy and I remain vigilant and on the lookout for wildlife. The warm sun is overhead, and my growling tummy has me thinking about lunch. Other than a small sack of dried figs and walnuts, there is no food to be found.

We take a break on a bridge abutment. Kassy points out an idyllic farmhouse, and I count the adjacent rice paddies. Five terraces stretch out like giant steps from the front of the house to the back of the barn. I've never seen such efficient use of a hillside. The terraces of spring green are aesthetically pleasing and make so much sense. I think about the steep slope of brambles behind my house in Washington state and imagine blissful terraces of silvery blueberry bushes.

I share my figs and walnuts with Kassy. She peels and splits another osettai orange. We both need all the energy we can get to navigate the next stretch of the busy highway, complete with three more tunnels.

The *Hoshigoe Tunnel* is 230 meters long and slightly brighter than the last two. This time, we have no sidewalk. Instead of a sidewalk, we follow a green line painted on the blacktop. There is also no guardrail between the green line and the flow of traffic. Terrific.

Kassy ditches her vow of silence and shifts to storytelling mode. I listen to a complicated story about her river rafting friends back home. She tells me about Diane, who is having an affair with Bob, the whitewater guide. Bob is engaged to Sue, and Sue is the owner of the rafting company. If I understand the narrative tension, Bob is risking his job to sneak around with Diane, and Diane is Sue's hairdresser. Apparently, poor Sue needs to hire better quality folks.

I don't know what Sue or Bob or Diane or their twisted love-triangle have to do with the Shikoku, but the convoluted story and Kassy's animation make me laugh. She carries on, introducing me to Greg, the diabetic with one leg, and another woman named Peggy who can't make it down the river without needing to pee over the side of the boat. I listen and allow kilometers of boring roadway to melt beneath my feet.

"To be continued," Kassy says as we approach another tunnel. We fall in single-file again, and Kassy leads me along the green painted line cutting through *Kubou Tunnel*. I'm sick of tunnels.

Usually, I'm a tunnel fan. When my kids were little, we took many road trips. When approaching a tunnel, they would squeal, "Honk the horn, Mom! Honk the horn!" It was a silly tradition, but if the tunnel was free of traffic, I always obliged. My kids are grown now and no longer in the backseat. But sometimes, to revisit the bygone days of motherhood, I still honk the horn.

At the other end of the *Kubou Tunnel*, I smell another dead piglet. I find his body, and Kassy and I lean over to inspect the poor beastie. We don't have wild hogs in Washington state, so this is a novelty. Despite all the hiking I did in Germany, I never ran into a wild boar on the trail. This is a good thing, of course. I always hiked with Jasper, and I suppose his doggie-scent kept the hogs away.

This little piggy is in better shape than the last. Its snout is long and black, and the turned-up nose is still intact. Most of its body has been eaten away by birds, leaving a darkly striped coat of orangish-red hair. I've always had a thing for pigs, and I do wish I could see an alive piglet, but only without the mama.

Kassy picks up the storyline again, but this time her focus is on the one-legged diabetic and his girlfriend, Laura. Once again, I have no idea where she is going with this, but I play along and enjoy her enthusiasm. Clearly, she is trying to entertain me.

Kassy drops her story at the entrance of the *Ichinosaka Tunnel*. After another 224 meters of walking in the dark, she doesn't pick it back up. Perhaps, she is too tired to continue. I try to amuse myself by continuing the thread in my head, but I can't recall who's who and who's doing who.

By three in the afternoon, Kassy and I are starving. Our rice gruel and rations of figs, walnuts, and orange were not enough to sustain us. We walk around a curve, and like a mirage, a giant red boat appears alongside the road. I can't tell if it's really a ship modified into a restaurant or if it's a restaurant built to look like an old ship. None of this really matters. It's a restaurant and restaurants have food!

As I pull the glass-paneled door open and walk inside, I can almost taste the tender udon noodles in salty broth. Kassy rubs her hands together in hungry anticipation. I scan the café tables and chairs, looking for signs of life.

"Sumimasen," I call out. "Sumimasen." But no one answers. An eerie feeling washes over me, and the hairs on the back of my neck bristle. "It's like a ghost ship."

"Let's get the heck out of here!" says Kassy. I don't argue. For the sake of my rumbling tummy, I take one more look around. I run my index finger along the cashier's counter, swiping up a greasy layer of dust.

Back out on the blacktop, Kassy looks absolutely defeated. She really wanted udon. And so, did I.

From the highway, I spot the top of a large orange and white pagoda, and I know the temple is nearby. Kassy starts another round of *Row-Row-Row-Your-Boat*, but this time, I sing along like a good sport, and we keep this up all the way to the steps of *Yakouji*.

According to my guidebook, 33 temple steps are designated for women, and 42 are for men. When I arrive at the gate, I don't see any signs indicating *his-or-her* directions.

I climb the first seven steps and bow before the gate. Once through the gate, I climb up another 30. The steps shimmer with small silver coins that I call yennies. These coins are Japan's equivalent to a U.S. penny. Visitors leave the yennies on the steps for luck, health, and wealth.

At the top of the steps, we find the purification station and bell tower. Kassy takes off to photograph the pagoda, but I hang back to wash up, ring the bell, and take in the view. *Minami town* stretches out below, promising a hot meal and a comfy bed.

From high above, I see the train station. I'll spend tonight and tomorrow in Minami and then hop the train to Tokushima, making my way back to Okinawa. My heart sinks a little. Even after a day of tunnel-hell, I am not ready to leave Shikoku or my pilgrim life.

Part Two
Ascetic Training

Part Two: *Ascetic Training*

Temple 24: Hotsumisakiji

The next break from work could not come soon enough. The days dragged on and on. Typically, I'm *all-in* when it comes to my job. However, this has not been the case since Shikoku wiggled into my heart.

To fill the henro void, I devoured everything I found written in English about the Shikoku – which wasn't much. My first trip was impromptu, and there were so many things I did not understand. However, I've used my down-time wisely to mentally prepare for *Ascetic Training*.

Self-discipline is a slippery slope, at least for me. I've long since mastered discipline in terms of my education and work ethic. My physical and mental toughness is a different story. I'll need to keep my emotions and my health in check.

I plan to incorporate the *Seven Gifts Needing No Wealth* into my pilgrimage and afterward throughout my daily life. The Japanese call this concept *Muzai Nanase*, which literally means "no money."

1) *Bohase* – is to lend your bed or shelter to another.
2) *Shozase* – is to give up your place or advantage.
3) *Shinse* – is body-service or the gift of labor.
4) *Waganse* – is to always show a happy face.
5) *Gonse* – is to use words that express kindheartedness.
6) *Ganse* – is to look upon others with gentleness.
7) *Shinse* – is to provide heart-service or to have a kind heart.

Last night, I flew into Osaka, hopped a bus to Tokushima, and then boarded a train to Kaifu station. I managed each leg of the journey thankfully without incident.

The single-car train glowed pink with twinkling lights and bouquets of silk cherry-blossoms. Gauzy rose curtains draped the windows, and paper lanterns swung above the aisle, keeping time with the clacking of the southbound train.

It was late in the evening, and apart from the conductor, there was not another soul in the car. For a moment, I was sad to be traveling solo. The festive train was high school-prom spectacular and just the kind of scene better shared with another.

I hated disembarking the party train for the lonely platform of Kannoura station. The night air swallowed me up in the darkness as I watched the twinkling pink lights melt away in the distance. I soothed myself with the knowledge that cherry-blossom season on Shikoku is in full swing! And tomorrow's hike would be spectacular.

I spent the night in a cabin connected to a surf-shop in the tiny village of Shishikui. The kind owner collected me from the train platform and has delivered me back here this morning. My plan is to continue south by train to *Hotsumisakiji*. The walking route hugs the coastline, and while I'm sorry to miss the scenery, I'm not ashamed to avoid the narrow tunnels, hot asphalt, and dangerous traffic. In this situation, the risks do not outweigh the rewards.

It's mid-morning, and below the station platform, a team of boys, clad in white knickers and black jerseys, swarm the baseball diamond like a hive of angry bees. That old familiar crack of the bat takes me back in time.

The coach cranks one out to left-field, and a little bee scoops it up and whips it to the shortstop. The shortstop turns on a heel and hammers it home. Perfection! The bat cracks again, and the right-fielder scrambles to catch the pop fly. He's got it!

I could watch these kids play all day, but the twinkling railcar from last night pulls up to the platform, and I hop on. The cherry-blossom overload is just as cute in daylight. If I were a sixteen-year-old bride, this would be my wedding venue.

Unlike last night, the train is full of passengers to share this festive display. More than a dozen white-clad Ohenro look up to greet me. We exchange nods, and I take the first open seat next to a young henro. His name is Uri, and he is from Poland.

"It's like a disco-tech, yah?" says Uri.

"Yeah! Makes me want to dance!"

Uri strikes a seated *Saturday Night Fever* pose and stretches out a long arm to bat a paper lantern. In silence, we watch the lantern bob and sway above our heads.

I feel downright cozy in the company of my temporary flock. Typically, when traveling by train in Japan, which is still new for me, I count the stops and continuously refer to my map. But now, I sit back and relax. When the train reaches our collective destination, I'll follow the flock.

The railcar chatter grows quiet as we turn and gawk out the windows at a massive, white statue of young Kukai. It's by far the largest Kukai I've ever seen. Uri tells me that below the figure is a temple used for training new priests. I know we must be nearing our stop in *Muroto*.

Apart from the training temple, Muroto holds many sacred sites associated with Kukai. These sites are known as the *Seven Wonders of Muroto*. The first wonder is a cavern and inner temple Kukai built in one night. Another is a rock he twisted to create a protective alcove for his mother to rest during a fierce storm. To the north lies his bathing pond.

Arguably, the most sacred of the seven wonders is *Mikurodo Cave*. During his teens, Kukai visited the cave during a period of ascetic training. Kukai said, "A shining star from the sky flew into my mouth." This is the cave where young Kukai achieved *enlightenment*.

Uri and I follow a Japanese henro up the hill to temple twenty-four. The poor guy is limping, and I want to go around him, but I also don't wish to be rude. After weeks of feeling warehoused in Okinawa, my legs belong to a racehorse twitching to catch the lead of out the starting gate.

Uri is a racehorse too. I feel him galloping closely behind, and I smell the peppermint gum on his breath. Twice, the toe of Uri's boot scuffs my heel. On the third scuff, Uri steps on the back of my shoe and gives me a flat tire.

Dammit! I hobble off the trail to make way for the stream of henro coming up the path. Somewhere, in the middle of the passing flock, Uri waves a long arm and calls out, "Sorry!" And then he disappears around a bend.

I fix my flat, collect myself, and prepare to take the hill. But the momentum has tanked. I'm all alone. Gone are the good vibrations of my temporary-tribe.

As it turns out, Uri's flat tire is my lucky break. Free from the crowd and not quite ready to resume the climb, I notice a side trail dimly lit with shimmering coins of sunshine dropping through the leafy canopy.

To my surprise, I stumble upon one of the seven wonders and enter the sacred grotto and inner-temple Kukai created in one night to shield his mother from a storm. Historically, the cavern is a special place for women. Until 1868, female pilgrims were not allowed to enter the main temple grounds. Instead, they gathered here to meditate and pray before proceeding along the women's road to the 25th temple.

I find a smooth stone and cop-a-squat, soaking in the accumulated energy of lady-henros gone by. I pull a few paper slips from my messenger bag and prepare the osamefudas for temple twenty-four and twenty-five. Using my lucky purple pen, I write my name and the day's prayer: *I wish for happiness in my marriage.*

In this divinely feminine space, I contemplate the woes and treasures of my sex. Yes, my matrimonial situation is less than ideal, but I have loved being a wife and a mother. I cheerfully shouldered the responsibility of keeping my family together. It's true – I have given much more love than I have received. But I know love, and I know how to love. Madly. Deeply. Truly. I light a candle, flip open my guidebook, and chant the *Heart Sutra.*

I enter the gate of temple twenty-four with hiking-sticks in hand and attempt an awkward bow. I'm out of practice. Typically, I collapse the poles and stuff them in my pack, leaving my hands free to properly tend to my tasks.

Once inside, I find the *Kane Ishi* or the bell rock. The deeply-dimpled boulder is another of the seven wonders. The rock is said to be a portal for communicating with ancestors. I grab a flat stone, the perfect kind for skipping across a lake, and test it out. My tap vibrates across the surface as if the rocky core were hollow. I strike again and listen and then hammer out a message for my grandmother.

Temple 25: Shinshoji

The narrow roadway leaving temple twenty-four is lined by small, granite lanterns. Each shrine is about chest high. I cross the road to check one out, and I'm surprised to find the image of Dr. Martin Luther King etched on an ebony placard below a lightbox. I walk a few paces and smile at the ever-familiar image of Mother Teresa. A few steps more, and I meet Nelson Mandela.

I meander down the hill, pausing at each shrine to examine the faces of passionate and graceful humans who have blasted their love-light on our often-dark world. Their selfless acts reach far beyond religion, culture, and creed. I'm grateful for the time and space to walk and reflect in the glow of their examples.

The seven-kilometer hike to *Shinshoji* should take less than two hours. The downhill route is roadside, but the ocean views are spectacular. I've always loved the Pacific Ocean, and my precious time in the Coast Guard strengthened the attachment.

The sun shines brightly overhead, but the wind whipping off the steel grey waves makes me shiver, forcing me to pick up the pace. Before long, my body falls into a rhythm. Old habits die hard, and I laugh once I realize I'm marching. My left foot strikes the ground, keeping time with a cadence only I can hear. I march all the way into town, pausing briefly to admire a long line of fishing vessels moored at the *Murotomisaki Port.*

The brightly painted orange and white gate of *Shinshoji* sits atop a long set of stairs. A dense crowd gathers at the base, forcing me to abandon my cadence and fall out of step. Typically, I'm not a fan of stairs, but my racehorse-quads, still twitchy and raring to go, pump out the set with ease.

A yellow ship's wheel graces the arch of the gate. My seafaring-heart swells. I think of my Coastguard shipmates, bow reverently, and enter Shinshoji.

Kukai founded this temple in 807 by carving a statue of Jizo. The Jizo depiction was not the garden variety Jizo surrounded by his army of babies. No. The one enshrined here is *Kajitori Jizo* or the *Helmsman Jizo*. Fishermen, fisherwomen, and their families pray to him for protection while out to sea.

After the purification ritual, I ring the bell to announce my arrival. Like the women's grotto, this temple warrants a wish aligned with the deity enshrined. I find a bench and scratch out a couple of new osamefudas: *I wish for the health and safety of my little brothers and sisters of the Coast Guard.*

Temple 26: Kongochoji

I had planned to bestow two little gifts on the first Jizo of this phase. So far, it hasn't seemed like the right time. I unzip the secret pocket in my messenger bag and withdraw two little toys – a shiny, red *Matchbox* car and a thumb-sized vinyl doll with long blonde hair and a blue cotton dress. The car is for my departed big brother and the doll is for my cousin.

I tuck the toys inside my shirt pocket to keep them close to me. I must wait until I find the perfect Jizo to make my offering. So, for now, Irv and Holly are my travel companions.

I weave my way through the neighborhood streets of Muroto and pause at a cigarette vending machine. I don't smoke. I gave up the habit decades ago, but in Japan, vending machines are my favorite roadside attractions, and this cigarette machine does not disappoint. While there isn't anything astonishing about the apparatus itself, the contents make me chuckle. Along with the well-known brands of Marlboro and Winston, this machine vends packs of *Hope* and *Peace*. Just imagine - Hope and Peace are but a match-strike away.

Up ahead, I see a familiar-looking henro. By familiar, I mean the henro is Caucasian, and therefore, it's probably Uri, the young guy from the train. I quicken my pace to close the gap.

Uri's wearing earbuds. I take advantage of his self-imposed isolation to sneak up behind him. I'm almost within flat-tire range, and I giggle at the prospect of revenge. It takes all the maturity I can muster to not step on the back of his boot.

Uri sets a rapid pace, and I do my best to keep up while going undetected. He comes shoulder-to-shoulder with the hobbling-henro from temple twenty-four. Uri pops out his earbuds, and I lean into my step to eavesdrop. I listen in, partly because I am bored and partly because I want to know what happened to the injured guy.

Cheerfully, Uri engages with the injured guy, a Buddhist monk named *TaiJo*. The monk speaks a bit of English and explains he injured his knee during a fall coming down *Burning Mountain*. I nod sympathetically, even though I'm not in the conversation, and neither has noticed me lurking a step behind.

Beyond *Konichiwa,* Uri doesn't appear to speak Japanese. From pilgrimages past, I've learned that a shared language isn't a prerequisite for making friends.

Uri points to a tree and says, "Tree!"

TaiJo says, "Ki!"

"Rock," says Uri.

"Iwa," says TaiJo.

Uri points to a faraway field, "Rice?"

"Hai," says TaiJo. "Gohan."

"Gohan!" Uri nods in appreciation.

Like me, Uri is a farm kid. So, I appreciate his fervor over a field of rice. I am forever admiring greenhouses and gardens stretching across the Shikoku countryside.

Uri wants to know the word for farmer. TaiJo doesn't understand, and unfortunately, there isn't a farmer within pointing distance. Uri stops walking and motions to the rice paddy.

I delicately fold myself into the conversation, like I've been there all along. I stare out at the rice paddy, making their duo a trio. They don't seem to even notice.

Uri pantomimes riding a tractor, and he's excellent at it. Sitting in a deep squat with his arms out, he grips an invisible steering wheel. He bobs up and down, motoring over all sorts of rocks and dips in his imaginary field. Uri makes little grunting sounds, like the chugging and grinding of tractor gears.

I love a good game of charades, but TaiJo looks bewildered. Suddenly, his eyes light up.

"Toire!" says TaiJo.

"Toire?" asks Uri.

TaiJo's face reddens as he joins Uri in the tractor squat.

"Toire! Toire!" Uri nods and offers a high-five.

TaiJo accepts the five but looks concerned. He drops his backpack and starts ransacking through the contents. Eventually, he produces a packet of tissues.

It doesn't take me long to realize *Toire* is not the Japanese word for farmer. Uri is a few seconds behind. But he makes up for lost time with a hearty belly-laugh.

TaiJo is the last to join our roadside giggle-fest. I realize it's horrendously uncouth, especially for a woman of my age. But after a lifetime surrounded by boys, I've yet to outgrow poop-humor.

"Good joke!" TaiJo smiles, but I'm not sure he fully embraces the gutter-level of our humor.

We leave the asphalt and take up a rocky trail into the forest. The climb is abrupt, but my legs are more powerful than ever. TaiJo, on the other hand, is suffering, and it shows. Uri and I pause several times to wait for our new friend.

We bow together in front of the silvered gate of *Kongochoji*. Uri lends a supporting arm to TaiJo. Slowly, the two ascend a long set of concrete stairs. I can tell by TaiJo's hesitation, each step sends a shockwave of pain to his injured knee.

At the purification station, I wash my hands and mouth, and when I turn around, TaiJo and Uri are nowhere in sight. I complete the rounds by myself and meet back up with Uri at the stamp office, but he hasn't seen TaiJo either. Unceremoniously, Uri and I part ways. I'm spending tonight at this temple, and he must find a suitable place to set up his tent. Like a late spring snowfall, our happy camaraderie melts away into a memory.

Temple 27: Konomineji

It's six in the morning. I should be deep in prayer, but I'm already looking forward to breakfast. Truthfully, I haven't been much of a Japanese breakfast fan. The problem has been the ever-present bowl of googly-eyed, white worms staring up at me. The dish sets my already queasy, morning-tummy a tilt.

The worms are actually krill – quite nutritious but not so delicious. Under a microscope, I'm sure they look like succulent lobsters. If I were starving to death, I'd dearly appreciate the wee maggots.

My tummy grumbles. Thankfully, the chanting of my fellow henros drowns out the sound. Perched on the backs of my feet, my knees grind painfully into the woven reeds of a tatami mat. It feels like I'm kneeling on a cheese shredder.

I'm supposed to be at peace. I'm supposed to be in prayer. All I can really do is shift my weight from side to side, alleviating the strain on my knees and the burn in my thighs.

It's moments like these I curse my lack of flexibility and overall fitness. Kassy could surely sit like this for hours. Kassy is a full two-weeks ahead of me. By now, she has probably entered the *Enlightenment* phase. I hope she is healthy and not feeling lonely. Most of all, I hope she is indeed enlightened.

Surrounding me, on this temple floor, are several ladies my senior. They sit in the same fashion, but they do it way better than me. I sneak a sideways glance at the old woman next to me. Her frail legs splay out to the side, and her bottom touches the mat. How is this possible? The young and the old sit in the same tucked position, still as statues, chanting together in a low melodic hum.

Between chants, a soft-faced monk catches my grimace. He looks upon me with sympathy and motions to a line of squat chairs in the back of the temple, but I'm far too proud. I brush him off with a kind smile and a shake of my head.

For the next 20 minutes, I dig my knees into the mat, forcing myself to remain still. I will not be beaten. I am the new bee in a foreign hive, but I will fit in, and I will hum along. My voice rises and falls and disappears into the collective buzz of my fellow henros.

I try to meditate, to focus on the meaning of today's pilgrimage. I want to say a prayer for Kassy, but I can't stop thinking about bananas. Oh, how I do hope there will be bananas at breakfast. I close my eyes and wrestle my monkey-mind. Kassy. Bananas. Kassy. Bananas. Bananas. Bananas.

A gentle hand taps my shoulder, and I realize the chanting has ceased. I open one eye. It's the old lady with the splayed legs. She offers a hand to help me to my feet. I smile and wave her away. It's not that I'm too proud to accept help, but she is a willow, and I am a cedar with a relatively robust trunk. I'm afraid to pull her down with me.

Stockinged feet pad their way across the tatami mats and out the sliding temple door. Once the last pair departs and I am all alone, I lift off my feet and into a kneel. A low moan rises from my toes and into my chest. The relief is pure ecstasy.

Next, I reach my hands out in front, lift my knees, and brace myself into a downward-facing dog. Ah, that feels divine! I rock side to side, arch my back, walk my hands to my feet, and slowly stand. It's a lot of extra steps, but I couldn't see it happening any other way.

My delayed exit from the temple earns me the last seat at the breakfast table. In front of me is a fat slab of gingered-salmon with crispy skin, a cake of tofu topped with bonito shavings, a poached egg in broth, steamed greens dressed in sesame oil, a square dish of soybeans tossed with strips of wakame seaweed, and an oval bowl of googly-eyed worms. But best of all, within an arm's reach, is a giant basket heaping with bananas. My meditation prayer has come true!

The route to *Konomineji* is 28.5 kilometers or roughly 18 miles. The path is primarily flat, with a small hill at the tenth kilometer and a precipitous 420-meter climb during the final four kilometers. Along the ascent, my guidebook lists a *Henro-Korogashi* – a kind of warning label, indicating a place where henros will likely fall.

Yikes. Today will be hard enough with trekking poles and two good knees. I wonder how my new friend, TaiJo, will manage.

The near 30k day is out of my comfort zone. Although I have hiked this amount and more, I'm older now and somewhat wiser. I listen to my body – at least most of the time.

There are no lodgings at Konomineji, so I plan to stop short of the temple to camp at a henro shelter. Although apprehensive, I'm anxious to try out my tent. I carried it all during the *Awakening* phase but never pulled it from my pack. It's time to put it to use.

Considering the task ahead, I ask permission to take another banana for the road. The hostess motions for me to wait, and she ducks into the kitchen. She returns with a rice ball wrapped in wax paper, a sliver of salmon in foil, two bananas, and an orange. I resist an overwhelming urge to hug this angel. Instead, I execute the most heartfelt bow I can muster. She returns the gesture with as much energy and warmth. And I feel loved.

The extra food adds a hefty amount of weight to my backpack. However, there are no facilities near the temple to purchase lunch or dinner. These gifts, along with a few dried figs and a handful of walnuts, will sustain me until tomorrow morning.

The walk along the coastline is blustery and lonely. Gusts of wind pepper me with roadside grit. I don't mind. The breeze is cooling in the afternoon sun, and my body feels strong. I credit the protein-packed meals and restful sleep of temple twenty-six.

I step off the trail in *Yasuda town* to hit the post office cash machine. Last night's stay was a little more expensive than predicted, but it was so worth it. I have read rants in online forums about how hiking in Japan makes for an expensive adventure. When compared to the Camino de Santiago, I must agree. However, where in the United States could I stay in a sacred space, sleep in a private room overlooking a pink sea of cherry-blossoms, participate in morning meditation, and enjoy beautifully prepared meals all for under $70?

At the post office, I wait in line at the cash machine behind a tall, fair-haired henro. Of course, I know who it is, and I am delighted. The morning has been a solitary affair, and I could use some company.

Uri completes his transaction, and when he turns around, he looks as happy to see me as I am to see him. He drapes a heavy arm over my shoulder, giving me one of those half-hugs I adore. I lean in and accept.

"I didn't think I'd see you again," he says.

"I'm like a bad penny," I say, but Uri doesn't understand the idiom. Perhaps, I should replace penny with *złoty* or *grosz*. I'm not sure which would be more appropriate in Polish.

"How was your night of camping?" I ask.

"Great, but I'm hungry!"

"Well, I got a banana with your name on it." I unzip my pack and fish out the treasure. I hate to give it up, but I also hate to see a starving kid. Uri peels and inhales it before I can secure my backpack.

Uri is tall and lanky and fair, like my youngest son Jaden. He doesn't necessarily remind me of Jade or any of my five sons. However, Uri falls within the right age bracket. My boys are in their early twenties and thirties. So, keeping company with that brand of youthful, masculine energy is as familiar as it is comforting.

Uri's pace is much faster than mine. Two of my choppy steps equals one of his relaxed strides. I do my best to keep up, but I know it won't last.

We take the cutoff leading up the hill, and my pace slows to a crawl. I can't catch my breath. I stop and pretend to tighten my shoe-laces. Bending over seems to help.

Ahead, Uri leans against a tree, patiently awaiting my recovery. Half of me is happy he waits. The other half wishes he'd go on without me, allowing me to wallow in my own misery at my own pace.

Uri pops a thumb in the air, "Okay?"

I return the signal, "Yup, okay." And I am. I'm more than okay. But sometimes, switchbacks turn me into a drama queen.

I catch up to Uri, and we march on. In some unspoken agreement, Uri shifts into low gear. Just above a whisper, he sings a little song. He sings in Polish. I cannot understand the words, but Uri's tune is sweet and simple, like a lullaby. So, I hum along.

We reach the henro shelter. I'm excited to see a water source and *his-and-her* outhouses. I'm ready to stop for the night, but my walking buddy is not.

"You can do it," says Uri. "Just a bit more."

He is right. I know I can. We have hours of daylight, and this section of trail is out and back. I can complete the rest of the climb today, come back and camp, and get a jumpstart on temple twenty-eight in the morning.

I ditch my tent, sleeping bag, mat, and toiletries in the shelter to lighten my load. Uri does the same. Together, we make our way up the hill.

The faint glow of twilight casts a pinkish hue across the temple grounds. A few eager frogs begin the evening's serenade. Comrade frogs will strengthen the chorus once the sun dips out of sight. Except for five adults gathered around a boy in a blue tracksuit, the campus is still.

I met tracksuit-boy, a kid in his early teens, on my walk to temple twenty-five. He travels with an extended family, and they walk a short distance and then pile into a long, white van. I saw him again last night, leaving temple twenty-six. He banged his head on the van window to get my attention. When I looked up at him, he smiled.

When we first met, he was so excited to meet me. He wanted to practice his English skills.

"My name is Kai," he said. "Like the sky."

Kai and I exchanged a few phrases, a bow, and even a high-five. The high-five was my dumb idea, and unfortunately, it proved more challenging than our language barrier. Kai struggles to control his hands and wrists. I hadn't noticed the problem before because he kept his palms pressed tightly together when he spoke. I assumed he was showing reverence. Like a big idiot, I held my hand high in the air. It took him several attempts to meet mine, but he never gave up.

Uri and I go our separate ways at the purification station. We agree to meet back up at the stamp office to make our way, downhill, to our campsite together. I'm happy I won't be alone on my first night in the forest.

Hesitantly, I wander toward the main hall. The family is chanting in a circle around Kai. I don't want to intrude, but Kai's mother glances up and waves me over.

By the time I join their circle, Kai has his hand in the air. "High-five," he says. And I oblige.

"High-five," he says again. We keep this up three more times.

In a dream, Kukai met a woman suffering from a terrible illness. He told her to travel to this temple and drink from its waterfall. She obeyed and was cured. Perhaps, Kai and his family have come to this same waterfall in search of a similar miracle.

Temple 28: Dainichiji

Uri and I break camp around six in the morning. Neither of us claims to have slept well. While I stayed warm and dry in my little tent, the accordion camp mat barely shielded me from the heavily pebbled ground.

I rub my lower back and roll my head from side to side, trying to work out the kinks. Uri looks no better as he staggers beneath the weight of his pack. Even still, he smiles at me with an air of smugness.

"You should have slept inside," said Uri. "There was plenty of room."

"I know, but I wanted to try out my tent."

"And how was it?"

"Fantastic!" I lie.

Of course, I should have slept inside, but I wasn't completely comfortable sharing space with a member of the opposite sex. While Uri is young enough to be one of my sons, he is not mine. I couldn't get beyond that fact. Besides, last night was good training – like a baby-step toward spending the night in the Shikoku forest alone.

Camping along the Shikoku is unnecessary. For the most part, so is being alone. I could have easily hopped a train or hitched a ride to shorten yesterday's walk. Sometimes, I like pushing beyond my comfort zone.

During a pilgrimage, discomfort is a valuable teacher and an integral part of spiritual growth and healing. I hope to never find myself completely comfortable. I want to keep pushing and growing and healing. The lack of homeostasis is addicting.

Uri and I backtrack down the trail from temple twenty-seven. It feels a little deflating, retracing our steps, especially because we have another long day on a short night's sleep. The 38-kilometer walk to Dainichiji is mostly flat, but it's way too much for me to complete in one day. My goal is to stop midway. Uri plans to make the whole trek.

I pause a moment near the *Tonohama* train station, thinking how nice it would be to fast-forward, but I'm not ready to leave Uri yet. We hardly talk, which I appreciate. His good vibes and silent presence leave me free to meditate and daydream.

This morning, I'm enduring an inner-debate. It's the old *I-miss-my-kids* versus *I-love-teaching* argument. Mine is truly a first-world problem. At 52, it's a privilege to contemplate retirement. I retired once already from the military; so, haven't financially needed a job in years. I work for the joy of working, but lately, there's a lot less joy and a ton more bullshit at my university. Perhaps, it's time. For the life of me, I cannot make up my mind.

Outside of *Aki City*, Uri and I rest in a henro hut and devour a stack of convenience-store rice triangles. I try to teach Uri how to open the ingenious package and peel back the cellophane, but he has no patience for it. He inhales six triangles before I open my second wrapper. I surrender my third triangle just to keep him from staring me down like a greedy beagle.

Uri reads the package label, conveniently printed in English. He pulls a face and sniffs the unopened triangle. "Salmon?" he says. "I hate salmon."

"That's fine." I hold out my hand. "Give it back."

"Why couldn't you get something less stinky, like pickled-plum filling?"

"Seriously, Uri?" I try to snatch the triangle from his hand, but he is too quick.

He struggles with the wrapper before taking a hesitant bite. His face contorts into another grimace, and then he sniffs, gags, and sniffs again. Finally, he stuffs the whole thing in his mouth.

"You're a little brat," I say.

"A brat?"

"Yes, like a spoiled-child."

I give him a good-natured shove. "Come on, Brat. Break's over."

The late morning sun is intense overhead, and the concrete path is ruthless underfoot. It's going to be a challenging day. However, our trailside breakfast and Uri's companionship will keep me well-nourished.

We walk side-by-side, talking and kidding each other more than usual. As a joke, I stick out my thumb to hitch a ride. Just like magic, a passing car slows down and pulls off the road.

"Great," says Uri. "You probably found the only murderer on the island."

I would never hitchhike in the States, and I probably wouldn't try it in Europe either. But something about Japan, and especially the island of Shikoku, breaks down and dissolves my human-related phobias. I feel so free and unburdened from the excess baggage of fear.

An old gentleman, dressed in henro garb, steps out of his vehicle to open the trunk for our packs. I'm thrilled, but Uri is hesitant. After a round-robin of bows and nods, I climb into the backseat, and Uri takes the front.

Our driver, and new best friend, is Mr. Osamu. He and I met back at temple twenty-four, but he doesn't seem to remember. We exchanged osamefuda slips. His slip is red, indicating he has completed the pilgrimage at least eight times.

At the stamp office of temple twenty-four, Mr.
Osamu had offered me a ride. Out of habit, I immediately
refused. He looked disappointed, and I walked away
feeling like a jerk. I had forgotten my pledge to gracefully
accept gifts and random acts of kindness, and in doing so,
I hurt his feelings. I'm thrilled to have a second chance to
make things right.

Sitting in the passenger seat of a car traveling in
the opposite lane than one is accustomed to, can be
frightening. Within the first few intersections, Uri is
white-knuckling the dashboard. He steals desperate
glances at me in the rearview mirror. I cannot help but
laugh. Our driver chuckles too, and that makes the
situation even more amusing.

Uri slams the ghost break to the floor as Osamu-
san sails through a red light. Realizing his error, the old
man shrugs and lets out a dismissive grunt. Osamu-san
taps the frames of his glasses and says to Uri, "No good."

I reach over and double-check my seatbelt. I tap
the back of Uri's headrest. He glances into the rearview
mirror, and I pantomime the pulling of a shoulder-
harness across my body. He nods and buckles up. Maybe,
the situation is not so funny after all.

Unscathed, Uri and I bail out of the car in the
parking lot of *Dainichiji*. We wait by the trunk to retrieve
our bags, but Mr. Osamu motions for us to follow him.
Uri and I point to the trunk and pretend to put on our
packs. "Later," says Mr. Osamu.

This is the second Dainichi temple along the loop.
The first one was temple-thirteen, where I had the
privilege of meeting the Zen Master Priest. To my delight,
she now follows me on social media and sometimes
comments or tags my photos with little hearts. I'm still
starstruck.

I follow Mr. Osamu and Uri up a short flight of roughly hewn, stone steps. It's all I can do to keep up with the two. Failing to match strides with Uri is no big deal. The kid is nearly a foot taller and decades younger, but Mr. Osamu is a different story. I tower over his small frame, and he is easily old enough to be my father.

At the purification station, Uri parts company with us and wanders off to explore the temple grounds. I stick like glue to Mr. Osamu, hoping to chant with him and observe how he moves through the rituals. I'm also worried. What if he forgets about our backpacks in his trunk? That would be a total disaster.

Temple 29: Kokubunji

Uri stares at me through the rear-view mirror. He mouths, "Now what?" I shrug and bite my lip.

Things got weird back in the parking lot of Dainichiji. When Uri and I tried to collect our backpacks, Mr. Osamu shook his head. "Later," he said. "Next temple." Then he hopped into his car and shut the door. There was nothing left to do but enjoy the ride.

I've decided to go with the flow. Uri is frazzled. Unlike me, he doesn't carry a messenger bag. His passport, extra cash, and maps are zipped in the top of his pack. With his backpack locked in the trunk, Uri is Mr. Osamu's hostage.

Fortunately, the uncomfortable ride to Kokubunji takes us less than 15 minutes. Again, Uri and I pile out of the car and wait by the trunk. Just as he did before, Mr. Osamu waves for us to follow.

"No," says Uri. My face reddens at his gruff tone. There's no reason to get confrontational, at least not yet.

Mr. Osamu holds out his car keys. "You keep," he says and hands the keys to Uri.

Uri tries to refuse, but it is pointless. Mr. Osamu is already across the parking lot. We jog to catch up and then follow him down a tidy path of stone pavers and beneath a veil of shimmering cherry-blossoms.

"Damn, he's quick," says Uri.

"I know! It's embarrassing."

"Why did he give me his keys?"

"To ease your mind – like a show of trust."

"He is a crazy old man."

"Maybe, but he can't leave with our packs."

"Sure. But I could steal his car."

"True, but you wouldn't."

"How does he know?"

"He just knows."

I stop to take a picture of Mr. Osamu before he reaches the steps of the purification station. His posture is impeccable, and his gait is effortless. He wears freshly pressed khaki pants with cargo pockets down each leg. The pants are hemmed above his black walking shoes, and I can see cream-colored dress socks. His white hakui is crisp and bright and not wrinkled and limp like mine. Perched atop his head, his conical hat bobs up and down with each step. He carries a white monk's bag over his shoulder, but he doesn't use the Kukai-staff or walking sticks. Clearly, he's in no need of the extra support.

In chops of English and Japanese, Mr. Osamu tells me there is a Kokubunji, or government temple, in each of the four prefectures. I know this already but listen politely. I'm thrilled he wishes to teach me.

Shoulder-to-shoulder, Mr. Osamu and I move through our rituals. Just like his gait, he is swift. We chant an abbreviated version together and step off to the Daishi hall. When we finish at the second hall, he pats my shoulder. "Good," he says. "Good Japanese."

When we meet up with Uri, back at the car, he has the trunk popped and his pack on his back. He stretches out his long arm to offer the keys back to Osamu-san. But the old man shakes his head.

"Later," says Mr. Osamu. "Next temple."

Temple 30: Zenrakuji

Uri glares at me from the rear-view mirror. He's giving me his best stink-eye. In response, I tilt my head and stick out my tongue.

It's true. I dove into the backseat of Mr. Osamu's car before Uri could protest. However, nobody forced Uri to climb into the passenger seat. He had his pack and could have taken off walking.

I'm enjoying my time with Mr. Osamu. It's nice to have a mentor. Before leaving the last temple, he told me he has walked the Shikoku three times and drove it another eleven.

"Last time," he sighed. "Eyes no good. Last time."

The ride to Zenrakuji is short. On foot, the stretch would have taken me an hour and a half. I'm thankful for the fast-forward, even if I've irritated Uri.

We leave our packs in the trunk, and again, Mr. Osamu hands Uri the keys. We hang back out of earshot to discuss the way forward. Uri is ready to walk and wants me to join him. Personally, I'm on the fence. I get a kick out of Mr. Osamu, but I did come here to walk.

"I'm having fun, Uri. Aren't you?"

"No. I'm scared. His driving is terrible."

"Yes, but only because his eyesight is bad."

"Exactly! We could die."

"Fair point."

Uri doesn't participate in rituals. He parts company at the fountain or bell, and we meet back up at the stamp office or gate. Growing up under the weight of dogmatic oppression, Uri had a falling-out with all things spiritual.

"I don't need the guilt or pressure," he shrugs.

"But why take a pilgrimage?" I ask. "The world's full of beautiful hikes."

"I don't know," he says. "I felt compelled to see Japan and visit the temples."

I nod my head in understanding. "Basically," he continues, "I'm a tourist in henro-disguise."

I get it. Part of me is also a tourist in henro garb. But no matter where I roam, I am a spiritual-being on a human-quest. This is what nourishes my pilgrim-heart and makes me a forever-peregrina, or in this situation, an Ohenro-san.

I like taking part in the rituals, especially with Mr. Osamu-san. It's essential to keep an open-mind. So far, nothing I've said or done has interfered with my faith. In fact, the opposite is true. In my brief encounter with Buddhism, I have uncovered principles of *compassion*, *kindness*, and *self-discipline*. Imagine a world full of these three elements.

Temple 31: Chikurinji

Uri and I are eating udon with Mr. Osamu in a noodle house with sticky tables and an even stickier floor. Our big plan to break company was thwarted once we reached the parking lot of temple thirty. Uri popped the trunk, and Mr. Osamu went over and gently shut it. He patted Uri's shoulder and said, "After lunch."

The rich udon broth is to die for, but the flies are killing my appetite. Osamu-san slurps and swats, and slurps and swats some more. Uri and I exchange glances, trying not to smile.

Uri leans over his bowl, trying to imitate his new mentor. Uri has almost no control over his chopsticks. Instead, he hunches even lower, and his sticks become bulldozer blades, ramming the tender noodles up and over the rim and between his parted lips.

My excellent chopstick skills are not worth much. It doesn't matter if I can snag a single grain of rice from the bowl. When dining with Mr. Osamu, speed is king. The men are halfway through their bowls already. I've got to pick up the pace. I lean in, but I flatly refuse to slurp.

In the space of 15 minutes, Mr. Osamu orders, eats, pays, and dashes out of the noodle house. Uri glances up. He looks agitated, but there is no time for discussion. Mr. Osamu is making a beeline for his car.

"Our packs!" shouts Uri.

We hop from our stools and chase after him. Once in the car, we realize the rush was unnecessary. Mr. Osamu tilts back the driver's seat and dozes off.

In the back seat, I study the snowflake pattern of white lace seat covers. Normally, I'd say the covers are proof of a Mrs. Osamu. But I've seen similar designs, protected by a layer of clear vinyl, in Tokyo taxi cabs.

Mr. Osamu snores. Uri rifles nervously through my guidebook. I relax and thumb through the photos of the last temple, enjoying the downtime.

The road to Chikurinji is jammed with traffic. Mr. Osamu, who we now lovingly refer to as Grandpa-san, makes progress in great lurches and sudden halts. The udon sloshes in my tummy, threatening to make a reappearance.

Traffic comes to a complete stop. Grandpa-san jumps out to assess the situation. I hold my breath as he walks around cars using the oncoming traffic lane.

The cars in front inch forward, but he doesn't return to the vehicle. The driver behind lays on the horn. Grandpa-san straightens, turns, and sternly marches to the rear. I lower my window all the way down to listen. I don't need language to decipher the stern lecture issued by our elderly companion.

The temple parking lot is a zoo. Buses spew out throngs of henros, and taxi cabs jockey for position. A parking attendant signals us to stop, but Grandpa-san misses the cue and nearly mows the man down.

Gone is our soup slurping, dozy chauffeur. I watch the softness of our driver's aging jawline harden to chiseled stone.

At the next intersection, Grandpa-san ignores another parking attendant. Instead of stopping, he hits the gas and cuts through a stream of cars. Uri grips the dashboard at the sudden change in Grandpa-san's demeanor. This is pure Ohenro adrenaline.

With a final whip of the wheel, Grandpa-san steals a parking spot from a white van. The passengers beat angrily on the windows. And I recognize my little buddy, the boy in the blue tracksuit.

I wave an apology to Kai's family. The van door slides open, and my young friend stumbles out to meet me. Kai and I exchange bows. In an unspoken agreement, we take off toward the temple gate, leaving Uri and the adults to sort out the hard feelings over a stolen parking spot.

Kai and I wait for the others at the top of the last set of stairs. He practices English, and we use my translator app to fill in the gaps. He seems to enjoy the conversation as much as I do.

Kai gives me a bookmark decorated with an origami Jizo, a trinket his mother made to give to friends he meets along his pilgrimage. I slide a prayer bracelet of soft-green aventurine beads from my wrist to his. In the slanting shade of a five-story pagoda, Kai and I become forever-friends.

Temple 32: Zenjibuji

Like temple twenty-six and a few others along the coastline, people visit *Zenjibuji* to pray for the safety of seafarers. Kukai visited this area in the early 9th century and carved the main deity, *Funadama Kannon,* or the Spirit of the Boat Kannon.

I want to make two wishes at each hall, one for my Coasties and one for Kai, the boy in the blue tracksuit. I don't know if double-wishes are greedy or frowned upon. I try to ask Grandpa-san if this is permissible. For some reason, he can no longer hear me. It's like there is a plexiglass plate between the two of us. Grandpa-san looks to Uri for translation – like Uri would have any idea of what in the world I'm asking.

I don't wait for an answer. I take matters into my own hands. After all, forgiveness is sweeter than permission. I light two candles, two sets of incense sticks, and deposit two coins to pad my dual-wish. I also abandon Grandpa-san's abbreviated chant and commit to the full-meal-deal, and then I repeat all of this at the Daishi hall for Kukai's blessing. Two wishes require extra effort on my part. It all seems reasonable to me.

After completing my rounds, I stop to admire a tall and slender statue of Kannon. I've noticed some depictions of Kannon are decidedly female, while others are androgynous. This statue, with an opened robe showing off pectoral muscles and a six-pack, seems rather masculine, but the face and hands are delicately feminine.

Perched atop her head, eleven faces of mixed-emotions greet me. Some expressions are angry, and some are peaceful. "I get it, girl. That's been my whole damn day."

To my surprise, my companions are not waiting for me outside of the stamp office. They are not at the gate. Instead, I find them sitting in the car. As I approach, Grandpa-san taps his watch.

Apparently, Uri has adopted a new grandfather, and I am now the third-wheel. Except for those moments chanting, shoulder-to-shoulder, Grandpa-san only has eyes and ears for Uri. I'm okay with that. We have formed a temporary Shikoku family. Like all families, there are moments of bliss and moments of dysfunction.

I take a backseat, and Grandpa-san and Uri return to the map that is spread out on the dash. Grandpa taps the center of *Kochi City*. The two of them discuss hotels. I scooch in closer, but Grandpa leans away. He waves a hand in the air like he's shooing a fly.

I sit back and try not to act annoyed. As a self-diagnosed control-freak, I'm uncomfortable handing over the reins to these clowns. Perhaps, I need to let go – to trust others. And then again, perhaps not.

Via translation app, Uri communicates his daily budget. Grandpa-san sucks through his teeth, making a hissing noise, and gravely nods his head. He makes a call, negotiates a rate, and writes the figure at the top of his notebook. I crane my neck to see, but Uri pops a thumb in the air, answering for both of us.

"Super! We can afford that!"

"We can afford what?" I ask.

"Grandpa found a place for 5,000 yen."

"One room? Two? Or three?" I ask.

"Does it matter?"

"Yeah, kind of," I can't help but roll my eyes.

And Uri shrugs.

Temple 33: Sekkeiji

It's seven in the morning, and I sit alone in this hotel lobby, waiting for Uri and Grandpa-san to emerge from their rooms. It's April Fools' Day, or at least it is in the United States. For years, I used this day to pull little pranks on my kids. The pranking grew in complexity as they grew in age.

When they were young, it was silly tricks like offering an empty wrapper of Juicy Fruit gum. Later, I scraped the sugary filling from between the sandwiched *Oreo* cookies, replacing it with toothpaste. Perhaps, my favorite prank was adding cocoa powder to melted glycerin soap and pouring the concoction into candy molds.

I remember my oldest son, Nicholas, asking if he could have one of my chocolates. I told him, "no," and then I left the kitchen. Hovering in the room next door, I waited. It wasn't five minutes before he was sputtering and hollering, as if he were being attacked by wolves.

The memory of Nicholas and the soap bon-bon makes me laugh aloud. The hotel clerk raises his eyebrows. I shrug my shoulders and smile.

When we arrived at our hotel last night, Grandpa-san gave a fist pump in the air, pointed to a line in his notebook, and tapped his watch. It was five o'clock sharp! Despite my double-wish dillydallying at temple thirty-two, Grandpa-san still managed to make his nightly rest stop as scheduled. Victory was sweet, and he glowed with pride.

Our lodgings in this bare-bones business hotel are pleasantly clean and cheap. Fortunately, the 5,000-yen quote included two single-rooms for Uri and me. At less than $48 US, I offered to cover our night. Uri graciously accepted, later confiding had I not offered; he would have gone the night without eating. And wow, did we ever eat!

Grandpa-san led us through alleys and across plazas, expertly weaving his way to a giant food court beneath an enormous circus tent. Vendors lined the choked aisles, offering everything from fried dumplings to sushi and bubble tea to sake. It was a foodie's paradise.

I gathered provisions while Uri stood in line for the beer. I picked packages of sushi and sashimi and a bento box with strips of teriyaki beef and chicken. Something told me Uri would prefer his dinner cooked. Grandpa bought a long, skinny fish complete with head and tail. The raw fish was smelly and slashed from stem to stern, stuffed with seasoned rice, and slit into bite-sized rings.

We found an open space at the end of a long table, occupied by a pack of ladies fresh from the office. Grandpa-san spoke to the women, and I detected his flirtatious tone. The ladies tittered like schoolgirls, covering their mouths, and leaning into his charm.

One of the ladies was proficient in English and served as our translator. We learned Grandpa-san is 81 years old and worked 30 years as a civil engineer, building dams all over Japan.

Considering Grandpa-san's failing eyesight and habit of running red lights, I asked the translator if he was married or had a family to check-in with daily. When our translator expressed my concerns, Grandpa-san bolted upright and slapped a palm to his forehead. He fished out his phone from a cargo pocket, said something to make the ladies laugh, and dashed for the exit.

"Oh, he is married," said the office-lady translator. "But he forgot to call his wife for the past three days." She smiled and took a sip of wine. "Your friend is in big trouble!"

When he returned to our table, Grandpa-san carried three mugs of frothy Guinness. He looked sheepish, like a kid who had just received a scolding. But he clinked glasses with the ladies and made them all giggle again.

We learned Grandpa-san suffers from a severe case of glaucoma and should no longer drive. Uri elbowed me in the ribs, but I maintained my composure. Well, that does explain a lot.

Our translator continued, telling us Grandpa-san is searching for a miracle. I raised my glass in a toast. Uri followed, and soon, we were clinking glasses with the office ladies, toasting to health and the miraculous recovery of Grandpa-san's eyesight.

I'm not sure how long we stayed out last night, but it was long enough to drink way too many beers. Whenever our mugs dipped below the halfway mark, Grandpa-san was up to fetch another round. When it came to beer, we had an international theme going on. Uri started us off with Japanese beer, and then we toured Ireland, Germany, Belgium, and China.

Uri staggers into the hotel lobby. He looks wrecked. We were all supposed to meet up at seven this morning. At half-past, there is still no sign of our companion.

Last night, Grandpa-san unsuccessfully tried to drink Uri and me under the table. He woefully underestimated our skills. It was all we could do to get him safely back to the hotel.

I nurse a can of hot black coffee, hoping to soothe my aching head. Uri sips a sports drink to replace electrolytes lost during our binge. I can't imagine how poorly Grandpa-san must be feeling.

Despite our overconsumption of food and drink, last night was a blast. However, this morning finds me ready to move on. I plan to visit the first temple with the guys and then make my own way.

Way behind schedule, Grandpa makes his appearance in the lobby and then herds us into the car. He looks over his notebook and shakes his head. I know he's wondering how to make up the lost 40 minutes of his meticulously scheduled travel plans.

The ride to *Sekkeiji* feels like our last. Grandpa-san sails through two intersections without stopping for the red lights. I let out a scream as a small fruit truck nearly T-bones us at a third intersection.

Once in the temple parking lot, Grandpa-san smacks his forehead with the palm of his hand and apologizes.

"Brain not working," he says.

Scared speechless, Uri bails out of the car. I tilt my head against my palms, still pressed tightly together in prayer. I make a light snoring sound, suggesting Grandpa naps while Uri and I explore the temple. He nods and tips back his seat.

Originally a *Shingon* temple, Sekkeiji is one of three *Zen* temples along the route. The others are back at eleven and fifteen. From what I've read, Zen temples are supposed to be austere in design and adornment. The campus does seem a tad stark, but as an outsider, I haven't developed an eye for such nuances.

I limp my way through the rituals at both halls. After, I meet up with Uri outside the stamp office. Still sipping his sports drink, he looks as bad as I feel.

As we offer our exiting bow at the gate, I promise never to overindulge along the Shikoku again. I didn't come here to party. And I certainly didn't come here to feel this crappy.

Temple 34: Tanemaji

In the parking lot of temple thirty-three, we left our Grandpa-san to nap. The leaving part was tricky. He clearly was not ready to separate. Grandpa-san shook his head and stamped his feet, but Uri and I prevailed. We promised to wait at *Tanemaji*.

"We will meet in two hours," I said, holding up two fingers and pointing to the clock on my phone. Grandpa nodded and set the alarm on his phone. Two hours should be perfect at my leisurely pace to walk the six and a half kilometers between temples.

After leaving Grandpa-san in the parking lot, Uri asked about the colorful placards suction-cupped to the car's windshield and rear window. The plastic placards look like a flower or maybe a four-leaf clover, and each petal is a different color – yellow, orange, light green, and dark green. This is the Japanese symbol and friendly warning of an elderly driver.

An upside-down arrowhead in yellow and dark green symbolizes a new driver. When I first moved to Okinawa, my driving was terrible. I had the worst time remembering which side of the road I was supposed to drive on, especially at intersections and roundabouts. Half as a joke and half as a sincere warning, I put both new-driver and elderly placards on my car. Later, as I grew more confident, I removed them and put them on a colleague's vehicle. She still hasn't noticed.

Uri and I are silent, taking in the expansive farmland and listening to the roadside gravel crunch beneath our feet. I'm feeling better, but Uri doesn't look as spry. I'm surprised because Uri is so young. I expected him to be more resilient. It just goes to show – age is but a number.

Happy to be on foot again, Uri and I weave our way through acres of greenhouses. We cut across rice paddies and fields of cereal crops. Despite the hangovers, we both seem right at home.

Tanemaji gets its name from five kinds of seeds grown in this region. *Tanema* means multi-species. According to legend, Kukai brought rice, wheat, two types of millet, and beans from China, and he planted them in fields surrounding the temple. I scan the horizon, wondering if any of today's plants might be heirlooms from the great Kobo Daishi.

As we arrive at the front gate, I hear a little beep-beep of a car horn. I look up to see Grandpa-san waiving out his window. His wave lacks the gusto we've come to expect, but Uri and I walk to the parking lot to meet him.

According to Grandpa-san, he is feeling 70% better. He certainly looks better. But I'm not ready to get back into the car with him.

"Shamrock of death," whispers Uri, pointing to the elderly-driver placard on Grandpa's rear window. I giggle and send an elbow to his ribcage. Uri is good company.

In front of the Daishi hall, Grandpa-san points out a statue of *Kosodate Kannon*. This is the birthing and child-rearing Kannon. Mothers, fathers, grandpas, and grandmas pray to Kosodate Kannon for the mother and baby's safety during the childbirth journey. Grandpa-san smiles and picks up a ladle with the bottom punched out. He explains that families leave the punched-out ladles to thank Kannon for trouble-free births.

Temple 35: Kiyotakiji

With reluctance, Uri and I load back into the car. Grandpa-san is persuasive because he clearly does not want to be alone, and we do not wish to break his heart; however, I worry our presence is overwhelming him. He needs more sleep.

Grandpa-san puts the car in reverse and backs out of the parking space. He's about to pull onto the main road, but the vehicle is still in reverse. I tap Uri's shoulder, and Uri nonchalantly reaches over and shifts the transmission into drive.

Why am I back in this car? It's scary, and I feel guilty for not walking. I'm in the *ascetic phase*. I'm supposed to suffer. It's supposed to be difficult!

An epiphany drops in my lap. Riding in the backseat is hard. Proxying control is hard. Keeping my mouth shut is also challenging. This whole misadventure is damn difficult. And sometimes, I do suffer.

I spent all yesterday negotiating carsickness. And I don't care much for being the third-wheel. I'm also not a big fan of feeling excluded from conversations.

Maybe, the most challenging part of my ascetic training is letting go of my itinerary and assisting another. Grandpa-san enjoys chanting and sharing bits of culture and Shikoku history with me. Uri treasures the camaraderie of our elderly companion, and clearly, Grandpa-san needs our help.

The ten-kilometer drive to temple thirty-five is tedious. With Uri's help, Grandpa-san maneuvers his car down a narrow road flanked by two ridiculously deep irrigation ditches. One false move, and we will be in the drink. The going is slow, and in the rearview mirror, I can see Uri holding his breath.

The farm road widens enough to allow an oncoming tractor to pass. Grandpa pulls over and kills the engine. He's sweating from the exertion, and I can see his 70% improvement has tanked.

"Too sick," says Grandpa-san. "Head not working."

Grandpa-san provides walking instructions to *Kiyotakiji*, our next temple. I'm reluctant to leave my pack, but Grandpa-san promises to wait for our return.

"Go. Go," Grandpa waves, shooing us like flies. "I sleep now."

Before we go, Grandpa-san surrenders his precious stamp book, leaving it in the care of Uri to collect a stamp. Uri? The same guy who has not once completed temple rituals or collected a stamp? I don't mean to be petty, but why wasn't I entrusted with the task?

The hike up to the temple gate is steep and long enough to burn off my irritation. Harboring negative emotions consumes too much energy. So, I give it up just as my thighs start to burn.

Once through the gate, I'm surprised to have Uri's company. Usually, he splits off to take photos while Grandpa and I tend to the rituals. I feel Uri's eyes upon me as I move through the purification station. He copies my actions and follows close behind as we move on to the bell tower. I swing the ramrod gentle enough to kiss the bell and politely announce my arrival. Uri grabs the rope and gives it all hell, and by proxy, he announces the arrival of Grandpa with a thunderous BONG.

I share the last of my incense, so Uri can light three sticks. And then, arm-in-arm, Uri chants along, tackling the difficult pronunciations and keeping pace as I trace my finger beneath the lines of the *Heart Sutra*.

At the stamp office, Uri proudly collects Grandpa's stamp. I inquire about incense, but there is none for sale. The monk working the desk holds up a finger, signaling me to wait. He disappears behind a beaded curtain. Moments later, he reappears with an opened pack.

"Ossetia," he says and sets the box of incense on the counter.

"Arigato, arigato," and I bow my way out the door.

Uri and I exit the temple gate together. He clutches Grandpa-san's book to his chest. I clutch my new-to-me box of incense.

"Race you," Uri bops the top of my head and takes off down the hill. To show off, he turns around and jogs backward. I know there's no way on earth I can keep up with the kid, let alone beat him in a race. I play along, leaning back into the slope and letting my feet fly out in front. Gravity pulls me down the hill, and the speed is exhilarating. At the bottom, Uri holds his arms out in blockade fashion to keep me from slamming into the side of Grandpa-san's car. He wraps me up in an awkward but heartfelt embrace. How I do love this sweet kid.

Temple 36: Shoryuji

Grandpa-san's health seems to have improved again after his short nap, but Uri and I have decided it's time to say our goodbyes. We both agree Grandpa-san would be better off if he had the whole day to rest. I leave Uri to the negotiations and wait by the trunk to collect our packs.

"No," Grandpa says. "After lunch is better."

Uri shrugs his shoulders, and I climb into the backseat. Truthfully, I'm starving, and another lunch with our dear companion sounds excellent. That's why I don't give Uri my famous eye-roll when he looks apologetically at me through the rearview mirror.

"It's just lunch," I whisper and pat his shoulder.

Grandpa-san takes us to a roadside market famous for its fresh seafood procured daily from local fishing boats. For me, it's a dream come true. For Uri, it's a bit of a nightmare. I help him shuffle through neat rows of transparent plastic bento boxes to find something that is not fish. The task proves more daunting than one might imagine.

Uri settles on pale strips of fried tofu heaped over white rice. How bland. He was banking on chicken. To make matters worse, the bottom of his container falls to the floor, showering our shoes and pant legs in a spray of rice. I can't help but laugh, but Grandpa is embarrassed, and the woman running the register shoots a stern look.

I dash back to the rows of plastic clamshells to fetch another tofu box. Uri wields a broom and dustpan, looking awfully sorry for himself. I don't understand the scene. What's the big deal? It was an accident, for goodness sakes. I bite my lip, pay for our lunches, and avoid making eye contact with the angry clerk.

We join Grandpa-san outside at a picnic table. He doesn't speak or even look up at us. He is still embarrassed over the mishap, or maybe he is merely ravenous. With his head down, he shoves large rounds of sushi into his mouth. It looks like hangover-eating, and I join in.

Uri picks at his rice. Grandpa-san leans back against the building and closes his eyes. I polish off my bento, but I'm still hungry.

I buy three pancakes from a street vendor. I don't think of pancakes as a dessert, but I want something sweet and don't want to go back into the store. When I return to the table with my paper sack of goodies, I offer a pancake to Grandpa-san and to Uri. Each refuses the offer, and I'm delighted.

I take a tentative bite of the first pancake, and I'm so disappointed to find it filled with starchy red beans. I move on to the next. First, I break open the pancake and examine the cream-colored contents. Hmm? What could it be? Maybe some sort of pudding or possibly cream-cheese? I take a nibble. Beans! Ugh! I break open the third. Yes. More beans.

After lunch, Uri and I wait by the trunk in anticipation of our departure. The weather is perfect for a walk, and the afternoon is young. Grandpa looks at us sheepishly and points to his map book at temple thirty-seven, about 75 kilometers from where we stand. Uri and I both shake our heads.

"I made a reservation. Nice place. You will like it," Grandpa says.

Uri hops back in the car. This is crazy. But I don't suppose there's any harm in spending one more evening together.

I turn to Uri and whisper, "I thought you had the terms of our release fully-negotiated."

"I dunno," says Uri. "I'm no good at break-ups."

We bow and enter the gate to *Shoryuji*. Grandpa-san pats the front of his trousers and says, "Toire." This is convenient because I need to do the same. He hurries up the path, and Uri lopes along at his side. I break into a jog to keep up. Despite Grandpa-san's earlier difficulties, the man is a pilgrim-machine.

I follow Grandpa-san into the bathroom, past a line of occupied urinals, and duck into one of the three private stalls. I always find it rather uncomfortable to walk behind the urinating men, but I'm getting used to it. I keep my eyes forward and move with purpose.

Grandpa waits for me outside by the exit. He pulls me toward the door and points to a set of symbols, and then he points to me. Next, he drags me around the building to the entrance. Again, he points to another set of symbols, but this time, he points to himself. Next, he points at me and then taps his crossed index fingers. I'm slow on the uptake, so Uri jumps in.

"Men's door," Uri points. "Women go around."

"What?" I'm shocked. "You mean I've been doing it wrong this whole time?"

Why hadn't someone explained this to me earlier? I've been wrongfully trespassing through the sacred urinal space for 30-some temples. Uri cracks up laughing. He giggles even louder when I tell him I had been using squat toilets backward until my moment of enlightenment at temple twelve.

Temple 37: Iwamotoji

Grandpa-san hugs the corners of the winding coastal road at what I'm sure are unsafe speeds. For the life of me, I cannot understand why I am not carsick. I'm almost always carsick, especially when confined to the backseat.

I credit my strong constitution to the giant glob of grated ginger from my bento lunchbox. Thinking the blob was mashed daikon radish, I popped the whole thing in my mouth. After the rice debacle, I didn't dare make a fuss or spit it out. Instead, I gulped it down, feeling the burn all the way into the pit of my stomach. To my surprise, the ginger stayed put and is serving me well.

Still showing signs of a hangover, Uri tips his head back into the headrest. In the rearview mirror, I can see his closed eyes. He's either sleeping or praying. My money is on the latter.

I shift my focus to the rugged beauty of Shikoku's coastline. Black haystacks jut from a deep blue ocean to meet an even bluer sky. There's not a cloud on the horizon.

The high road winds inland, and I'm treated to a tidy grid of rice paddies flooded with sparkling water below. I wonder if rice grows year-round on Shikoku. These fields are either newly planted or newly harvested, as not a tiny green shoot across this vast grid is visible – at least not to the naked eye.

Once inside the temple gate of *Iwamotoji*, we are greeted by the cutest, patina-green dragon spitting into the bowl of a carved boulder. Eight tin ladles with bamboo handles are strewn about the rock. Grandpa-san reaches for two and hands me one. Uri takes off, as he usually does, to explore the temple grounds.

The main deity or honzon of this temple is Fudo Myoo, the *Immovable King of Brightness*. He is part of a greater grouping of *Myoo* or *Bright Kings*. Each king has different tools to signify purpose.

With one hand, Fudo Myoo holds the sword of wisdom to cut through ignorance and obstacles of the physical and emotional realms. With the other hand, he holds a lasso to rein in evil. While his chubby body is childlike, his face is fierce. Like a wild hog, he has tusks, and he bites down on one side of his lip. One eye is half-closed, giving the universal *stink-eye*. I have a remarkably similar expression my kids call the *Mom-glare*.

Images of Myoo are set against a backdrop of flames and are typically housed where fire rituals or *Goma* take place. I feel fortunate to have participated in a fire ceremony back at temple six. I would have enjoyed the experience more had I understood the symbolism and ritual beforehand. Sometimes, spontaneity rules.

A legend tells of a monk returning from China on terribly rough seas. The monk called upon Fudo Myoo for protection, and Myoo delivered the monk, the ship, and the fellow passengers safely to the shore.

The monk on the ship was no other than young Kukai, whose footsteps I am following around this lovely island. During my pilgrimage on Shikoku, should I find myself in need of protection, I hope Fudo Myoo will answer my call.

Temple 38: Kongofukuji

This morning finds me eating breakfast again with Grandpa-san and Uri. It's the usual temple fare, served up in nine tiny dishes. Before me awaits a small slab of fried mackerel. There is also a hardboiled egg and some flaked bonito alongside a blog of mashed daikon. This time, I will first test the blob to ensure it is daikon and not grated ginger. A little square of tofu, sprinkled with green onion circles, floats in a golden broth. There are two precious bites of steamed greens, a smattering of pickled veggies, a dried plum, a never-ending rice bowl, and a tidy stack of dark green nori strips wrapped in cellophane.

I am ravenous, but I wait patiently until all my fellow pilgrims are seated. While I may have been the last one to pick my stiff body up from the tatami mat after our early-morning meditation, I am the first to sit down at the table. Call me an opportunist.

Yesterday, after lunch, I was irritated to learn Grandpa had booked our lodging without talking with us first. However, this morning, I have nothing but praise for the old trickster. His actions were a little underhanded but thoughtful. The nightly rate was beyond Uri's budget, but Grandpa covered Uri's share, and the two of them bunked together for the night.

My little room was well-equipped with multiple futon mattresses, pillows, and thick comforters. I stacked the futons and several quilts together, making a dreamily comfortable pallet. There was also a kettle and an array of packaged miso soups, rice crackers, teas, and cookies. With such a private and bountiful little banquet, I opted to skip the formal dinner and fellowship to enjoy a little me-time in the bathhouse.

This morning, I'm seated across from an Italian henro wearing a big smile and a crisp blue and white checked button-up. "I make a present for you," says the Italian. He digs around in his man-purse, looking for something that must be quite small. He raises his eyebrows, signaling the find, and then giggles a little peal of joy. Next, he holds out his closed fists for me to choose.

I tap his left fist, and he rolls his hand over and opens his palm. I smile and pluck up a set of steamer clamshells. Inside the shells, in blue marker, he has written the words, *I love you.*

I hold the shells and work the hinge like a puppet's mouth opening and closing. I'm no ventriloquist, but I do my best, "I love you too!"

My response pleases the Italian, and he giggles some more. He offers his other closed fist to the lady henro sitting next to me. She receives an I-love-you-clam too. The gift makes her blush, and although her English skills are well-developed, she does not return the sentiment.

In the lobby, I say goodbye to Uri and Grandpa-san. This time, I mean it. Standing on tippy-toes, I throw my arms around Uri's broad shoulders, and he picks me up in a giant bear hug. After exchanging farewells and contact information, I bow reverently to Grandpa-san. I will miss these guys, but I'm so excited to strike out on my own.

Alone, at last, I begin my road-hugging hike to Kongofukuji. With nearly 83 kilometers between me and the next temple, I realize the journey will take the better of three or maybe even four full days, unless, of course, I hop on public transportation or stick out my thumb again. I'm not planning to do either. I've waited too long to hike, and my legs are restless for the road.

I'm less than five-kilometers in when out of nowhere, a spring downpour catches me unprepared. I scramble for shelter and take refuge beneath a covered bus stop. As I'm stretching the rain shield over my backpack, I hear a beep-beep of a car horn.

Grandpa pulls up to the curb, rolls down his window, and from the passenger seat, Uri yells, "Hey lady, how about a lift." My trail angels have returned, but I take a moment to contemplate.

"Sure!" I shout. "Why the heck not? What's one more day?" I slide across the bench seat and reposition myself back in my old familiar space. Grandpa nods his head and grunts with approval.

Despite the unrelenting downpour, the drive is relatively uneventful. I'm guessing Grandpa-san slept peacefully last night. In fact, we all seem refreshed. We are clean and relaxed from the previous night's bath, and our clothes are freshly laundered. Yet, I find myself in a state of discontent, self-shaming over how readily I tucked back into the comfort and safety of Grandpa-san's car.

Shoulder to shoulder, the three of us execute a well-choreographed bow and pass through the temple gate. We stop to admire a statue of a massive sea turtle. Immediately, I think of my youngest son, Jaden, who was born in Hawaii and nicknamed *Baby-Honu*, the Hawaiian name for sea turtle.

In Hawaii, the sea turtle is a symbol of wisdom and good fortune. I wonder if the same is true in Japan. All I know is I cannot see a turtle and not think of my youngest son. As a little boy, Jaden was so pokey, trailing behind his older brothers, stopping to smell the flowers, and taking on life at his own pace. He's still that way, and as a family, we have a lot to learn from our Baby Honu.

Grandpa-san tells us a legend of Kukai and a great sea turtle. I piece together his collage of English and Japanese words and get the gist. It seems Kukai was stranded, either in a flood of rough seas or marooned upon a small island. When he called out to the universe for assistance, a giant green sea turtle came to his rescue. The turtle carried Kukai on its back, delivering the grateful monk safely to shore.

The serendipity of morning events is not lost on me. Grandpa-san rescued me from the flooded streets and delivered me safely to the temple. I am thankful to be back in the company of my companions. There will be plenty of time to go it alone later. After all, I'm not even halfway around the island.

Grandpa-san and I move through our rituals. We weave our way around koi ponds, shining like mirror-glass in the mid-morning sun. At the main hall, I light an extra three sticks of incense for Jaden, my turtle-boy. I light one for his past, one for his present, and another for his future, and I pray he continues embracing life at his own sweet tempo.

Temple 39: Enkoji

Grandpa-san removes his conical hat, henro vest, and monk's bag before loading back into the car. He gently places all three items onto the passenger seat. His shoulders relax, and his brow softens. Our hard-charging henro transforms into our easy-going tour guide.

Grandpa-san leads us down a narrow pathway across the road from the temple gates and through a leafy forest flanking the coastline. Through a break in the trees, I see a dazzling-white lighthouse jutting skyward from a jetty wall of black basalt.

I have a thing for lighthouses. I always have. I pause to snap a photo whenever the view is irresistibly good. Grandpa and Uri march on without me, but we meet back up at the base of the lighthouse.

I try to explain my fondness of lighthouses - how I grew up along the Oregon coastline and retired from the Coast Guard, and how lighthouses are woven into the historical fabric of my childhood and my military service. My uninterested companions turn and head up the trail without me. I linger in the solitude and the majesty of the lonely lighthouse. I allow myself the brief indulgence of marinating in my own history. I return to the car feeling grateful and refreshed.

The 55-kilometer drive to *Enkoji* goes off without a hitch. Either Grandpa-san's skills have improved, or I am less of a drama-queen. This blissful state of affairs is probably a delicate combination of both.

Grandpa-san is on the ball today. He claims his eyesight has miraculously improved. All of this is somewhat ironic, especially as we enter temple thirty-nine, famed for its healing eye-washing well.

Gyoki founded Enkoji in 724 by carving a statue of *Yakushi Nyorai*, the healing buddha, commonly depicted holding a medicine jar. The temple draws suffering henro, searching for miracle cures for an array of eye-related ailments. Grandpa-san is no exception.

He scoops the water into a cupped hand and splashes it across his eyes. He kneels closer to the well, fills up both hands, and lowers his head into his palms, bathing his eyes in the cool water.

When it's my turn, I hesitate. I question the sanitation of the well, wondering how many eyes have been washed in these waters. And if any of my fellow henros suffer conjunctivitis – the dreaded pink-eye.

In truth, I don't need an eye-healing treatment, but I'm here, kneeling before this magical well. I may never have this opportunity again. Yes, I'm nearsighted. Thankfully, I don't suffer from anything serious like glaucoma or cataracts, or macular degeneration.

It's an odd coincidence that Kassy, my first companion, and Grandpa-san both suffer from glaucoma. Uri serves as Grandpa-san's second set of eyes. And I often served as Kassy's.

Enkoji is the last temple in the *Ascetic phase* of my journey. Thanks entirely to Grandpa-san, I am way ahead of schedule; however, I feel a sudden need to return to Okinawa. I miss Jasper. I also want to put distance between the end of this phase and the beginning of *Enlightenment*.

Despite my objections, Grandpa-san insists on going out of his way to drive me to the *Kochi airport*. His kind gesture cuts a full day of ground transportation off my to-do list. Now, all there is left for me to do is hop on the short flight back to Okinawa.

We say our goodbyes curbside. I know I will never see Grandpa and Uri again. We take one last selfie. Flanking our mentor between the two of us, I smile at how Uri and I tower over this tiny but ever-so-mighty Ohenro-san.

I wrap my arms around Uri's shoulders, and as before, he takes me up in a giant bear hug. No matter how much I want to hug my henro-grandfather goodbye, I resist the urge. In my heart, I know he would not welcome that level of affection from me. Instead, I simply bow.

Grandpa-san reaches out a warm hand and pats the top of my head. His touch is more than enough to open the floodgates to my tears. I laugh, wipe my eyes, and dash through the doors.

Once safely inside, I watch as the car pulls away from the curb, and Grandpa-san and Uri disappear into *Enlightenment*.

Part Three
Enlightenment

Part Three: *Enlightenment*

Temple 40: Kanjizaiji

After only a few days in Okinawa, I was dying to get back on the trail. I woke before the sun, hopped a plane and a train, and now I'm standing at the gate of *Kanjizaiji*. Ahead of me is the cutest pair of aging henro, a husband-and-wife team. Their images should be crafted into sets of salt and pepper shakers and sold in every gift shop around the island. They are simply adorable!

I follow the couple to the main hall, and we form a huddle to chant the *Heart Sutra*. The syllables fumble from my lips as if pronouncing them for the first time. This is the price for participating in Grandpa-san's abbreviated rituals.

Once through the sutras, I hang back to admire a large statue of Kukai. He carries a staff in one hand and a begging bowl in the other. Time has left a deep patina of green on the statue's surface. In the morning light, with the brim of his hat pulled low, his face is but a shadow. Above his sandals, someone has tied a set of white leg-warmers. I think about the 80s and smile.

I meet back up with the salt and pepper couple and sheepishly ask permission to take their photo. I end up taking two, one with my phone and one with theirs. Ours is a friendly exchange with lots of smiles and a volley of excessive bows.

Once outside the gate, the wife presents me with an osettai of green tea and a brilliant tangerine. We exchange another round of bows. I leave them waiting on the bus as I head off to find the next temple. This is such a promising start to my *Enlightenment*.

Temple 41: Ryukoji

Nailing the morning's first temple puts pep into my step. I feel fantastic. And that's important because there are 50 kilometers between me and the next temple.

The phrase *nailing the temple* is not my own. Historically, real nails were once involved in the process. Instead of the paper osamefuda strips used by modern henro, a thin shingle of wood called an *Uchi* was carried as the henro calling card. Visiting henro nailed their Uchi to gates and temple walls. As the popularity of the pilgrimage grew, the act of nailing a temple became a destructive practice.

Other than getting an early start on my day, I haven't planned my attack. My off-the-cuff strategy, or lack of strategy, is to walk until I get tired. Hopefully, I'll find a place to sleep within the next 20 or 30 kilometers. If not, I'm prepared to camp.

The scant week between phases has done little to prepare me for *Enlightenment*. I'm not sure what to expect. Here I am, walking roadside through urban sprawl, and while I do feel energetic, I'm not particularly enlightened.

My sense is that this phase and the others are like moving through the towns and villages along the Camino de Santiago. It is silly to expect to walk from one temple to the next and feel a sense of enlightenment or, dare I say, *Nirvana*. It's not the physical trail that manifests change. I don't think the process is contextual to time or space. Instead, spiritual growth develops over the entirety of the journey and beyond.

I've met a good handful of Camino peregrinos who felt a generalized let-down upon reaching Santiago de Compostela, the celebrated end of the Camino. They expected a *Wizard-of-Oz* epiphany at the culmination of their pilgrimages. But this isn't how it works.

There is no parade at the end of the Camino. No wizard nor pope behind a velvet curtain magically pops out to grant wishes or provide answers to life's most pressing questions. Wishes and answers are found along the way – or may materialize days, months, or even years following a pilgrimage. At least, this has been my humble experience.

I hope to be fortunate enough to learn as much about myself and my world from the Shikoku 88 as I did from the Camino. The *Way* is forever on my mind, even today, as I find myself trudging along a busy highway in Japan. The eucalyptus forests and the medieval villages of Spain are always with me.

Moving in and out of my Camino haze, I hardly notice the blue mini-van pass and pull to the road's shoulder. A grandmotherly-woman steps from the driver's seat and waves. I return her greeting. With one fist pointed toward me, she extends and retracts her fingers several times. I recognize the hand signal. It looks like *go-away,* but I know she means *come-here.* So, I do as she commands.

The woman slides the side of the van open, and I'm surprised to see a load of car-seat-strapped kiddies in the two back rows. The front seat is occupied by a younger lady, leaving no open space for me.

Looking impatient, the driver flips her hand faster, saying, "Please, please." But what she really means is, *Get in the damn van! I don't have all day.* So, I get in the damn van, squeezing by amply-sized hips in the narrow space between the driver's seat and the first row of car seats.

I have no idea why the grandmother offered me a ride. I wasn't hitchhiking, and she clearly does not have space for me. Besides, who picks up a vagabond with a vanload of kids? I'm not an ax-murdering psychopath, but how does she know that? This is one more example of *things-that-never-happen-in-The-United-States.*

A curious toddler, dressed in a blue and white sailor outfit, reaches out his dimpled fist and latches onto my braid. He gives my hair a tug, and I let him. Little by little, as if playing a game, his jerks become more aggressive. Eventually, I grab his hand and wrench it open. Of course, he lets out a scream as if I'm killing him. The woman in the passenger seat flips around and slices me in half with an accusing glare.

For the next 20 minutes, I ride in silence, crammed between the seats, with a monster-child tugging my hair out by the roots. However, I am grateful - grateful for the company of this rotten kid and grateful for the kind woman who rescued me from the busy highway.

In the parking lot of Ryukoji, the driver slides open the van door to let me out. The toddler screams again as I pry open his tiny fist to free my braid. This time, both ladies witness my actions. In tandem, they cover their mouths and laugh. This sends the screaming little boy into joyful peals. It doesn't take long before all the children are giggling, including myself.

As I bow my goodbye to the driver, she holds up her open palm, signaling me to wait. She retrieves a white paper sack from the hatch of the van, "Osettai!" she says, and we exchange bows.

After completing my temple rounds and collecting my stamp, I sit on the steps outside the gate and unwrap a homemade rice triangle from the white paper bag. Also included are a cookie and a juice box. This must be some daycare kid's lunch. The triangle puts all the convenience store *onigiri* on my gastro-resume to shame. I'd gladly put up with that little brat pulling my hair for another hour if it meant another bag of deliciousness.

I'm halfway through my triangle when I realize how appropriate the osettai really is. According to my guidebook, Kukai met an old man in this area carrying a great bag of rice. Kukai believed the old chap to be *Inari-Myojin*, the god of rice. To honor the Inari tradition, Kukai built this temple to pray for an abundant rice yield. Contemporary henro still pray for rice, but they also come to pray for business success. Even though I'm already outside the gate, I take a moment to say a little prayer for the harvest.

Temple 42: Butsumokuji

Nourished by delicious rice and toddler giggles, I set off for Butsumokuji. The hike is less than three kilometers or nearly two miles. It runs parallel to an expressway, but I'm treated to a smooth path, separated from traffic by a median strip of tulips in full bloom. The blossoms are close to the ground, and with my backpack, I don't dare stoop low enough to inhale the scent. Instead, I imagine the fragrance. It's the one held by most early bulb flowers, an earthy and spiced crispness belonging to the first day of spring.

I love tulips. In Washington, they grow in spontaneous clumps around my house. These median tulips are a platoon of hyper-uniform, single red blooms. Evenly-spaced in squads, the rows run six deep and for as far as my eye can see. The contrast of red flowers and blacktop is a visual stunner. Although I prefer much less structure, I can't help but be utterly impressed by the commitment and discipline it must take to accomplish such a tidy and terribly temporary spectacle.

The tulip trail guides me all the way to the temple gate of *Butsumokuji*. According to legend, Kukai arrived in this area not by way of a tulip trail but by way of a cow. Kukai met an old man who offered him an osettai ride on the back of his cow. And here I thought crammed into a minivan of toddlers was odd. Anyway, I digress.

So, Kukai was riding on a cow and being led by the old man. When the trio stopped to rest beneath the shade of a camphor tree, Kukia noticed something gleaming from one of the branches. Upon investigation, Kukai discovered a jewel. He recognized the stone as one he had thrown all the way from China.

In the trunk of this jewel-bedazzled camphor tree, Kukai carved the image of *Dainichi Nyorai* or Supreme Buddha of the Cosmos. Kukai placed the jewel between the deity's eyes and then constructed a temple. Initially, henro visited this temple to pray for peace and prosperity in the home. Now, the temple is used as a place to pray and memorialize departed pets – and maybe even cows.

For as long as I can remember, I've kept a dog. In early childhood, *my dog* belonged to everyone in the family. On my 13th birthday, I was gifted *Babe*, an Australian Shepherd puppy. Babe was followed by *Rags* and then *Pete*, also Australian Shepherds. Next, I adopted *Uh-Oh the Wonder Dog*. Then along came *Scotty*, the rat terrier. And now, there is my loyal Labrador, *Jasper*. I take a moment to remember each companion before writing all their names on two prayer strips.

Lately, I've been worried about Jasper. Something isn't right. The heat and humidity are tough on him. Along with the concrete jungle of Okinawa City, apartment life has done little to maintain his vitality. He's aging faster than I think he should. His once thick coat is growing thin and dull. He's still as happy as ever, but I've noticed a fogginess in his eyes and a general loss of oomph. So, before making my exit out the gate, I say an extra prayer for Jasper's health and longevity.

Temple 43: Meisekiji

Thanks to the grandmother in the blue minivan, I have more than enough energy left in my tank to tackle the ten-kilometer romp and nail yet another temple. My hunger is satiated, so I won't need to wander off course in search of food. To make matters even better, the monk working at the last stamp office was kind enough to call ahead and book me a hotel for the night. So now, all that's left for me in the world to do is simply walk. How perfect.

From temple forty-two, the path continues through an old cemetery dotted with lichen-speckled monuments of granite. I stop before an ornate headstone with a hefty inscription. How I do wish I could read Japanese. I try my translator camera app, but it's not working. The marker's size and grandeur lead me to believe that buried here is someone of great importance. I touch the cool granite, trace a few characters with my fingertip, and then make my way up the trail.

It's before noon, and the sun is coming up over the rocky hill in front of me. At the top of the hill, I see a golden statue of Kukai. I snap a quick photo and go back to milling my way up through the headstones.

As I draw nearer to golden Kukai, I realize the figure is not a statue at all. He moves! Thinking the sun is playing tricks on me, I stop and watch for a few seconds. The figure slowly raises his staff in my direction and starts down the hill. The light behind this Kukai-doppelganger sets his brocade-covered thatched hat and white vest aglow.

I step aside to allow this living Kukai to pass. He nods and plants a gnarled and badly-twisted walking stick firmly before him, causing the multiple rings atop the staff to tinkle like chimes in the wind. Once he has passed, I pull out my phone to take another picture. Like a mirage, he disappears amongst the long shadows of gravestones. I blink my eyes, wondering if I had imagined him. But then another tinkle of chimes assures me I am not going mad.

Gone are the tulips and ancient headstones, leaving the roadside walk more than a tad monotonous. To pass the time, I play kick-the-can with a large chunk of flat bark – cedar, perhaps.

As a kid, I played this little game with a soda can on my way home from school. Now that I'm older, I don't like the ruckus caused by the tin can skittering across the blacktop. For aural and aesthetic reasons, my favorite device as an adult is a pinecone.

I've kicked a cone all over the Black Forest in Germany. And I've kicked all over Spain, France, England, and Switzerland. Shikoku seems to have a shortage of cones this time of year. Fortunately, this bit of bark is an adequate substitute.

I pause a moment at a trail detour sign. The monk back at the last temple warned me of the detour. The original trail cuts off into the woods, but apparently, it is in a poor state of repair following a rainy season and subsequent erosion. The suggested detour leads down this main roadway, but it adds another five kilometers. I was confident about the original 10k, but I'm not so sure about 15.

The monk spoke English well. When I asked him if the trail was at all passable, he smiled and said, "For me? Yes, of course." I raised my eyebrows in response to the positive news. He quickly sized me up and continued, "For you? I think no."

Yes. I have a couple of decades on the cheeky lad, no doubt. But what does he know of my goat-like trail skills? While I'm no match for Kassy, I am feeling sure-footed today. So, out of spite or ordinary laziness, I ignore the longer detour route and the monk's recommendation in favor of the original trail through the forest. At the base of the trail, I contemplate yet another warning sign. I don't need my translator app to decipher because along with the characters is a picture of a stick-figure henro sliding down a bumpy trail on his stick-figure backside.

From the safety of the graveled trail base, I assess the situation. Jagged swaths of exposed clay mar the crumbling trail as it winds up through a towering bamboo forest. It's a little more rugged than predicted. Physically frozen in a state of indecision, I start constructing a risk-assessment based on what-ifs.

Out of nowhere, I hear a faint tinkling of wind chimes. I turn and see my golden Kukai. I'm startled and do a poor job covering my fright. His eyes twinkle, and an impish grin spreads across his leathered face. He's delighted. I can tell. But he offers an apology in the form of a bow.

I point to the warning sign. "Very dangerous?" I ask, not knowing if he understands a lick of English.

My Kukai smiles and replies in English. "I go this way." And with that, he steps in front of me and takes off up the trail. I stand a little dumbfounded until he turns around and nods. Taking this as an invitation, I scramble up the hill after him.

The going is slow, as my guide kicks footholds into the worst part of the trail for me to use. It's an incredible kindness. We don't speak, but occasionally, the old man turns around to make sure I am okay. I follow closely behind, trying to walk in his footsteps to reduce further damage to the trail.

It doesn't take long before we have traversed through the worst of the erosion zone. I stay behind my trail-Kukai, anyway, allowing him to lead me through the forest and onto a hilltop clearing of scrub brush and windblown pines. I smell the familiar musky odor of wild hogs and deduce the narrow path we follow is a hog trail and not a henro-route. But I'm not overly concerned.

The old henro, in many ways, reminds me of my paternal grandfather. As a child, I walked behind my grandfather along the many forested trails zig-zagging through our family farm. And like my grandfather, trail-Kukai stoops to pick up branches, large stones, and other debris obstructing the path. Every now and again, he steps over a small stick, leaving it for me to gather and toss trailside.

My guide is a frail-looking old man of at least 80 years. However, as the trail levels, it's all I can do to keep up with him. His long legs, clad in white cotton pants, are positively birdlike. He carries a small, gray daypack with a recycled mayonnaise jar full of water strapped to the side. On his feet, he wears a sloppy pair of black sneakers with Velcro straps. The shoes are at least two sizes too large, exposing his bare heels with every step. Who is this odd little man leading me through the forest? And why am I so at peace in his company?

Once out of the forest and back on the main road, my Kukai leads me to the *Hanaga Tunnel* entrance. The tunnel is yet another death-defying-passageway without sidewalk or guardrails. He slows down and moves into the middle of the single-lane roadway, and I take up position alongside him.

Enjoying the tunnel's coolness and temporary respite from the afternoon sun, we walk without talking. Darkness folds around us, and my guide retrieves a small flashlight from his vest pocket. Swinging the light back and forth in time with his stride, he warns oncoming traffic the tunnel is presently occupied.

Fortunately, we don't encounter traffic in this first tunnel. However, in our second tunnel, we must press against the sooty wall to allow a small lorry to pass.

Outside the final tunnel, we stop for a rest in a shady henro-hut occupied by two teens with shaved heads. They speak with my guide, and even though I cannot follow the conversation, they seem to be on familiar terms. There is much laughter and what I assume to be bantering or teasing, back and forth. It's a lively exchange, and I'm sorry I cannot participate.

Intuitively, I know this is the end of the trail with my Kukai. After a painfully brief rest, I thank him and bid him farewell. He simply nods, turns around, and goes back to his animated conversation with the boys.

I walk alone for the next hour, feeling grateful and a bit dumbfounded by my experience in the forest with my golden guide. The kind old man escorted me through the worst parts of the trail and kept me safe. I never felt uneasy, as I often do with strange men. There was something so peaceful and trustworthy about him. I feel blessed to have crossed his path.

It's well after four o'clock when I enter the temple grounds. Although against the rules, I head to the stamp office to catch it before it closes for the evening. Once my book is officially stamped, I'm free to take my time at both halls.

Meisekiji was established during the 6th century, and *Senju Kannon*, the deity of 1,000 arms with an eye in each palm, is enshrined here. The temple name means daybreak and stone.

According to legend, there once was a beautiful goddess who carried large stones as an act of penance while she prayed. She worked all night long, but upon daybreak, she disappeared behind the shadows of her stacks of rocks, just as my trail-Kukai had disappeared this morning into the long shadows of gravestones.

Temple 44: Daihoji

Outside of my hotel, I stop to admire a dewy *sakura* tree sparkling in the morning sun. I've seen so many gorgeous cherry-blossom trees since starting my pilgrimage; however, I've never beheld a sakura tree of this intensity. This tree's mossy trunk is badly twisted and over-burdened beneath a sea of scarlet blossoms rippling like waves over its spindly branches. The tree is ancient and terribly frail, and yet, it's still a showstopper.

Step by step, I'm learning to become more comfortable with my own aging process. I've met so many senior henro along the way that are like the stunning sakura tree. Their bodies are weathered and frail, but they are still strong enough to bloom and share their beauty with the world. Kassy and Grandpa-san and my golden Kukai are a few timeless examples of the senior health and vitality I've witnessed along the way. When I am in my 70s and 80s, I hope I will have the oomph and courage to embrace my independence and continue seeking the light through peregrination. What a gift that would be to my soul.

As I make my way out of town, I shift focus from my future self to the present. I promised myself I'd meditate on my current state of happiness during this stretch of the route. Simply put, things need to change. The family situation feels too big to tackle today. Besides, I'm only part of the equation. So, I'll focus on work.

My tentative plan is to return to Europe and continue with my university. I put in the transfer request months ago, but I can't get a straight answer. I've explained the hardship of working with a service dog in a country where accessibility laws are quite different and service dogs are rare. I fear my appeals are falling on deaf ears. I love Japan, but life was simpler for Jasper in Europe because he could go everywhere with me. His constant companionship and physical support made my life better, as well. He's kept me upright and moving for nearly seven years. In his absence, I must rely heavily on trekking poles. While I'm surprised how well I'm doing without him, I'd prefer him at my side.

If my transfer request is denied, as I'm worried it will be, I'll have some decisions to make. It's wonderful to have the time and space to meditate on all the potential what-ifs of my employment future. I mean, it's kind of poetic when I think about it. Before walking my first Camino, I had medically retired from the military. The Camino gave me the confidence I needed to leave my sofa and embrace my current professorship. And now, maybe the Shikoku will provide me with the courage and grace to retire and return home.

I miss my sons, and my grandchildren aren't getting any younger. Technology helps bridge the distance, but there is no substitute for a homemade birthday cake made by Mom, or a family gathered around the table to share a Thanksgiving meal. I haven't baked a cake or roasted a bird in many years. These sound like trivial things to sacrifice for the opportunity to travel the world, but these little things are important to me. Maybe my pilgrimages will serve as bookends, marking the beginning and the ending of my rambling ways.

It takes me a full two days to walk the 70-kilometer trek from temple forty-three to forty-four. Typically, I don't walk more than 15 to 20k per day, especially if the trail runs roadside. The hard surface wreaks havoc on plantar fasciitis and shin splints, but I'm feeling better than expected.

Outside the gate of *Daihoji,* I admire a giant pair of straw sandals. I look down at my sneakers and feel thankful. Straw sandals are the traditional henro footwear of choice, and I've seen several Japanese henro wearing similar versions. I cannot imagine the abuse my arches would take, plodding along without my trusty pair of trail-runners. The giant sandals are remade every 100 years. My shoes won't survive beyond this adventure.

Fortunately, I make the stamp office before it closes. As before, I bend the rules and collect my stamp before going through the proper rituals. After stamping my book, the lady behind the counter looks me up and down and then makes a little *tsk-tsk* sound before stacking a sandwich, two tangerines, a bottle of water, and a generous handful of hard candy in front of me. When I bow and thank her, she shakes her head and continues the tsk-tsk-ing.

I leave the stamp office a tad confused but head about my business of lighting incense sticks and chanting. The dipping sun showers a stand of white cherry-blossom trees in a wash of golden light. I've seen this magic trick before, back when I first met my trail-Kukai.

Before departing, I visit the bathroom, making sure I enter through the women's door. When I catch a glimpse of my reflection, I laugh aloud. No wonder the woman at the stamp office *tsk-tsk'd* me. I look like a madwoman! Having slept in my tent, I hadn't given any thought to personal hygiene. My face is streaked with dirt and sweat, and my hair is a bird's nest. I lean in closer to the looking glass and pick a handful of dry grass from my sloppy updo. I'm overdue for a comfy bed and a proper bath.

Temple 45: Iwayaji

I spent most of yesterday and the day before in a self-reflective haze. I spoke with almost no one. So deep was my preoccupation, I failed to realize I had reached the half-way mark of my journey. Last night, I nailed the 44th of 88 temples, but I wasn't cognizant enough to recognize the significance.

My hopes of a bed and a bath also went unrecognized. Instead, I pitched my tent trailside again. Fortunately, I had the gifts of food and water from the lady at the stamp office to serve as my supper. I wolfed down the thin sandwich of white bread, mayonnaise, and a slice of processed poultry. After peeling and eating the tangerines, I scavenged through my pack and devoured the last few figs and a handful of trail-mix.

I woke up hungry. Except for a few hard candies, I'm out of food. The continuing state of diminished personal hygiene is now obvious, even without a stamp-lady or a looking glass. I absolutely must find a better place to sleep tonight.

Rationing the little water left in my bottle, I make my way to the forty-fifth temple. The hike is less than 10k, beautifully forested, soft underfoot, but also rugged and steep. The candy helps, but by the time I see the front gate, I'm feeling shaky and dangerously low on energy.

I rest for a few moments on a bench next to a vending machine. I down two bottles of lemony *Aquarius* and feel my spirits lifting. I don't know why we don't have Aquarius in the States. It's a lifesaver on Shikoku.

I'm excited to experience this temple. According to my guidebook, Kukai trained in an area beyond the temple grounds. The training area is accessed by first paying respects to 36 statues called *The Immortal Youths* and then passing through a wooden gate and climbing rocks, ropes, ladders, and chains. I doubt I'll venture beyond the Immortal Youths, but I am intrigued.

It is said Kukai was led to this place by a lady-recluse. He carved two statues of *Fudo Myoo* to establish the temple. This area is considered a *nansho* or a difficult place. This is probably why Fudo Myoo, the fierce protector, was chosen to serve as the main deity.

I enter the gate and discover a temple unlike any I've visited thus far. At first blush, it looks shabby and needs a general sprucing up. After poking around, I'd redescribe it as *wild* or authentic.

There are all sorts of nooks and crannies to investigate. First, I enter a dark cave, dimly illuminated by a few sputtering candles. My phone's flashlight feature floods the cave with barely enough light to give me the confidence to continue.

I baby-step my way toward a grouping of small statues depicting Fudo Myoo. Scraps of paper, coins, candle stubs, and colorful ends of burnt incense litter the altar like confetti. I toss a coin, listen as it settles amongst the rest, and make a wish for continued protection.

Next, a toppled arrangement of soot-covered statues, too blackened to recognize, rest upon the remains of charred orange crates. Evidently, a candle or two burned out of control, destroying this makeshift altar.

Deeper into the cave, I find a pile of broken pottery, burnt shingles, and rusty scrap metal. In a heap, several Jizo statues are strewn about. What happened here? I fight an urge to upright the Jizos before moving on.

I trip over a large root in the middle of the narrow passageway and come down hard on both knees. My phone flies out of my hand, and I scramble after it in the dark. I do not understand this cave experience at all!

I'm not sure if I'm supposed to be in here. The cave entrance was wide-open, and I didn't see a sign indicating visitors were not allowed, but this surely is not a safe space. I should turn back around, but my curiosity pushes me deeper into the darkness.

The candlelight grows brighter as I near the end of the cave. On an altar of stone sits a large Jizo. Tied around his neck are several red baby bibs and, on his head, someone has placed a red brocade hat with white satin trim. Flanked by bouquets of fresh flowers and greenery, the statue is illuminated by two fat candles sputtering on tarnished brass holders. There is a cinder box to burn incense, a wire basket to collect coins, and a green plastic tote holding ladles. The dippers are damp, and I see by the puddle in Jizo's stone lap, an offering of water was recently made. I pick up a ladle to follow suit, but I cannot find a well or bucket of water. Instead, I burn a stick of incense and stumble toward daylight.

My bizarre cave experience is one of those times I wish I had a traveling companion. If Uri or Kassy had been with me, we could have scared the pants off each other. We also could have bounced ideas back and forth to piece together some of the mystery.

The main hall is shadowed by towering rock formations. I light my incense sticks, drop a couple of coins, and work my way through the *Heart Sutra*. To the right of the hall, an enormous wooden ladder leads to another cavern cut into a giant rocky haystack. A little boy is working his way up the rungs. In the distance, I hear a woman shriek and scream something in rapid-fire Japanese. The little boy releases an exhausted sigh and slowly climbs back down the ladder.

Again, curiosity gets the better of me. Hand over hand, I climb the sturdy rungs to see where they lead. The climbing part is easy, but I hold my breath when making the transition from the final rung to the timber-planked platform. Vertigo and ladders make for strange bedfellows. So, I creep along on all fours. When I finally look up, I realize I am not alone.

Tucked against the stone wall sits a young man with a shaved head. I try to return to the ladder without disturbing him, but he opens his eyes and cocks his head.

"TaiJo!" I am so surprised. This is the young monk that Uri and I met on our way to temple twenty-six. I never expected to see him again. I get to my feet, dust off my knees, and pat my chest with both hands. "Christine," I say, hoping it's not too silly to wish to be remembered.

He nods, but I'm not convinced. Our meeting, although funny in a sophomoric way, was nearly 20 temples ago. To help jog his mind, I hold my hand over my head and say, "Uri."

TaiJo's eyes light up as he connects the dots. "But where is your friend now?"

I shrug my shoulders and motion that he is far ahead of me, which I'm sure is true. "How is your knee?" I ask.

He lifts a backpack from his lap to show me a sturdy and confining brace. "No good," he says.

"Oh, I'm sorry. Are you in much pain?"

TaiJo nods, and we sit in silence for a moment. The cavern is clearly another shrine. Silver coins glint from crevices and crumbling ledges carved into the rocky façade.

In one corner, a faceless figure constructed of crude wooden blocks with an onion-shaped head stands behind a fruit crate filled with wishes, coins, and trinkets. The red baby bibs wrapped below the onion inform me this is a shrine to Jizo.

I want to hang out with TaiJo, but I also don't want to be *that girl* – the girl who thinks she's cool enough to keep company with a Buddhist monk. Although, to be perfectly honest, I am a little starstruck by TaiJo and his whole Zen vibe.

To avoid being a pest, I offer TaiJo a nonchalant wave goodbye before getting on all fours and backing my way toward the ladder. Once on solid ground, TaiJo calls from the platform, "Christine-san! Wait!" I am thrilled.

TaiJo accompanies me to the Daishi hall, where I finish up my ritual. He doesn't offer to chant with me. Instead, he mills around out of earshot and waits.

We walk together to the stamp office. I'm here to collect my stamp, but TaiJo is here to collect the key to the wooden gate leading to Kukai's training area. The area is dangerous, and the locked gate prevents amateur-henro from accessing the wilds of Kukai's old stomping grounds.

Since injuring his knee, TaiJo has become a public transportation henro instead of a walking one. He asks me to join him beyond the temple grounds to assist with the uneven trail or call for help if he is injured.

"Why don't you wait and come back after your knee is better?" I ask.

"Wait?" TaiJo looks at me like I'm crazy. "Why wait? We live now."

When TaiJo asks the woman behind the desk for a key, she arches her pencil-thin eyebrows and says, "Ehhhh?" This is the Japanese version of "Seriously?"

The woman sizes up the unlikely duo, shakes her head, and hands TaiJo the key. I buy a fat packet of color-coded osamefuda slips to offer the 36 Immortal Youths. Specific colors are gifted to certain youths. Hopefully, matching the proper color with each statue won't be overly challenging.

TaiJo and I disappear beyond the temple grounds into a lush pine forest. We enter through an opened wooden gate, making me question the key-collection ordeal.

A few steps beyond the gate, we find the first Immortal Youth. In front of the knee-high monument sits an upcycled, plastic food tub, like the kind used for yogurt or cottage cheese. The tub is filled with red paper slips. Easy! Pulling the first red slip from the top of my stack, I fold it neatly in fourths and drop it in the tub. TaiJo reaches down, collects my strip, unfolds it, smooths out the creases, and puts it back into the bucket. I don't ask why, but I also don't fold my next strip.

The steep trail zig-zags from statue to statue. A few times, we must use a taut rope to pull ourselves up a rock scramble to find the next youth. It's challenging for sure, but I don't think it's particularly dangerous. So far, TaiJo hasn't needed my help.

It takes the better part of an hour to find all the statues. I love the process. It's a cross between treasure hunting and reverse-trick-or-treating. Every time we find another figure, TaiJo chants a few lines, and I drop a slip into a bucket.

When we hit the last statue, I am satisfied. Throughout the ups and downs of the trail, I kept my fat stack of slips in order. I stayed true to the color-coding, and there are no leftovers.

TaiJo leads me to another wooden gate sandwiched inside the narrow opening of cave walls. The old gate is rickety, and one of the bottom panels is heavily dry-rotted. The rot leaves enough space for a raccoon or other beastie to pass beneath.

To the left of the cave is a vermillion statue of Fudo Myoo. Except for the vibrant color, he looks like other depictions I've seen along the way. He is as fierce as always, but his brilliant red hue adds to his intensity.

Chanting in front of Fudo Myoo, TaiJo places the paper sleeve, given to him by the stamp-lady, in the collection box. She gave me one too. "To keep you safe," she said. The sleeve is decorated with a red symbol on one side and three lines of characters on the other side. It reminds me of the kind of thing used to bundle a pair of chopsticks. I reach into my pants pocket and touch the thick paper. I decide to hold on to mine as a souvenir. Who knows when I'll need a keep-me-safe token?

TaiJo unlocks the brass padlock and swings the rotting gate open. We stand together for a moment, assessing the small cave and the rocky climb to the narrow exit. Without discussion, we both dump our backpacks. There is no way all of me, plus Little Miho, will make it through the slit of light at the end of the cave.

TaiJo leads the way. Despite the clunky knee brace, he hops from boulder to boulder and climbs around on all fours. Exactly how he thought I might assist him, I'm unsure. Perhaps, the worst is yet to come.

TaiJo extends a hand, attempting to pull me through the cave opening. It's like being born. I enter the opening headfirst. I'm able to get my shoulders out, but my butt is stuck. TaiJo pulls harder.

"Yee-Ouch! You're hurting me!" I pull back into the cave, freeing my hips from the sharp bite of jagged rock.

"You so fat," says TaiJo with a laugh.

"Thanks, asshole!" I snap back.

"Asshole, asshole," chants TaiJo. "I like that word!"

I'm laughing too hard to explain his new vocabulary word. I'm sure he wouldn't be tossing it out if he understood the literal meaning.

I take a moment to regroup and strategize. TaiJo sits on a rock on the other side of the birth canal. He is laughing and singing, "asshole, asshole."

The cave opening widens the higher I climb. Hand-over-hand, I make my way high enough to allow my ample backside to pass through. It's still a tight squeeze. I make it without ripping my pants or skin.

Once on the other side, I wish I hadn't labored so hard to get through. Before me is a crumbling path perched high on a craggy bluff. A rusted cable affixed with iron hooks into the rock face serves as a handrail of sorts.

TaiJo skips ahead, barely touching the railing, while I death-grip the cable and move along at a snail's pace. I'm trying to avoid looking down, but it's impossible not to. I scan the trail for the next stable place to step. I'm without my walking sticks and so unsure of myself. I'm also terribly afraid of heights.

TaiJo clangs one of two enormous chains against the rocky face of our next obstacle. Each link of the chain is larger than my hand. I follow the double-strand straight up and over a behemoth stone haystack. The surface is mossy but thankfully dry. I expect TaiJo to take the lead and scamper up the chains, but he does not. Instead, he motions for me to go ahead.

"Promise you'll catch me on the way down."

"No way. You too fat. You crush me."

"Thanks, Asshole."

Down below, I hear TaiJo chanting his asshole-refrain, but I do my best to block him out. I don't know why I've decided to climb this rock, but as it turns out, I'm pretty darn good at it, and I'm much stronger than I thought. I hold both chains and scan for a toehold. When I find one, I kick into it and push myself up the rock. I worried I wouldn't have enough upper-body strength, but my legs are doing most of the work.

I summit the haystack and stand on a small patch of grassy bramble next to a ladder of silvering beams and steel brackets. The ladder looks well made, but time and the weather have taken a toll. Several rungs show signs of rot. A few have been replaced, and some are missing. Worse than its state of disrepair, the ladder leans against another impossibly vertical rock formation. I yell down to TaiJo, "Are you kidding me?"

He ignores me and starts up the chains. I watch him for a moment. He obviously does not need my help.

The ladder's feet rest on a narrow ledge above a sheer cliff. To mount the ladder, I face the cliff, grab a side rail with my left hand, plant my left foot on the first rung, and swing my body 180-degrees over the cliff before contacting the other rail. Rung by rung, I make my way to the narrow summit where Kukai once roosted for days in deep meditation.

Circling the tip-top of Kukai's roost is an iron railing. I hang on for dear life as I inch away from the ladder to make room for TaiJo. Inside the circle is a tiny shrine no larger than an ordinary birdhouse. Wrapping one arm around the bar for stability, I release a hand to scavenge in my satchel for an osamefuda slip. I didn't come this far to leave without making a wish. Thankfully, I've already inscribed my day's meditation. *Grant me the Courage and Wisdom to negotiate life's obstacles with Grace.* Now, isn't that ironic?

When I jotted down my intention this morning, I was referring to my job and age-related struggles, like sailing through menopause without losing my mind. I had no idea the obstacles would be so physical. However, I must say, sitting atop Kukai's roost, I have handled this situation brilliantly.

I kept my wits about me, and my body was capable of more than I had expected. Climbing up to Kukai's roost, and pushing my physical abilities, may not have been the wisest choice. But I can't help but be incredibly proud of myself.

Back on the ground and through the other side of the cave womb, TaiJo squares off in front of me and bows. "You surprise me, Christine-san. I never think for you to climb the chains. I think you only wait for me."

"Wait?" I smiled, "Why wait? We live now."

Temple 46: Joruriji

Last night, TaiJo and I hopped a bus from temple forty-five to *Matsuyama City*. Using his monk-connections, TaiJo found shelter at the temple, and I crashed at a small inn across the street. The inn was quaint and family-run – more than a business hotel, but not a traditional Japanese inn with a hot bath. However, I did enjoy a long shower and a home-cooked meal of miso soup, fried salmon, pickled plums, and rice.

Although TaiJo and I hadn't made plans to meet back up again, I'm happy to find him waiting for me inside the gate next to the purification fountain. Refreshed and ready for the day's adventure, I follow him through the rituals, doing my best to keep up with the steady pace of his chant.

Joruriji was founded by Gyoki in 708 after he carved a statue of *Yakushi Nyorai*, the Buddha of healing. In 812, Kukai paid a call, restoring the ramshackle buildings to their original glory. Wildfires claimed the temple in 1715, but it was restored once again in the 1800s.

According to my guidebook, somewhere within the temple compound, there is a tree that is 1,000 years old. I'd very much like to see it, but TaiJo is acting rather impatient with me. I'm stuck making a choice between a great-granddaddy of a tree or my new Buddhist-monk-of-a-friend. I really dig nature, but the fangirl in me chooses the monk.

Temple 47: Yasakaji

The next temple is 15 minutes away. TaiJo and I make quick work of the path connecting forty-six to forty-seven, but I can see my companion is in severe pain today. He hops along, leaning heavily on his walking stick, babying his injured knee.

Once inside the temple grounds, I stop to gaze at an information sign, like I always do. I scan the dates and font. It takes me a few moments to realize I'm literally reading the sign. It's in English! And now that I think about it, the last temple's information sign was also in English. How odd. I wonder why the language has changed.

According to the sign, this temple was founded during the 7th century. The original campus included a large temple, 12 lodging houses, and 48 branch temples. It's nowhere near that expansive now. Like so many temples along the way, the original was destroyed by wildfires.

Before getting into my henro-routine, I take a moment to admire the landscaping and overall setting. The temple is set high in a draw, surrounded by heavily-forested hills. Cherry-blossoms in full bloom shimmer in the morning breeze and form a soft-pink frothy wave flowing down the hillside. Overhead, a pine bow trained on a long bamboo pole creates a handy overpass for squirrels. Everywhere I turn, the gardening is nothing short of immaculate.

In front of the main temple, I admire the largest conch shell I've ever seen and probably will ever see in my entire life. Tucked back on the temple platform and protected by a guardrail, I'm not permitted to touch or get a closer look. I think the shell is real. Apart from its size, it certainly looks real.

Attached to the one end of the shell is a large metal tip, like a megaphone. The shell rests horizontal, but from stem to stern, it's longer than I am tall. I ask TaiJo if he thinks the shell is real.

"Why would it not be?" he questions, a little too dismissively.

"Why would it not be?" I parrot his answer. "Have you ever seen a shell this big in your whole life?" TaiJo shrugs and limps away toward the Daishi hall.

I could stay in these temple grounds all day long, but TaiJo is impatient with my loitering. The air is cool and moist and carries woodsy hints of pine and cedar with a touch of floral. I'm in sensorial-heaven. I inhale three deep breaths, hoping to capture the memory of all I see and smell.

Temple 48: Sairinji

The four-kilometer stretch to temple forty-eight cuts through suburban-sprawl, and the going is tedious. TaiJo limps along, and for the most part, he's making good time. We walk without talking. Our silence allows me the freedom to bounce around in my own head. This is one of the many treasures of pilgrimage. Not often do I find myself free and unobstructed by technology, social obligation, or work-related noise. The wide-open headspace is nothing short of addicting.

My empty stomach growls loud enough to make TaiJo smile. Without talking, I follow him into a convenience store and load up on rice triangles, cold drinks, and trail-mix-like snacks. I say trail-mix *like,* but I should say trail-mix *unlike.* Because the contents held in this cellophane package is unlike any trail-mix I've ever eaten. I recognize the wasabi peas, salty soybeans, and candy-coated peanuts. But what's with these itsy-bitsy dried fish with their googly eyes and wee gaping mouths?

Outside the store, we sit on the stoop and devour our catch. I hand TaiJo my open bag of trail-mix. He pours the mix directly in his mouth, like a teenager drinking from a milk carton. I let out a little scoff of disgust, and he offers me a guilty but not-so-sorry grin. I'm old enough to be his mother, and I imagine, in the past, his own mother scolded him for such behavior.

At the temple gate, TaiJo splits off, leaving me to happily read another sign in English. According to the sign, Gyoki established Sairinji in 741. Kukai popped by to give the place a remodel in 807. The campus buildings burnt to the ground around 1630 but were rebuilt in 1700. Reading in English is so much fun!

Legend tells of Kukai visiting this area and finding the villagers suffering under a relentless drought. Responding to their pleas and prayers for relief, Kukai thrust his walking staff into the ground and up bubbled a spring of the purest water. The spring continues to feed the pond in front of the temple.

I cross the bridge leading to the middle of the pond where a statue of Jizo sits. According to my book, this Jizo is said to grant one wish to each person who makes a water offering. Next to Jizo is a stone bowl of water and a ladle. I dip out a cupful, pour it across Jizo's lap, and make my wish for continued health and happiness.

I meet up with TaiJo in front of the bamboo of *familial piety*. It is believed if one prays into this bush, one will achieve a happy home. My domestic life is long overdue for a tune-up. I waste no time entertaining doubts.

Temple 49: Jodoji

Temples forty-six through fifty-one are clumped within a short day's walk. TaiJo and I hadn't agreed to hang together, but I was hoping to continue in our silent companionship. However, his knee is killing him, so he hopped a bus. I'm not ready for public transportation – not even with a local guide.

Without language skills, knowing when and where to get on and get off the bus is only half the battle. Although highly organized, I find the Japanese bus routine difficult to manage. Passengers enter the bus from the backdoor, take a ticket, and pay when exiting the front. The last time I hopped on the bus, I forgot to collect a ticket, and then I didn't have enough change to pay my fare. I had large bills, but nothing small. The frustrated driver shooed me out the door with a scolding that I was happy not to have understood.

I plod along on my own now, making quick time in the absence of my wounded comrade. I like this pace, but I do miss his presence. I don't feel particularly motherly to the young monk. At 25, he is the same age as my fourth son, Garret. Like hanging out with Uri, I find comfort in his brand of youthful energy.

Garret and the rest of my boys are on my mind as I enter the gate of *Jodoji*. I take a seat next to the concrete pedestal of a ginormous Jizo. And I write out a few wishes for my sons.

Temple 50: Hantaji

After another short slog through suburbia, I enter the gate of *Hantaji*. Gyoki established this temple in the middle of the 8th century, and Kukai is known to have studied and trained here.

This temple is frequented by budding academics praying for success or assistance on a particular exam. Others visit to pray for prosperity in business ventures or marital unions. I find myself interested in all three motivations, and so before hitting the purification fountain, I jot down a different wish on three separate osamefuda slips.

Since I no longer bear the burden of exams and final papers, I make my first wish for my students. Most of my adult students are nontraditional. Many must balance demanding military careers and family responsibilities with their academic goals. Some speak English as their second or even third language, and several might be classified as *hard-to-serve* by mainstream academia, but I think they are all amazing. They need all the help I have to offer. A wish for success will only serve them well.

I dabble in small-press publishing. Right now, it's merely a hobby. The side-hustle provides an outlet for my own travel writing, but I also do a fair amount of coaching and editing. The big-picture aspirations are tiny, and I like it that way. So, I make a wish for a tiny amount of prosperity – enough to satisfy but not enough to overwhelm. I've walked the workaholic road long enough to know I do not want to follow that route through my latter 50 years.

My final wish is for my husband and me. Not to be cliché, but our relationship is *complicated*. I wake up every morning and declare my love and commitment. I decide to be married. Jim, however, does not. Sometimes, loving Jim is easy. At other times, it's a lot of work.

After two decades of marriage, maybe this is the way it works for most couples. Or perhaps, love has run its course, and we are nearing our expiration date. I comfort myself by writing off his behaviors as symptoms of a midlife-crisis. However, we are going on a decade of crisis, and it's getting harder to self-soothe. I scratch out a wish for love's revival. The prose is thin and reads as if it were written by a heartbroken teenager.

Temple 51: Ishiteji

The walk from temple fifty to fifty-one irritates me. I'm crabby and sick of the punishing concrete. And the current stream of traffic whizzing by does nothing to improve my mood.

I reach *Ishiteji*, hoping to find a peaceful refuge, but I'm out of luck. Loads of elderly bus-henro belch through the gate in front of me. I'm lost in a geriatric sea of conical hats and walking sticks. Accompanying the busloads are an equal number of tourists.

The crowd is so thick that I contemplate skipping this temple and moving on to the next. I dig around in my satchel until I feel the brocade-covered stamp book. As if reading braille, my fingertips study the gilded flowers set against a silky backdrop of teal. I flip open to the expecting page and stare at the blank parchment.

Can I give myself permission to leave one page of this book blank? Sure. I suppose so, but will I look at this book in 20 years and remember why I chose not to collect the stamp? Will I be sorry? And will I remember the reasons? – that I was annoyed because others dared visit the temple at the same time – that I was sick and tired of traffic and concrete - and that the crowd and the traffic and the concrete were not the real problems – because the real problem is that I'm not dealing with any of my real problems. In this moment of clarity, I flip my book shut and march toward the purification fountain.

At the main hall, I light three sticks of incense. I also complete the full series of recommended chants and ask *Yakushi Nyorai*, the healing Buddha and deity of this temple, to grant me the wisdom, courage, and grace to create the life I desire.

Temple 52: Taisanji

I left temple fifty feeling resolved. But now, I'm feeling sorry for myself again. Sorrow has accompanied me all day. And I'm tired of sorrow's company.

Usually, walking is my prayer, and pilgrimage is my church. The heavy traffic and crowds feel like infringements – like trying to convene with God during a hailstorm of conversation and road noise. But I also don't want to be alone in my own head right now.

So, when I see TaiJo waiting at the bus stop outside of temple fifty-one, I feel a great relief. I give him a tentative wave, and he returns it with enthusiasm. It is the green-light I need to join him.

I don't want to impose on TaiJo. I'm sure he is on the pilgrimage to do serious work. However, when I plop next to him, he sighs and relaxes against the bench. Perhaps, TaiJo needs out of his own head too.

I follow TaiJo onto the bus, mimicking his every move like a trained monkey. He has no idea he serves as my unofficial bus mentor. We sit together in silence, but on the inside, I am bubbling over with gratitude for his companionship and transportation guidance.

The three-hour walk melts into mere minutes as the bus rattles along toward *Taisanji*. TaiJo pulls a cable, signaling the driver to stop. When he stands, I stand. I follow him toward the front, pay the driver, and exit without altercation, confusion, or embarrassment. Bus-success is sweet!

We bow at the gate and enter together. I pause in front of a towering bronze statue of *Sho Kannon*, the goddess of mercy, set against a lush backdrop of cedar and bamboo. I feel the tension leave my neck and shoulders, and I am delivered from the hustle of the city to this hilltop-oasis.

In the deity's hand is a lotus blossom, representing the *Buddha mind*. The irony of this symbolism is not lost on me. After meeting back up with TaiJo, it took less than 15 minutes to shift from my angry-monkey mind to a more peaceful version of me.

A relaxing tingle vibrates through my body, radiating out the top of my head. I arch my back a bit, enjoying the sensation like a gentle tickle to the inside of my arm. I lean into the energy and wrap myself in the protective cloak of whispering leaves, evergreens, and birdsong.

Temple 53: Enmyoji

TaiJo limps to the bus stop, and I follow. The short walk is shy of a full kilometer, but he struggles. With each step, he releases a barely audible gasp.

We wait on a bench together, and I offer him some ibuprofen. He holds up a hand in refusal. I persist, "These help with the swelling – and the pain."

"Pain is important."

"I get it, but you don't have to suffer."

"Suffer?" He cocks his head.

"Suffer is when your body hurts or when your heart hurts," I tap my chest to help drive the meaning.

TaiJo is silent for a moment, nodding his head. "Suffer is important."

"Suffering." The English professor in me just won't die. "Suffer, suffer-ed, suffer-ing."

"Hmmph," TaiJo grunts. "Suffering is important."

"Exactly," I praise.

"Exactly," rebounds TaiJo in a mocking tone.

The ride to *Enmyoji* takes less time to complete than the walk to the bus stop. But it gives me a chance to practice my bus skills. I'm two for two and feeling proud.

Enmyoji is our eighth temple of the day. The low-hanging fruit of monotony is ripe for the picking. We stumble through the rituals, but I cannot focus. One temple runs into the next, and I am failing to find anything particularly special about the experience.

While waiting in line for my stamp, I scan through my guidebook for fun facts or tidbits of inspiration. Eureka! I've found something!

Hidden in plain sight, somewhere on this campus, is a statue of the Virgin Mary. Disguised as Kannon, the figure of Mary was secretly venerated by the hidden Christians of Japan. How intriguing!

TaiJo is as curious about the statue as I am, and we set out to explore the campus. It doesn't take long. A wealth of fresh-flower offerings at the base of a well-worn and rather unassuming stone monument ends our quest.

TaiJo reads the nearby information sign, printed in Japanese. The inscription refers to the statue as the *Maria Kannon*. I'm interested in knowing when the figure was carved, but unfortunately, no dates are offered.

"What do you do?" asks TaiJo.

"What do you mean?

"As Christian. What do you do?"

I shrug my shoulders. "I don't exactly know. Some Christians might pray."

"Chant?"

"Yeah, in a way."

I think for a moment. I'm not a Catholic, but I prayed the rosary while hiking with a Catholic family on the Camino. I only know the part that includes *The Lord's Prayer*, and so those lines were assigned to me.

"Some Christians might pray the rosary."

"You chant it for me?"

"I only know a little part."

"Chant a little part," he urges. "Please."

So, I do.

TaiJo cocks his head, "Teach me."

"Our Father, who art in heaven," I point to TaiJo, and he repeats my words. Line by line, I lead this Buddhist monk through my Sunday-school tradition.

Temple 54: Enmeiji:

Last night, TaiJo and I rode the bus to *Imabari City*. I stayed in a somewhat sketchy business hotel, and TaiJo used his connections to score a bed at the temple. I love staying on the actual temple campus, but those stays are few and far between. A night spent in a temple is a treasured cultural experience I am grateful to receive whenever the opportunity presents itself.

Most temples along the Shikoku do not offer accommodations for ordinary henro; however, according to TaiJo, there are free beds or sleeping spaces set aside for pilgrimaging monks or mendicant henro. I am neither monk nor beggar. So, when TaiJo offered to find space for me, I politely refused.

Before parting, we didn't make plans to meet up - just as we never have before. However, after entering the *Enmeiji* gate, I am crestfallen to not find him waiting for me. We barely speak to one another, but I have enjoyed his steady companionship.

The main deity in this temple is *Fudo Myoo*, the ever-fierce guardian. So, I write out two osamefuda slips, asking Fudo Myoo to protect TaiJo and prevent further injury to his knee. TaiJo has surrendered his pilgrimage to public transportation, but the effort still involves a lot of walking, stair climbing, and negotiating uneven terrain.

I make my way to the bell. With a gentle swing, the battering ram kisses the bell, and in a low hum, announces my arrival to Fudo Myoo. The bell, created in 1704, is like most of the bells I've encountered along the way; however, this one carries a quirky story.

According to legend, this bell has been historically attractive to thieves. Whenever a thief successfully removes the bell, it cries out without being touched. Instead of the usual bong-bong, this bell peals, "*Inuru-Inuru*," or "home-home." Of course, this oddity frightens the thieves. After each theft, the bell has always been returned to its rightful home.

Temple 55: Nankobo

Like the last eight temples, temples fifty-four through fifty-nine are clustered within a day's walk. It's a 19-kilometer stretch or about 12 miles. Apart from a steep climb up to temple fifty-eight, the elevation remains relatively constant. So, it's no big deal.

The real *big deal* I'm facing is the monotony. Part of the problem is I no longer have TaiJo to fuss over. The other part of the problem is that the temples are running together again. I'm ashamed to admit it, but I'm bored.

Yesterday knocked the wind out of my pilgrim sail. I was in and out of eight different temples, chanting the same things twice at each location. That's 16 repetitions and 32 wishes printed on slips.

The good news is my pronunciations are improving. I no longer bury my head in my guidebook, tracing a finger under each line. When I'm stuck in a total white-out snowstorm of henro, I stand in the middle and chant along without my book. It's like singing along with the car radio. I may not know each word of a favorite song, but I chime in with relative consistency.

Feeling bored is a disgrace. I used to tell my kids only boring people get bored. Now, I'm the boring person. I'm a spoiled brat in the backseat of a station wagon bound for Disneyland.

The language, food, customs, people, and beautiful temples are so far beyond my upbringing. Even though I've lived in Okinawa City for the past nine months, it's nothing like Shikoku. In fact, one of my main reasons for embarking on the Shikoku pilgrimage was to embrace Japanese culture free from the invasive American military influences infecting Okinawa.

But alone in my skeezy hotel room last night, boredom got the best of me, and I booked a flight for tomorrow morning back to Okinawa. It's dumb to leave right now because my university is on spring break. I have all this free time, but I need space to readjust my attitude. I'll return in a few days, fresh and ready to continue. Besides, I really miss my dog.

Approaching the gate of *Nankobo*, I'm looking for something that makes this temple stand out from the one before. Thankfully, I don't have to look hard. The front gate is magnificent, and unlike any other, I've beheld. Intricately carved of wood and lavished with gold leaf, four fierce guardians protect the entryway.

I bow at the gate, express my gratitude, and find my way to the purification fountain. On a bench near the fountain, I scratch out several osamefuda slips with today's revised intentions. My new focus is to *Embrace the Beauty of Shikoku and Appreciate Life's Blessings*.

At the bell tower, I pull back the battering ram with all my might, release it, and prepare my body for the shock of reverberations. Typically, I don't like to make a fuss. I try to tap the bell as lightly as possible – coming in like a lamb and not a lion. But today, I need to shake things up. I also pledge to complete each temple ritual without shortcuts – even though my jaw still aches from yesterday's overexertion.

Temple 56: Taisanji

Walking on sidewalks that flank busy streets is rarely inspiring. Few hikers I know would argue, but I'm more than a hiker. I'm a henro, and so I must find the silver-lining.

And that silver comes in the comforting familiarity of the golden arches. Since I'm not homesick enough to face down a McDonald's cheeseburger, I continue for another block and opt for a symbol of Americana even more familiar to me than Micky-D's. I pop into a 7-Eleven store and immediately feel at home.

From 10 to 18-years-old, 7-Eleven was my second-home. I spent much of my time behind a cash register, or stocking shelves, or sucking down a cherry Slurpee like a ravenous hummingbird.

Of course, Japanese 7-Eleven stores stock different items than the store I grew up in during the 70s and 80s. The setup and basic ambiance are the same. Unlike other convenience stores in Japan, my bankcard always works in 7-Eleven cash machines. This place is beyond comforting, and I stock up on my favorite Japanese comfort food, salmon-filled rice triangles.

I shove the last bite of rice in my mouth, and with a happy belly and clear focus, I bow and enter the gate of *Taisanji*. Before getting down to business, I stroll through the campus, looking for unique splendors to set this temple apart from the past 55.

I stare down a pathway of dull gray pavers skirted by a dusty swath of weedy pea-gravel. Hmm. This might take some imagination.

I scuff along the pea gravel, searching for a pine tree Kukai planted way back in 815. Of course, I expect to behold an old granddaddy of a tree, wizened by time, and twisted by the centuries of typhoons known only too well to this island's flora and fauna. Instead, I find a beautifully manicured, garden-landscape variety – a tad spindly and no taller than two of me stacked end to end.

According to legend, every time the pine withers away, a new one pops up in its place. Eyeing the puny evergreen, I figure this is as good an explanation as any.

The honzon of Taisanji is *Jizo Bosatsu*, my favorite bodhisattva to date. While I have a thing for Jizo in general, I like the whole bodhisattva concept. In Japan, a bodhisattva is called bosatsu. Unlike Buddha, a bosatsu has yet to achieve enlightenment. Instead of crossing the threshold, these loving beings hang back with the rest of us, delaying *Enlightenment* out of compassion for mere mortals like me. I find this incredibly endearing. Whenever I behold Jizo, surrounded by an army of fat babies, my heart melts a little each time.

Temple 57: Eifukuji

At the gate of *Eifukuji*, I check-in with myself and conduct a mini-inventory. The gentle climb up *Mt. Futo* and away from traffic noise was enough to reset my attitude and prepare me for the much steeper haul to temple fifty-eight. I'm feeling refreshed and energized, and grateful. I marvel at the shift in perspective. Even my body feels fantastic. What a difference strolling through nature can make for me.

I wash my hands and mouth, all the while admiring an angry-looking dragon perched on a rock, spitting water into the stone trough. A fat section of green bamboo balances on the far side of the trough. When I finish with my purification, I replace my dipper alongside the other ten perched on the bamboo beam.

I wait behind an old woman trying to ring the bell to announce her arrival. She is tiny and frail in a shriveled-raisin way that happens to great-grandmothers who are lucky enough to live a long and loving life. She's wearing henro-white, but her black sneakers are laced in neon pink. I think of my grandmother and smile.

On Shikoku, age is not such a big deal. I think about my first henro-friend, Kassy. She walked me into the ground day-after-day. Yes, she struggles with her eyesight, way-finding, and using technology. After all, these are age-related inconveniences. However, these issues didn't hamper her spirit. She's out there somewhere now, many temples ahead, finding her way and ringing temple bells to announce herself to the world.

The wide brim of the old woman's sedge-hat makes it difficult for her to see what she is doing. She doesn't seem to possess enough upper-body strength to move the battering ram. I want to step up to the platform and help her out, but I resist the urge. After all, she didn't get to temple fifty-seven without figuring out how to ring a bell. I don't want to take away from her experience. And so, I wait.

Each time she swings the rope, I lean toward the bell as if willing the log to connect. After her eighth attempt, the softest hum vibrates the air. She's done it! And when she turns around and looks me in the eyes, I can see she is as excited by her success as I am. We exchange bows, and now, I can leave the temple with a full heart.

Outside the temple, the little lady of the bell is loading into a taxi. She offers a shy nod, and I return the gesture. I watch the cab pull away, stop, and then back up again.

The cab door flings open. The lady hops out, and with remarkable speed, shuffles toward me. I can't help but smile as I watch her neon pink laces dance with each choppy step. Short of an arm-length apart, she stops and thrusts a white paper bag to my chest. "Ossetia," she says. "Yum-yum."

I peek inside and see two dusty mochis, one baby pink and the other seafoam green. Her gift is thoughtful, and I am ravenous. I need all the energy I can get to haul myself up the steep incline to *Senyuji*. I bow with genuine gratitude, and we exchange osamefuda slips.

She examines my name printed on the slip. It takes her a while to pronounce, but she sounds it out bit by bit, "Ku-ri-tsu-n" That's as close to Christine as I can expect.

I examine her slip written in Japanese. Fortunately, I've been working on my characters. While it does take me much longer to decipher, I give it my best, "Mo-tsu-mo-to san."

I must be right on the money because she beams. She holds my osamefuda slip between her pressed palms like it's a treasure. "Aw, Kuritsun-san, you smart."

We exchange a few rounds of bows and compliments until the cab driver politely taps his horn, telling us it is time to wrap it up. She puts a hand over her mouth to conceal her laughter. Then, she backs all the way to the cab, bowing as she goes.

I watch the cab pull away again, and I think of my grandmother. She would have loved to see Japan and all these temples. Over the final few years of her life, I was teaching overseas and didn't make enough effort to see her often. I visited a few times every year, twice in the summer and once at Christmas. I took comfort knowing she was there, waiting for me to come back home.

My children are all busy adulting, and my grandkids are busy being kids. My parents are absorbed in their own lives. During the first year of my absence, I'm sure my presence was missed. By now, everyone is carrying on as they should. In the absence of my grandmother, I feel like no one is missing me at all.

Temple 58: Senyuji

Sorrow is hitching a ride on my back again, so I change my headspace and focus on the mochi. In Japan, I've learned it is rude to walk down the street while eating or drinking. On Okinawa, I see Americans do so every day, but I never see an Okinawan do it. So, I keep the top of the white paper sack folded down until I'm in the forest and out of sight.

I don't love the taste or the texture of mochi. I wish I did. However, I do think they are beautiful. I also appreciate how difficult they must be to make. Who knew rice could become a stretchy, fleshy substance?

A piece of Mochi does not look at all like it tastes. To me, mochis look like dreamy puffs of marshmallow dusted in powdered sugar. I always expect a cream or fruity filling, but it's almost always red beans.

I bite into the pink one and shout, "Beans! Beans are not dessert!" But I devour it in two bites and snatch up the green one.

It takes half a bottle of water to wash the mochi down. My hunger is satiated, but I'm left with gritty bits of red bean granules wedged between my teeth. I take another swig of water, swish it around, make sure the coast is clear, and spit. If walking while eating is rude, I cannot imagine how I might be judged for spitting.

The climb up to Senyuji totally kicks my butt. However, to my surprise, I cover the two-and-a-half-kilometer stretch in near-record time. It must be bean power!

Once inside the gate, I stop to admire a statue of Kannon towering over me. This temple's main deity is *Senju Kannon*, the thousand-armed deity with an eye in each palm. However, is statue does not look like the other Senju depictions.

Kannon is the main deity at 39 of the 88 temples on Shikoku. Since I am new to all that is Buddhist, keeping my deities in order is no easy task. I think the Kannon towering before me with the baby in her arms is *Kosodate Kannon*, the motherhood and childbirth deity, like the one I saw with Grandpa-san back at temple thirty-four.

Forever a mother, I am always worried about my sons. For the most part, they each do a fine job navigating life's obstacles. They are grown men now and don't necessarily need me fussing over them, but I take a moment anyway to write out a wish for each one.

Temple 59: Kokubunji

As I bow at the gate of *Kokubunji*, I realize this is not only my last temple of the day, but it is the final one for this trip. I'll be returning home to Okinawa bright and early in the morning.

Clearly, I acted hastily last night when I made my flight arrangements home. I was irritable and bored, but the day's beauty and the little bell-lady have revived me. I have so much more in the tank. Thankfully, the flight to Okinawa is short and relatively inexpensive.

I'll make a quick pitstop at home and fly back within a few days. Besides, my henro-whites could use a proper washing machine and an iron. Jasper and a balcony of plants will be happy to see me.

This is the third of four Kokubunji stops along the Shikoku route. The first two were back at temples fifteen and twenty-nine. The final one is ahead in the *Kagawa Prefecture* at temple eighty.

I wash up at the purification fountain. Most fountains feature a dragon spitting into the trough below. This one has a black ginger pot with gold leaves around the neck and gold characters across the belly.

A large bowl is carved into a deeply rippled black rock. Perched above the waterline sits the pot. The pool below is currently still, but I imagine when the fountain cycles on, the water bubbles out from beneath the lid and down the sides of the squat vessel.

Yakushi Nyorai, the Buddha of healing, is the honzon enshrined at this temple. So, I write out another prayer for TaiJo's knee. I had hoped to run into him, but I am no match for public transportation.

Before starting my pilgrimage, I assumed it would be *my feet* in need of healing prayers. This was certainly the case on the Camino – but not on Shikoku. My plantar fasciitis is almost non-existent, and I remain blister-free. It's truly remarkable, considering my long history with both maladies.

As I'm in no hurry to rush off to another temple, I take my time and wander through an old cemetery. Amongst the headstones, I find the *Vase of Yakushi*, a giant ginger jar carved from black granite and adorned with gold. And now I realize the significance of the pot set in the center of the purification fountain. It's the tiny doppelganger to this beauty. It is believed if one touches the pot while praying, one will be cured of any sickness. Since I'm not currently sick, I say a prayer for my continued good health.

Once out of the cemetery, I find a statue of Kobo Daishi. The figure is shorter than I am, but it seems to be a true-to-size depiction of Kukai. He holds a bowl in one hand, and the other is stretched out as if to receive a handshake.

By the discoloration of the statue's hand, I assume shaking is the thing to do. I don't want to jump to conclusions. So, I use my translator app to read the sign next to the statue: *Shake hands with the master and make only one wish. Don't do this more. The master is also busy.*

I can't think of a wish. According to the sign, I need to get it right the first time. I take a raincheck for now, planning to return once I gather my thoughts.

At both halls, I examine silvering wooden elephants, with delicately carved tusks, adorning the beams and roofline. I move through my rituals, reciting every syllable with as much precision as my foreign tongue can muster.

Behind me, I hear the strike of a match. Lingering in an envelope of earthy sandalwood smoke, I hear another strike. High-notes of rose tickle my nostrils. Aw, it must be a husband-and-wife team. My heart pings as I remember the old couple waiting at the bus stop back at temple forty. They seemed inseparable and unified in their quest – and so very married.

In the haze of smoldering incense, I realize how much I am missing my husband – how much I want to be like the couple at the bus stop – Inseparable, or at least, unified. My heart breaks a little as I contemplate our marital health. How did we drift so far apart? And can we close the chasm or maybe build a bridge?

I make my way back to the statue of Kukai. With a firm handshake, I make my wish. It's an elaborate wish, a run-on-sentence-of-a-wish, but it is only one wish.

Temple 60: Yokomineji

The morning after completing my visit to temple fifty-nine, I hopped a flight back home. I was just outside the Okinawa airport when I received a text message from my hubby. To my surprise, Jim was making his way to Tokyo to join me on the Shikoku. My goodness! Kukai works fast. He granted my wish in less than 24 hours.

I had enough time to pop over to the dog sitter and take Jasper for a walk while my henro-whites were in the washing machine. It was a quick turnaround, but I didn't mind. In the space of about eight hours, I was back in the air, headed to Tokyo to meet up with Jim. And now, we are in a rental car making our way toward *Yokomineji*, the sixtieth temple.

I'm thrilled Jim decided to surprise me. The logistical inconvenience of his surprise is no bother at all. However, I am apprehensive. Jim is not the hardiest of travel companions. He prefers western hotels with regular mattresses. This limits us to business hotels unless I can talk him into a tatami mat on a temple floor. He doesn't eat fish – none at all. Apart from ramen and teriyaki chicken or beef, he doesn't eat Japanese food.

I know cultural differences are hard for him to embrace, but he seems willing to try. When he stays with me in Okinawa, which is about six weeks on and six weeks off, I make accommodations to ensure his comfort. I want him to stay put and not pop back to the comfort of the good old *USA* whenever he misses a cheeseburger. However, I must admit that when he does go home, I feel a sense of relief, a kind of freedom – like no longer walking on eggshells to keep him happy.

We work out our survival strategy during our ten-hour drive. It's best to hammer out a plan now to avoid fighting once we are on the trail. I want our time together to be memorable — and not merely remembered by a massive blowout over something silly.

Since Jim is more comfortable in western hotels, I agree to business hotels unless the rare opportunity for temple lodging arises. The experience outweighs the discomfort of sleeping on a futon. Thankfully, he agrees.

Jim does like rice, so I will surrender every bowl of rice along the Shikoku. In turn, he will happily surrender every morsel of fish, raw or otherwise. Whenever possible, we will drop by a convenience market, so he can load up on fried chicken and hot dogs. I'm fine living on my rice-triangles if that's what it takes.

We hit a roadblock about coffee. Unfortunately, the morning cup of joe isn't a Japanese tradition. Sure, we have a coffeemaker in our Okinawa apartment, but getting a freshly-pressed or brewed cup bright and early along the Shikoku isn't an option. He turns his nose up at the vending machines stocked with every kind of canned coffee — hot, cold, black, strong, light, cream, sugar, cream & sugar... The options are stunning. I can't fix this situation. Coffee is available. Yes, it's in a can, but it is delicious. If he can climb down from his caffeine-infused high horse, I think we can manage!

Jim hasn't shown much interest in Japanese culture. When I first asked him to join me on the Shikoku, he refused. I asked one more time, but I didn't pester. I learned my lesson from the Camino. He didn't want to walk the Camino, but I begged him. When begging failed, I deployed a well-crafted guilt trip. All-in-all, we had a reasonably good time, but it came at a stressful price.

I don't want to sacrifice my joy along the Shikoku. He's come here on his own accord, and he seems ready to overcome some self-imposed limitations. Who knew a carefully crafted wish and handshake with Kukai would create such a turnaround?

We crash in a business hotel for the night. It's mildly skeezy and cramped, but I keep my complaints to myself. In the morning, we make the short drive to *Yokomineji.* The plan is to ditch the car as soon as possible and rely on our feet and public transportation. Hopefully, finding a place to return the car will not be too difficult.

The morning air is cool and damp, and the winding uphill drive to the temple is heavily forested. We enjoy peekaboo views of a green river looping through the valley below. The river looks like a taffeta ribbon in the wind.

In the parking lot below the temple, Jim scores his first can of vending-machine coffee. Tipping the can to his lips, he takes a sip and grimaces, "Ugh! That's nasty!"

I examine the can. "Well, it's black and extra strong." I plunk some more change into the machine and retrieve another can, but this time with cream and sugar. I watch with a raised eyebrow for the verdict.

"It's not the worst coffee I've ever had," he says.

"Well then, let's chalk it up as a success."

We walk the wooded-trail from the parking lot to the temple grounds. Jim admires the pine trees and granddaddy cedars. "I never knew Japan was so... so green." I nod my head and smile. So far, so good!

Like my buddy Uri, Jim isn't interested in participating in temple rituals or collecting stamps. So, we split up at the purification fountain. He takes off to explore the grounds, and I head to the hall, housing *Dainichi Nyorai,* the highest of the enlightened beings.

I catch up with Jim standing in front of a statue of Kukai. Pointing to the foliage in the backdrop, Jim says, "Look, that's *mountain laurel.*"

"Yup, that's a *rhododendron.*"

I grew up in the west. Jim grew up in the east. He says mountain laurel, and I say rhododendron. He says buggy, and I say shopping cart. It reminds me of the words to an Ella Fitzgerald & Louis Armstrong song. *You say to-may-to, and I say to-ma-ta…*

Frankly, I don't care what he calls the shrubbery behind Kukai. I'm thrilled he is taking in the beauty and making connections. Maybe he will find comfort on this rural island, just as I have.

Temple 61: Koonji

We find ourselves weaving our way through a busload of elderly henro. Jim is clearly charmed, as he always seems to be by senior citizens. He smiles and bows, making the old ladies giggle and cover their mouths. When it comes to elderly women, he's really a bit of a flirt, but I love this about him.

When we first started dating, he met my grandmother. The kindly way he spoke to her, so genuine and reverent, sealed the deal. I knew I wanted to marry him. That was a long time ago. We've certainly had our ups and downs, but I'm happy to see a shimmer of the golden-boy I fell in love with.

Deploying my crowd-beating strategy, I strike out for the stamp office before completing my tasks. When I present my book, the monk behind the counter turns me away. His English is perfect – a little too perfect. Not only does he refuse to stamp my book, but he also does a decent job of shaming me.

With my tail between my legs, I leave the office and queue up at the purification station. Jim settles in on a bench, enjoying the parade of grannies and grandaddies. He looks content, so I chill-out and take my time.

Koonji is in sharp contrast to the other temples I have visited thus far and not in an esthetically pleasing way. Gone are the charming pagodas and old wooden halls with carved elephants or lions holding up the rafters. While the original temple was founded in the 6th century, the current architecture of the main hall reminds me of a community college built in the 1970s. Everything is constructed of poured concrete – gray, square, and drab.

Once I have properly completed my duties, I wait my turn at the stamp office. I pass my book to my old pal, but he gives me another stern look and shakes his head.

"I did both temples. Honestly, I did!"

"I know this. I watched you."

"Okay. Then may I have my stamp, please?"

His eyebrows narrow. Out of nowhere, he starts chewing like a cow. If that's not odd enough, he looks like a terribly angry and rabid cow.

"No chewing!" he barks.

There is an awkward silence. The ladies behind me shuffle backward out the door, leaving me alone with the mad cow. It takes me a moment.

"Oh! I get it. You are talking about my gum."

"No eating! No drinking. No chewing. It's disrespectful."

I do something I have not done since getting caught with gum in elementary school. I swallow it. Next, I open my mouth and stick out my tongue to show the empty cavern of my disrespectful mouth.

"I am truly sorry. I didn't know. Now, may I please have my stamp?"

The monk's composure doesn't soften. However, he sweeps my three coins from the counter and collects my book. With perhaps a little more force than necessary, he slams down three vermillion stamps on the page. I hold my breath as his paintbrush strokes out the graceful lines of calligraphy.

I bow, thank him in Japanese, and baby-step backward toward the door. He nods his head and says, "Remember, NO GUM!"

Temple 62: Hojuji

Along with my reprimand for gum chewing at temple sixty-one, the surly monk advised me to skip temple sixty-two. In terms of operating hours and stamp fee, *Hojuji* is not participating in the 88-temple standardized procedures. The monk warned me Hojuji could be an unwelcoming place for henro – and coming from him, that says a lot.

To solve the problem of the wayward temple, a makeshift stamp office is set up in the parking lot of temple sixty-one. I size up the long queue of henro snaking across the parking lot to the tent. I don't feel like waiting to collect a stamp for a temple I won't visit.

I can't see the point of collecting a parking lot stamp – especially after getting busted for my crowd-beating strategy. Instead, I'll try my luck at Hojuji. How bad could it be? If the situation turns sour, I can always return to the line for my consolatory-stamp-of-nothingness to fill the gaping blank page in my book.

In the parking lot of temple sixty-two, I prepare for battle. I straighten my hakui, wrap my prayer beads around my wrist, and unfurl the royal purple collar. I gave up wearing a sedge hat so many temples ago because it was uncomfortable and impractical in the wind. Instead, I wear a white scarf to cover my head.

Standing on the sidewalk, I take inventory. Everything looks good, and I'm not chewing gum. I ask Jim to hang back until I give him the all-clear sign. He's not in henro garb, and I don't want to be turned away because my hubby is a tourist.

Once inside the temple gate, I see a placard with a camera inside a red circle with a slash running through it. Okay. No pictures. Got it. I put my phone away, so I won't have the urge.

The temple grounds are serene. Apart from a monk raking gravel, I am alone. When I finish my duties, the monk puts down his rake and makes his way over to the office. He speaks English and apologizes for the 600-yen stamp fee, which is twice the going rate. To compensate, he gifts me with a little tea-towel embossed with an image of *Hotei*, the laughing bodhisattva.

I wave for Jim to join me, and the monk proceeds to give us a tour. At the main hall, he stops. "You must take off your shoes here." Jim and I comply, awkwardly bracing against each other to complete his request.

"Come with me," he says quietly, raising a finger to his lips as he mounts the stairs to the upper platform. "This is *Juichimen Kannon Bosatsu*, a precious artifact not normally seen by the public."

Intuitively, I pull my camera from my pocket but then remember photos are prohibited.

"It's okay, take pictures," he encourages. I hesitate, but he insists.

The ancient carving is about three feet tall and includes two gold hinged-doors that open to form an altar.

"Normally, these doors are shut," he says. "But today, you are lucky!"

Jim and I thank him for his kindness, but he is not done with us yet. Apart from the brilliant gold leaf, the wooden relic has darkened with time, making it near impossible to pick out features. So, our instructor points to some specifics.

"Juichimen Kannon has eleven faces," he explains. "Some of these faces are so angry. Others are smiling, and some are full of mercy." I nod and pay close attention, but I cannot discern one emotion from another.

He points to a gold lotus blossom in her left hand. Initially, I thought she was holding an artichoke. Thankfully, I didn't pipe up and share this dimwitted observation.

It's nearly closing time when our tour is complete. Our guide escorts us to the temple gate, and we exchange a round of well-wishes and bows. I reach in my pocket and offer him a square of dark chocolate wrapped in gold. He accepts with a smile."

"Ah, chocolate and gold," he says. "My two favorite treasures."

Temple 63: Kichijoji

Ditching our rental car is somewhat of a logistical nightmare. Last night, Jim and I tucked into a cozy *izakaya* to hash out a plan. In Japan, an izakaya is an informal, family-run gathering place to enjoy drinks and snacks after the workday. So, over a platter of yummy mochi-chicken bites and icy drafts of *Asahi*, we found a return center in *Ozu City*, a two-hour drive in the opposite direction.

We poured over bus and train schedules. Logistically, it didn't make sense for both of us to make the trip backward. So, this morning, Jim dumped me curbside at *Kichijoji*.

Alone again, at last, I bow and enter temple sixty-three. It must have rained last night because the temple grounds are damp and fresh. A canopy of dewy cherry-blossoms sparkles like diamonds in the morning sunshine.

I hit the purification station and admire yet another adorable dragon. This little fellow sits upright on his back haunches and holds a sphere in his front claws. Water shoots from between his fangs and splashes gently in the concrete trough below.

I'm the first henro here, and it's so quiet. To preserve the peace, I forgo announcing my presence via belfry and report directly to the main hall. I whisper my way through the sutras, enjoying the complex arrangement escaping my lips in breathy puffs.

Close to the main hall is a tall black boulder, heavily speckled with lichen. Towards the bottom of the boulder is a hole slightly smaller than my head. According to legend, if I close my eyes, make a wish, and walk from here to the stone with my outstretched staff, and somehow manage to thrust the stick through the hole, without looking, my wish will come true.

I contemplate the path. It is a short distance and relatively free from obstacles. While I don't own a proper Kukai-staff, I do have a set of handy-dandy hiking-poles. So, I close my eyes and whisper my request. "I wish for a successful rendezvous with my husband this afternoon."

Although we scrutinized our plans, a little luck could prove useful. With an outstretched hiking-pole, I wobble my way toward the target. I catch a toe on a rock, stumble forward, and find myself hugging the boulder for support. When I open my eyes, I'm surprised to see my hiking-pole sticking smartly through the hole. "Now, isn't that amazing?"

Temple 64: Maegamiji

I walk for nearly an hour, stopping to admire spring's gift of daffodils and scarlet tulips poking up through the tall grasses lining the narrow roadway. The late morning sun shines warmly down, hitting me somewhere between my forehead and crown. My whole head tingles as individual strands of hair stretch skyward, like sunflowers, to worship the light.

As I near the temple, I no longer need to watch for route markers. Instead, two tidy columns of soft pink cherry-blossoms guide me to the gate. It's a dreamy sort of welcome, the kind I would expect when climbing into the pages of a fairytale.

Before the gate, I linger to translate a sign with my phone. Gone are the placards printed in English I enjoyed several temples ago. I don't necessarily need to know each site's historical relevance but knowing adds a layer of richness to the experience.

For the most part, the temple signs expound upon the information already included in my guidebook. However, my book includes fun-facts not always found at temples. For instance, on the 20th of each month, this temple opens the doors to three *Gongen* statues for a public showing.

If I understand correctly, a Gongen is an incarnation – a manifestation of a Buddha who has come to guide people toward salvation. When standing before a Gongen, a henro can rub an ailing body part, and the part will heal. Unfortunately, I'm here too early. It would have been a waste of Gongen energy anyway because all my body parts are feeling fantastic.

Temple 65: Sankakuji

The trek to *Sankakuji* is 45 kilometers. This is more than double my walking comfort zone. So, I leave temple sixty-four, find the rail station, and wait on the next train to help me close the gap.

As I wait on the platform, a text from Jim tells me the car return was successful and that he is also awaiting a train. With any luck, the holey-boulder back at temple sixty-three will grant my wish for rendezvous, and Jim and I will meet up somewhere between here and the Sankakuji bus stop. And then together, we will complete the trek to temple sixty-five.

There's a lot that could go wrong, especially considering our mutual inexperience with public transportation. I've checked and double-checked our plans, plotted the route in my guidebook, and pulled up the directions on my phone, but I still lack the confidence needed to relax and enjoy the journey.

Right on schedule, the train heading for *Niihama City* arrives. I hop on and quickly find an empty seat. Behind me, I hear someone call out, "Christine-san!"

I turn around and am over-the-moon to see TaiJo walking up the aisle to sit next to me. Immediately, my shoulders relax. I don't know how it is possible, but once again, I have my trusty friend and transportation mentor by my side.

In our brief relationship, TaiJo has never been one for small talk. However, he does say his knee is much better. I'm thrilled, but I don't tell him I wrote healing prayers for his recovery on my osamefuda slips. I think this might embarrass him. Instead, I sit and happily steep in my own gratitude.

When TaiJo and I disembark, I'm shocked to see Jim waiting for me at the station. I think it's a total miracle – some sort of divine intervention from the powerful holey-boulder. Jim's explanation is less than mystical. Apparently, for an extra 100-yen, one can jump an express train instead of the slower one TaiJo and I selected that stops at each station along the way.

Jim is as surprised to meet TaiJo as TaiJo is to meet my husband. "Oh, Christine-san. Your man is young and handsome," TaiJo gives me a broad smile.

"Yes, TaiJo. He is handsome. But we are the same age!"

"No. No. Jim-san is so young," TaiJo teases.

It's silly, but I get a little defensive about the age thing every now and again. More often than I care to count, people mistake Jim for one of my sons. It's not that I look particularly old for my years. It's just that this guy doesn't age. He doesn't get fat either, which is even more annoying.

TaiJo guides us to the bus stop. When the bus arrives, Jim and I follow him aboard, mimicking his actions like obedient ducklings. The men sit across from each other and immediately hit it off, chatting back and forth. I close my eyes and listen to the conversation. I'm happy to have met back up with my buddy, and I'm thrilled Jim is showing such interest in the life and times of a young Buddhist monk.

After a steep hike, the three of us stand together before the gate of Sankakuji. This is the first temple I have visited where the bell is built right into the gate. I'm not sure how to handle the situation. Do I bow first and then ring the bell? Or would the opposite be appropriate?

I wait for TaiJo's guidance, but he executes a quick bow and skips the bell altogether. Jim follows at his heels, but I hang back to swing the rope. When I walk beneath the humming bell, my ears are treated to a gentle tickle that makes my whole-body shiver with delight.

My reunion with TaiJo is short-lived. He is staying at Sankakuji this evening. He will spend a few days here, mentally and physically preparing for the next phase of his pilgrimage. *Nirvana!*

Part Four
Nirvana

Part Four: *Enlightenment*

Temple 66: Unpenji

In the parking lot of temple sixty-five, Jim and I pour over the guidebook, figuring out how best to tackle the rigorous hike to *Unpenji*. The shortest distance drops us in a valley, up a small hill, back into another valley, and then up a ridiculously steep mountainous path, all of which I'm sure would be incredibly beautiful. However, we won't make it before the stamp office closes. In fact, we might not make it before nightfall.

An alternative option would be to backtrack toward temple sixty-four, cross an expressway, and find a bus to get us within walking distance of a ropeway. Riding a cable car up the mountain would be breathtaking and peaceful; however, we are still faced with the problem of getting back down from temple sixty-six before dark. I bring up the option of camping, but the idea is quickly shot down.

I can't blame Jim for not wanting to sleep trailside. While he packed a sleeping bag, he doesn't have a pad or pillow. I offer to surrender my comfort items, but he brings up the inadequate size of my tent. Technically, the tent is designed for two people, but these must be very tiny people.

Before the start of my adventure, I practiced camping on the balcony of my Okinawa apartment. Jasper and I slept together for one uncomfortable night. So, if the tent cannot easily accommodate a lady and her Labrador, it will undoubtedly yield a restless night for my broad-shouldered husband and me.

We are about to surrender our plans and find a local hotel for the night when a long white van packed with henro ladies pulls up alongside. A woman hops out and gives the little hand signal that looks like "Go away!" but really means, "Come here!" It would make so much more sense to me if she turned her wrist over with her palm facing skyward, but that's just not the way it's done in Japan. Jim is clearly confused, but I grab his arm and jerk him toward the van.

As we board, there is not an empty seat to be found. Somehow, the ladies manage to pack themselves tighter, providing two edges in the aisle. Jim looks uncomfortable but stable. My sliver-of-a-seat accommodates less than a third of my ample-backside. With each bump or curve, the seat tries to buck me off. Each time my butt hits the floor, the ladies giggle with delight. But I'm thankful and only too happy to provide comedic relief.

The van drops us in front of the ropeway. Jim and I cram into a cable car with our new tribe of chortling ladies. Packed in the middle of the crowd, I worry I will not be able to see. This is rarely a problem for me in Japan. I'm not tall, but I'm a full head taller than the other women. Jim towers above us all. Most of the ladies don't even come up to his chest. So, with a bird's eye view, we ooh and ahh over the heavily-forested valley below.

Our car glides up the mountain. With each dip and stutter, the ladies squeal like children on a Ferris wheel. The combined energy is uplifting as they chatter their way up the mountain. While it's not the peaceful ride I had imagined, it is heaps of fun.

The amoeba of ladies carries us from the cable car, oozing toward our first look at *Nirvana*. There is a unified gasp as we attempt to make sense of the scene. I feel a tight squeeze on my arm, and I look down into the misty eyes of the woman who first invited us to join their adventure. While I may not understand the significance of this final phase of pilgrimage, she clearly does. In response, my heart opens the floodgates, and I blink back tears of wonder. The motherly woman squeezes me tighter.

"Unbelievable," croaks Jim. He looks at me with dry eyes, but I know him well. He's choked up too and clearly in awe. We stand shoulder-to-shoulder, weighted down by the majesty and palpable gravity of this sacred place.

The amoeba lurches forward. My new mom holds tightly to my arm, silently commanding me to join in their worship. I relax and proxy control. She leads me down a path flanked by hundreds of curious statues. Somewhat comical, the life-size statues of wizened monks welcome us to *Nirvana*.

Jim peels off from the pack to explore the statues. I watch him approach an old man with eyebrows hanging down to the sidewalk. He moves on to another with a mustache of the same length. He explores the smooth stone head of a seated monk. His hand grazes over a protruding brow and then across the lumps and bumps of a phrenologist's dream.

Standing before the hall enshrining *Senju Kannon*, the 1,000-armed bodhisattva, I simplify my intentions. Apart from my name, I write only *Wisdom, Courage*, and *Grace* on my osamefuda slips. Possessing these three attributes will carry me forward, allowing me to navigate the unchartered waters of my changing life.

Amidst a joyful noise, I chant along without my book. At an octave lower than the rest, my voice pops in at lines I know and fades into a whisper with the more difficult ones. Even though I have read a poorly translated version, I don't comprehend the words I am saying. Comprehension hardly matters. The collective energy feeds me and promises to sustain me throughout these final 22 temples.

Jim meets back up with our group outside of the stamp office. A big part of me wants to break off and explore, but my henro mother has yet to release me. I allow her to lead me back to the ropeway, into the cable car, down the mountain, and back into the van.

I exchange osamefudas with my temporary mom. Her slip is gold, signifying she is somewhere between her 50th and 99th pilgrimage. As her last maternal act, she slips two granola bars into the pocket of my hakui. "Ossetia," she says and reaches up to pat my cheek.

The driver dumps us in the parking lot of temple sixty-seven. The ladies are calling it a night and heading off to their arranged lodgings. Jim and I bow, saying *sayonara* to our new friends.

Temple 67: Daikoji

Jim and I bow at the gate of *Daikoji* and dash inside. I have about 20 minutes to make the rounds and collect my stamp before the office closes. The campus is beautiful, and I hate to rush.

I leave Jim at the bell tower to consult the guidebook for potential lodging. I know there is a henro house near, but these accommodations are supposed to be made well in advance. Worst case scenario, I'm sure I can call a taxi and have the driver deliver us to another business hotel.

Even though I am in a hurry, I cannot help but stop and admire a gorgeous evergreen. The pine tree is planted in a graveled square in front of the hall dedicated to *Yakushi Nyorai,* the Buddha of healing. Painstakingly manicured, the pine looks like a supersized bonsai tree.

Next to the main hall, soft mounds of cherry-blossoms bathe in an egg-yolk glow. Without my glasses, the blossoms look like a vibrant row of snow-covered hills awash in the evening sun.

In the stamp office, a monk asks me a question in Japanese. I respond, "The United States."

"Oh," he says with surprise. "You speak Japanese?"

"No," I blush an apology.

"If you don't speak Japanese, how do you know what I said?"

I shrug, trying to think of a viable answer. "Hmm, I suppose I've heard the question before."

We ponder the phenomenon for a moment, and then he laughs, "Perhaps, in your first life, you were Japanese!"

"Perhaps," I smile and segue into matters concerning my current life. With a quick phone call, the monk secures a family-run inn known as a *Minshuku.*

Ordinarily, it is frowned upon to book a minshuku this late in the game. This is because minshukus customarily offer dinner and breakfast. It is presumptuous to expect last-minute accommodations. What if the family hasn't been grocery shopping lately? However, the monk reassures me the proprietors will appreciate my business.

Outside the temple gate, Jim and I search the grounds for a camphor tree planted by Kukai in the 9th century. I'm not exactly sure what a camphor tree looks like, but I remember the leaves from the small branch used back at temple six to honor my grandparents in the fire ceremony.

We nearly bump into Kukai's camphor on our way down the steps. How we walked by this goliath on our way up is beyond me. This is the cost of being singularly-focused on my stamp book.

This great-great-grandaddy of a tree makes me think of my grandfather's holly tree planted in front of the family home when my father was a baby. Each Christmas, I would cut low-hanging boughs, and with gloved-hands, construct a classic albeit prickly wreath to grace my grandmother's door.

Jim and I make our way to the inn. It's a short walk, but our tummies are grumbling. We eat the granola bars given to me in the parking lot by the lady from the van. I savor the last crumbs, thinking about the many mothers who have sustained me along the way.

Temple 68: Jinnein

Last night's stay at the *Minshuku Shikokuji* was a dream. Our hosts were so kind I forgot to feel bad about the last-minute reservation. Dinner was delicious. Jim had to help me to my feet from the squat table where I devoured his portion of fresh sashimi as well as my own. Thankfully, there was also miso soup, bottomless rice bowls, and generous baskets of tempura and bowls of pickled vegetables – all of which Jim loved.

We waddled back to our sleeping cell for the night, an upstairs room with sliding walls of rice paper panels. I stacked three futons and two thick comforters to create a cozy pallet. Of course, Jim complained about his uncomfortable sleep, but the guy sawed logs like a proper lumberjack all night long. Next time, I'll record his snoring as proof that the futons are just as comfy as a western bed.

Breakfast was simple but perfect – boiled eggs, bananas, and rice. This is precisely the kind of meal we need to get us through a long day of walking. We plan to sleep at temple seventy-five tonight. It is 34 kilometers and several temples away.

I hadn't planned on walking this far today, but late last night, while I was kept awake by the lumberjack sleeping beside me, I perused social media. I found a post from Kassy. At first, I was thrilled because I taught her how to post during our *Awakening phase*. Her daughter even sent a private message to thank me.

Unfortunately, Kassy's social media update was not good news. She has injured her foot or maybe an ankle and cannot continue her pilgrimage. To make matters worse, she's been stuck at temple seventy-five for days because she cannot walk, cannot communicate her problem, and has no idea how she will get home.

I wish Kassy would have contacted me. My hunch is she has forgotten how to use the message feature on her phone. I almost send her a text to let her know help is on the way, but I think better of it. It will be more fun to surprise her tonight.

Once inside the Jinnein temple gate, I sit on the bell tower steps and write out a day's worth of osamefuda slips, praying for Kassy's quick recovery. During this final stage of *Nirvana*, I had planned to focus on the elements of *Wisdom*, *Courage*, and *Grace*, but these prayers will have to wait until I reach Kassy and assess the situation.

Despite the rush, I complete my morning rituals in the prescribed order without the shortcuts I learned from Grandpa-san. I'm in and out of the gate in the space of about 20 minutes. It feels hurried, of course, but it also feels necessary.

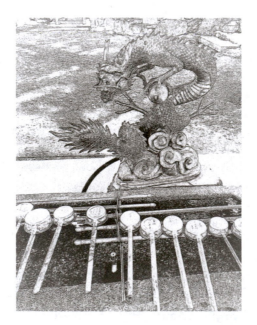

Temple 69: Kannonji

Kannonji and *Jinnein* are next-door neighbors. It's hard for me to discern one campus from the next. Since I've just purified myself and rang the bell to announce my arrival at the neighbor's temple, repeating these steps seems like overkill.

I'm still clean as a whistle, and I'm sure my announcement was heard over here. So, I head straight to the main hall and get down to business.

The deity housed inside is *Sho Kannon*, the crowned bodhisattva holding a lotus flower. Back at temple sixty-two, I mistook the lotus for an artichoke. Thankfully, I kept my thoughts to myself.

In Japan, the lotus flower symbolizes the *Buddha Mind*. Lately, I have been rather monkey-minded, especially when attempting to meditate. Maybe the lotus might be a good tattoo, a reminder to focus. I kind of have my heart set on some cherry-blossom ink after completing my pilgrimage; perhaps I should reconsider.

Jim waits for me outside the stamp office. It feels odd collecting a stamp while the ink from the previous temple is still damp. I typically recycle the same slip of blotting paper used to protect the adjacent page, but I don't want to risk smudging. The lady behind the desk reads my mind and hands me a bit of newspaper for my book and two fresh bananas for my hubby and me.

Temple 70: Motoyamaji

The walk to *Motoyamaji* takes less than an hour, but it is down a busy roadway. Exhaust spewing from the morning traffic is all but choking me. Jim spots a footbridge crossing the river and connecting to a path moving in the same direction. It's a few extra steps, but I'm sure it will be worth it.

Jim and I hotfoot it across the lanes of traffic and up and over the bridge. We find ourselves on a bike path running adjacent to the river, separated by a wide swath of greenspace. How perfect.

Overhead, dozens of fish-shaped windsocks flutter and snap in the breeze. The colors illuminated by the morning sun are dazzling – bright pink, red, blue, green… At my apartment, I have a faded orange fish. I found the windsock alongside the road while walking Jasper. I took it home and hung it from my balcony, thinking it looked rather festive. Now, walking beneath these brilliant ones, I realize there's nothing particularly festive about that tired old windsock.

From our path, I can see a long row of cherry-blossom trees across the water. Behind the shimmering pink waits a multi-storied pagoda. This must be Motoyamaji. We quicken our pace.

And then, out of nowhere, we find ourselves in a blanket of gnats! I have a bug net in my pack, but I don't dare stop to get it. We cough and gag our way through the swarm. Once we are safe, Jim picks the bugs from my hair, and I try to fish out the little rascals stuck in his beard. But it's hopeless.

It's terribly rude to spit, but I do not chastise Jim. His infraction is perfectly understandable, considering the circumstances. I am no spitter. So, I swish water around in my mouth, freeing the wee beasties from between my teeth, and swallow them down. Why not? I have already eaten more gnats than I did grains of rice at breakfast. Ugh.

We are still laughing and coughing up bugs as we enter the temple. It's hard to get serious after that experience. But we do our best to sober up.

At the purification fountain, I wish I could dump a few ladles over my head to wash the bugs out, but I know my actions would be frowned upon. Instead, I move through my rituals and make a wish for Kassy's recovery.

In the stamp office, an older monk looks me up and down. I'm sure I must be quite a sight.

"Oh, you walked through the park," he says.

"Yes, yes we did." I wipe away a tickle on my brow and produce three more smashed gnats.

"Very pretty in the morning," He says.

The monk lowers his eyes, pretending to focus on his calligraphy; however, I can see the strain as he fights back a grin.

Temple 71: Iyadaniji

Walking toward temple seventy-one, I admire a garden of chamomile, calendula, and some other herbs I do not recognize. In a neighboring plot, rows of tall plants with elongated green and reddish leaves reach out for the mid-morning sun. A few more steps and a waft of peppermint wraps around me like a blanket of snow. I can almost taste the red and white striped candies kept in the glove box of my grandfather's Gran Torino.

I'm noticing a pattern. Gracing the front of nearly every house are small plots of herbs. These must be tea gardens. An old woman squatting between rows looks up and smiles. Hers is a near-toothless grin. I stop for a moment to return the greeting. She holds up a handful of spring green tendrils and gives me the *come-here* signal.

Climbing down into the ditch and then carefully stepping over tidy rows, I squat down beside her. She hands me the greens, and at first whiff, I know it is lemon balm. To make a fair trade, I give her a gold-wrapped square of dark chocolate. She tucks the treasure in the pocket of her blue and white gingham apron. She offers another smile, only broader this time.

Invigorated by such an intimate exchange, I hop over the ditch to join Jim, and we head down the narrow road. My heart is wide-open. I love the temples and countryside, but it is these little moments with the people of Shikoku that mean the most.

The rural neighborhood fades and yields to a more suburban one. I marvel at tidy landscaped plots, chock full of with flowering shrubs and sculpted bonsai trees. Usually, I'm not a huge fan of walking through suburban neighborhoods, but this one is a horticulturist's dream.

This neighborhood looks newer than most. It is exceedingly well-planned and impeccably groomed. *PTA* signs dot the walkway along with other signs reading *SOS*. I'm guessing the SOS means *Save Our Schools*. What I don't understand is why these signs are not written in Japanese. Of course, SOS is internationally known. Can the same be said about PTA?

Alongside the road and in front of each home, yellow footprints are spray-painted on the blacktop. "Hmm," says Jim. "I bet the feet mark the spots where children are supposed to wait for the bus."

"Bet you're right," I reply. "It's all so organized."

"Yeah, that's how I always imagined Japan," Jim says. "Well, at least until we got to Okinawa."

Jim is far from in love with Okinawa. It's not at all what we had pictured back when we first discussed accepting my current post. For me, my classroom, and the beaches, and all the yummy food have made island life a wonderful experience. Beyond golf, there is nothing there for Jim.

A transfer back to Europe might improve our situation. We are hanging on by a thread. But we *are* hanging on. Perhaps, this is the best we can do for now.

The 12-kilometer walk to *Iyadaniji* disappears beneath our feet, and we are both a little startled to find ourselves suddenly before the gate. We bow and enter, and I pause before a stone statue of Kukai. At the top of his filigreed staff hang 12 metal rings.

Way back between temples forty-two and forty-three, I met my own private Kukai, the kindly old henro who guided me safely around a washed-out trail and escorted me through two dark tunnels. He carried a similar staff with the same filagree, but only six rings hung from the top of his.

I don't know the significance of the rings, and unsurprisingly, my quick *Google* search fails to quench my curiosity. All throughout this adventure, I've had to accept that many questions will remain unanswered.

To my delight, the Daishi hall, where one venerates Kobo Daishi or Kukai, is housed in a cave! Thankfully, I am alone, and so I chant as loud as I can, listening as these lyrical syllables leave my mouth and bounce off the cave walls. I'm tempted to holler out a loud *yip-yip* or *echo-echo*, but I stick to the script.

On my way out of the cave, I notice something I had not seen when I first approached the candlelit altar. An old monk sits against the cave wall in a large rattan chair. He shakes his head from side to side as I hustle toward the exit.

Temple 72: Mandalaji

The old monk in the cave story gives Jim a good chuckle. Of course, I'm embarrassed, but this is so *not* out of the realm of my ordinary. My one regret is that I may have offended the monk. I didn't intend to be disrespectful; however, after visiting seventy-one temples and chanting the same chants over again, I'm growing lax in the manners department. I'm probably due for another attitude adjustment.

The short walk through the woods to *Mandalaji* is refreshing. It's so good to be out of the suburbs. The dirt trail is padded with decomposing bamboo leaves. It's soft underfoot, like a nap of a luxurious carpet. Soft-purple blossoms on leggy branches of wild azaleas reach through a forest of gold bamboo to greet me.

The trail curves past a small pond and then parallels a large lake with dark green water. We stop at the boat ramp for a short lunch break. Swarming black turtles snap up from the water's surface, devouring misty clouds of mosquitos hovering above. I contemplate tossing the turtles the last few grains of rice from my triangle, but I'm too hungry to make such a sacrifice.

Before the temple, I examine some sort of fruit tree covered in hundreds of little orange paper packages. The paper seems to be folded around small pieces of fruit. It's not an orange tree. It's nothing familiar to me, like an apple, peach, or a cherry tree.

I'm so tempted to unwrap just one paper, but after my echoing faux pas at the last temple, I've promised myself to be more cognizant about my personal footprint along the Shikoku. So, I must be satisfied with a guess. And my best guess is lychee.

The peaceful walk through the bamboo forest did nothing to prepare me for the throng of people inside the temple gate. More than a time or two, at popular temples, I've been swept up in a great white wave of henro, and I didn't really mind, but this crowd is different. While the crowd is clearly Japanese, no one is wearing white. No one is lighting incense, and no one is chanting.

I cut my way through the masses to take care of business. At the hall enshrining *Dainichi Nyorai*, I try to whisper my way through the *Heart Sutra*, but I cannot concentrate, and I lose my place. I try again, but then a young woman pops between me and the hall and snaps a photo – right in my face. Unbelievable! Purely out of self-preservation, I channel Grandpa-san and revive his abbreviated rituals.

I meet Jim outside the temple office. He has researched the mystery tree and shows me a picture of a lychee tree on his phone. The leaves look the same, and the shape and size seem to match the description.

"Thanks," I say. "Looks like a lychee, alright." Jim tucks his phone back into his cargo pocket. "Now, let's get the hell out of here!"

Temple 73: Shusshakaji

Shusshakaji is just a short jaunt from the last temple, but it is up a steep hill. The hot afternoon sun fries the top of my head and sends squiggly lines up from the roasting blacktop beneath my feet. I huff and puff up the hill, gulping mouthfuls of pea-soup air. Jim, who is traditionally in better shape, struggles more than I do. He has yet to acclimate.

The unforgiving heat and humidity of Shikoku could make this such a miserable walk in the summertime. I wouldn't be able to handle it. In fact, I'm kind of worried about walking in mid-May. If I stepped up the pace, rented a car again, or relied on public transportation, I could knock the rest of the temples out in a few days, but I'm not ready to end my pilgrimage. I still have much to learn and even more to ponder.

One of the significant advantages of completing the Shikoku in spurts, as I have been doing, is I'm allowed to ruminate over each section and make-meaning. The breaks between sections relieve the doldrums of walking roadside, day after day, with only an occasional woodland, riverside, or mountainous pass.

Boredom is part of pilgrimage, at least for me. I grew restless many times along the Camino de Santiago. I think every Peregrino does. When my head is on straight, I use the time wisely, embracing the tedious bits with my own brand of *walking meditation*.

But I can't usually meditate in the company of others. This is what frustrated me about walking with Kassy. There was too much chit-chat. The same is true today.

While Jim is known to be a man of few words, he has been particularly chatty this trip. But this good. At least we are talking to one another. I can feel the gap caused by our living on two different continents, growing smaller with each step. There will be plenty of me-time once he returns stateside again.

We pause before a large statue of Kukai. In one hand, he holds his staff. In his other hand, he holds a beggar's bowl. Someone has been thoughtful enough to climb Kukai's pedestal and fill his empty bowl with a brilliant orange that is more vividly orange than I knew orange could ever be.

I see this all the time – fruit left for Kukai and other deities. At Jizo's feet, worshippers leave candy, juice boxes, milk, cookies, and other childhood favorites. My practical mind wonders who collects the offering before it rots. Even deep in the woods, several kilometers from town, I have seen gifts of the most perfect tomatoes. So far, I've never seen produce rotting or half-eaten by birds or squirrels. The offerings are nothing less than stellar. How is this possible?

The cool water of the purification fountain feels lovely on my face and heat-swollen hands. I dip extra ladles to inconspicuously cool off. I want to dump one over my head, but I stick strictly to the script. Hands and mouth only. Even Jim takes part in this refreshing ritual, but I don't catch him before he brings the ladle to his lips and sucks down a cupful. Gross!

In the stamp office, an old woman with badly gnarled and arthritic hands struggles to pick up the calligraphy brush. I look away to give her a little privacy. I hear the first whisper of ink and turn to watch the graceful black lines filling up the page.

Temple 74: Koyamaji

Jim and I walk down the hill from temple seventy-three and past the still throbbing crowd of temple seventy-two. While it's a short walk, less than an hour, to *Koyamaji,* the heat is getting the best of us. We drag along through the suburban sprawl, searching for an oasis of green.

We stop at a vending machine, grab cold sports drinks, and seek refuge beneath the welcoming canopy of a cherry-blossom tree, graciously reaching out her branches to protect us. The soft-pink blossoms buzz with life, and industrious bees not hampered by heat set about their daily chores.

The vibrations of worker-bees wiggle down through the canals of my ears, making me feel a little dozy. We sit on our backpacks and lean against the slender trunk mottled by splotches of seafoam lichen. I close my eyes, allowing the busy bees to transport me back to the apple orchard behind my grandmother's house.

My grandmother was always well-supplied in apples. She made pies and applesauce, but I loved her apple butter. Darkened with generous dashes of cinnamon and clove, she cooked it down into a thick and creamy spread.

As I'm about to sink my teeth into a hot buttered biscuit slathered in appley goodness, Jim nudges me. "Hey," he says. "Better get going."

Jim helps me to my feet, and I try my best to swallow my annoyance at being cheated out of my dream-state biscuit. Fishing around in my satchel, I find a cellophane package of wasabi peas. Roasted peas are nothing like apples, and wasabi is nothing like cinnamon, but it's all I have.

We share the peas, washing them down with lemony *Aquarius*. The citrus and radish-like heat are an odd pairing. But the combo fills a void and provides some much-needed energy.

The gate of Koyamaji is guarded by two ridiculously cute shisha dogs crouched on adjacent eaves. The half-dog half-lion creature plays a significant role in Okinawan mythology, protecting the islanders from all sorts of nasty evils. I've seen them all over Okinawa and always in pairs. One has an opened-mouth, and the other's mouth is closed. Like gargoyles, pairs of shisha grace rooftops, pillars, gates, and cinder-block fences. I even have a small terracotta set flanking the entryway of my apartment. I've only seen a few here on Shikoku.

We leave the Shishas and enter the temple of bunnies. Now, this is a first! Unfortunately, my guidebook offers no explanation to the multiple rabbits perched on the rooftops and atop the hall housing the deity *Yakushi Nyorai*, the Buddha of healing.

After completing my tasks, Jim and I explore the grounds, hoping to discover what is up with all the rabbits. A whimsical statue of a mama rabbit hugging her baby provides a clue. I've always thought of rabbits as a sign of luck or fertility. Perhaps this temple is a designated place where couples come to pray for success in baby-making. Or anxious grandparents wish for grandchildren. Since Yakushi Nyorai is the Buddha of healing, perhaps this is also the place to overcome reproductive problems.

Jim and I search for information signs to use our translator apps, but the process is a bit like hunting for Easter eggs. Tucked against a large palm, I find a small and unassuming shrine, a dollhouse version of a temple. Next to the shrine is a laminated piece of paper illustrated with a pink rabbit, a cartoonish pregnant lady with an enormous belly, and an old grandmother being hugged by a child.

The clipart illustrations confirm what I had initially expected, but I use my app anyway. *God – Gynecological Healing – Easy Delivery – Memorial for all women's worries.*

Wow! All women's worries. Where has this shrine been all my life? I assume the concerns in question are health-related and not about glass ceilings, reproductive rights, and other equality concerns.

I'm clearly not interested in personal fertility. That ship sailed long ago. With five grandchildren, I'm not about to overstep my bounds to pray for more. I am concerned about menopause and hormone imbalance, and breast cancer… I could go on and on. Instead, I seize the moment and make a prayer in the form of proclamations.

With hubby out of earshot, I work my way down from top to bottom. "I have healthy, beautiful breasts." I pause as an elderly couple walks behind me. "My ovaries are magnificent! My fallopian tubes are magical. My uterus is a wonderful space. And my cervix is simply perfect! My vagina is… is, hmm." I can't think of an appropriate adjective. "Well, my vagina is – is as it should be!"

Temple 75: Zentsuji

My heart drops a little as we approach the massive temple grounds and see a long line of tour buses in a crowded parking lot. *Zentsuji* is our eighth and final temple on today's docket. However, I don't have it in me right now to explore.

According to the step-counter on my phone, we have walked nearly 40 kilometers or 25 miles. And I feel it! The step-counter is relatively accurate.

Today's distance is a personal record! I'm proud of my accomplishment, but I'm also sweat-stained, stinky, and beyond exhausted. I decide to waylay the temple rituals until tomorrow morning. I'll complete the rounds just as the stamp office opens for the day. It makes no sense to fight the crowd this afternoon.

Jim offers no argument, so we cut through the temple grounds to the dorm, which is more like a giant *Holiday Inn* than the quaint temple lodgings I've enjoyed thus far, but I don't care. All I need now is a hot bath and a futon. Besides, I really want to find my injured friend, Kassy. I imagine locating her will be no easy task, especially with the popularity and grand scale of this campus.

A female monk receives us in the lobby. Up until now, I have not seen a female monk. I'm not sure of the proper vocabulary. I suppose she could be a nun, but she looks just like her male counterparts milling about the lobby, assisting other henro and tourists.

She is dressed in a robe of burnt orange. Her hair is shorn, making her intensely dark eyes even more expressive. Without a sound, she directs us to a storage space for our shoes and hiking-poles. She hands us each a pair of satin slippers. I prefer my arch-supporting flip-flops, but I can tell by her gentle yet firm demeanor that this is a slippers-only establishment.

Jim manages to stuff two-thirds of his foot in the dainty slipper. He hands them back, but she shakes her head. He tries again, exaggerating to make his point. In response, the monk pops up on her tiptoes, like she is wearing stilettos, and wobbles away. Jim pushes the ball of his foot into the slippers, pops up on his own set of high-heels, and wobbles off behind her. How I wish I could record a video for our sons' delight.

She leads us into an elevator and then down a corridor. She pauses in front of two restrooms, pointing to the women's and then to the men's bathroom. She stops again to show us the laundry room and the long trough to brush our teeth. And then, without uttering a word, she hands Jim a key and points to our door.

Once inside our room, we collapse on the tatami mats, too tired to drag out the futons and make a proper pallet. Jim dozes off, and I wiggle out of my clothes and wrap myself in a crisp cotton *yukata*, which is like a casual version of kimono.

I leave Jim sleeping and head off to find the public bathhouse. It's nearly the dinner hour, and baths are not busy this time of day. In fact, I'm usually the only early bird. I need a long soak, but I don't want my tattooed body to cause offense, and I really don't want to face the humiliation of being kicked out of the facility either.

To my luck, the only other woman in the bathhouse is Kassy! There must be at least a hundred sleeping quarters in this inn. But here she is, and I thought it was going to be a challenge to find her.

I wash up first. Seated on a three-legged stool, I fill a basin with water to soak my feet. I go about my business, soaping myself from head to toe and lathering up my hair.

When I'm finished, I slide into a kiddie pool of hot water and crab-walk my way over to where Kassy is seated. She sees me, smiles briefly, and then looks away.

"Kassy!"

She looks over again and gives me a blank stare. I know she suffers from glaucoma, but surely her eyesight can't be that bad. I move directly in front of her.

"Hey, friend. Don't you recognize me?"

She blinks, looking painfully confused.

"Kassy, it's Christine. Remember?"

I see a lightbulb click on, and Kassy's face softens. "Well, yes. Of course. But what on earth are you doing here?"

"We've come to save you. I read about your injury on *Facebook*."

"You did? Really? I couldn't tell if my post worked."

"Well, I promise it did, and that's why we are here."

"Who's we?"

"Jim and me."

Kassy reaches out and grabs my arm. "Oh, I'm so happy. He needs to share in your adventures."

"Agreed. We are actually having fun! But enough about me. What's going on with your ankle?"

"It's my foot – a stress fracture, I think."

"Can you walk?"

"Not very well."

"How long have you been here?"

"I'm not sure. I've lost track of time."

Over cups of instant ramen and cans of vending machine beer, Jim, Kassy, and I discuss options. Kassy clearly cannot put weight on her injured foot. However, she isn't ready to abandon her pilgrimage.

"Kassy," I announce, "You're coming home to Okinawa with us. We'll take care of you."

"Good idea," Jim agrees. "We'll find you a doctor, get some x-rays, and go from there."

Kassy clasps her hands and holds them over her heart.

"So, I take that as a yes?" I ask.

Kassy nods.

I woke early this morning to a case of terrible cramps. I can barely stand. The cramps are familiar, but it can't be what I'm thinking. It just can't be.

I drag myself from the futon and to my feet. "Holy cow! You've got to be kidding."

Jim rolls over. "You okay?"

"No!" I'm beside myself. "I'm not okay!"

"What's going on?"

"My stupid period started."

"What?" He sits up. "I thought you were done with all that months ago."

"Yeah, I thought so too."

"Maybe it's all the walking?"

"Walking? No. It was those damn bunnies."

Jim scratches his head. "Bunnies?"

"Yeah. Temple seventy-four – the place with all the damn rabbits. I said a prayer for my lady parts, and I guess it was answered!"

"Should've been more specific," mumbles Jim.

He tugs at the comforter and rolls back to his side. I pace around, trying to make sense of the situation. Jim is exactly right. I should have been *way* more specific. This isn't the first time an answered prayer has gone sideways.

I pop a couple ibuprofen caps and take off to complete my rituals. What else is there to do? I'm the one who stood before a shrine dedicated to women's health and made my proclamations.

I walk around a towering five-story pagoda, profoundly enjoying the stillness of the morning. Based on the pulse of yesterday's crowd, I never expected to be alone, but here I am. All the information signs I come across have a doppelgänger in English, so I take my time to read each one.

There are dozens of monk statues like I saw at temple sixty-six. I'm not sure if I'm supposed to find them amusing, but I do. The figures are so animated with exaggerated features, like enormous ears or bulging tummies or impossibly shaggy brows growing down to the ground. I run my hand over a few stone heads, feeling the cool lumps and bumps passing beneath my fingers. I look for a placard that might explain what these funny fellows are all about, but I find nothing.

To my surprise, Jim meets me in front of the main hall. He stays by me as I light the incense sticks for my past, present, and future. I make a proclamation for Kassy's speedy recovery and sweeten the deal with a few extra coins in the offertory box. And why not? I somehow willed myself out of menopause, so I ought to be able to do something about her foot.

Temple 76: Konzoji

Kassy wants one more day of pilgrimage. Injured or not, who can blame her? Leaving the trail 13 temples short of the goal is tragic.

Jim and I divvy up the contents of her backpack, which has grown heavier than remembered. Along with way too much gear, she has collected souvenirs. She also has a hefty stash of osettai oranges.

I insist on transporting Kassy via cab. We don't know the extent of her injury, and I don't want her to cause further harm. She has her Kukai-staff, but it's not enough to keep the weight off her injured foot. She needs crutches.

Even traveling by cab, the process crawls along at a snail's pace. Jim offers Kassy a piggyback-ride through *Konzoji*, but she flatly refuses. I can't blame her, but I would have enjoyed the photo-opp.

In front of the hall housing *Yakushi Nyorai*, the Buddha of healing, Kassy wraps an arm around my shoulder so I can help her up the steps. It's fun to chant side-by-side with her again like we did during the first 23 temples. Despite her injury and obvious pain, she is still mucking it up and making jokes. Her humor at a time like this is admirable.

I feel like a jerk for treating her poorly during our *Awakening phase*. I was selfish. I was so set on a solo-situation, I failed to see the beautiful gift dropped into my lap. She has taught me much about growing older with *Grace*. Kassy has more to teach me. In return, the least I can do is offer my home and services whenever she is in need.

"Kassy," I grab her hand. "I am sorry for acting like a brat."

She looks confused. "I don't remember you being particularly bratty."

"Well, trust me. I was a brat. I didn't want to walk with you, but I couldn't outwalk you, and whenever I stopped, you stopped. I was selfish and lacked patience."

"Well, that's understandable."

"It is?"

"Sure. Do you think I wanted to walk with an American? Especially one from my home state?"

"But that's not all. I was also angry and embarrassed when you tried to get your backpack transported."

"But you were right. There isn't a system here, like there is on the Camino."

"I know. But still, it was none of my business. Besides, had you managed to transport your pack via monk-power, you might not be injured right now."

"Is this why you've invited me to your home?"

"No. I'm inviting you because you are my friend, and I treasure you."

"Oh," she wraps me up in a hug. "And I love you too."

"Okay, that's enough," I push away after an awkwardly long embrace. "Now, can I carry you down the steps?"

"Why not?"

Kassy throws her arms around my neck, and I swoop her up honey-moon style. "This is kind of romantic," she laughs.

Temple 77: Doryuji

The founding story of this temple is based on a tragic event. In 749, a powerful man named *Doryu* was lord of this land. Doryu accidentally shot and killed a nurse who was passing through his property. In great remorse, Doryu carved a statue of the healing Buddha, *Yakushi Nyorai*. He then enshrined the deity in a small hut. About one-hundred years later, Kukai came along and expanded Doryu's efforts.

Thankfully, our cab driver pulls beyond the temple gate and into a handicapped zone. He drops us a few steps from the hall. This kind of access is common amongst suburban and inner-city temples but much less common at the rural and remote sites. While challenging, I think most of the pilgrimage could be managed on crutches or maybe even in a wheelchair.

Since we have neither crutches nor a wheelchair, Jim and I flank Kassy for support. She wraps her arms around our shoulders, allowing us to occasionally lift her up and down the steps. Despite our best efforts, she can't seem to keep the weight off her foot.

We try moving through the rituals properly, but the strain on Kassy is too great. To pick up the pace, I introduce Kassy to Grandpa-san's abbreviated chants. She doesn't mind and admits she's developed a similar routine.

Despite the adjustments, the effort is proving too much. "We need to call it a day," I say.

Kassy's faded-blue eyes plead with my own. "Oh, come on," she says. "Just one more."

Temple 78: Goshoji

Gyoki founded *Goshoji* sometime during the 8th century. A hundred years later, Kukai rehabilitated the dilapidated buildings and enshrined *Amida Nyorai*, the Buddha of light. Much later, the temple was converted by the *Jishu sect* to spread the teachings of *Nenbutsu*.

Despite my ongoing research and current progress as a henro, my understanding of Buddhism, in general, is still extremely limited. However, in my laywoman's terms, the Jishu sect and Nenbutsu principles center around a specific devotional formula as a means of achieving salvation. Maybe I'm oversimplifying, but for a Sunday-school kid raised in a rural Methodist church, this concept is not at all out-of-the-box.

I try to explain my interpretations to the present company. Kassy stares at me blankly, occasionally wincing in pain. Her head is obviously elsewhere, but out of politeness, she pretends to listen. Unabashed, Jim has no trouble displaying his disinterest and walks away mid-lecture.

Like my henro-friend, Uri, I think Jim also suffers post-Baptist-trauma or something of the sort. He was like this on the Camino, too – willing to walk alongside and carry my toiletries, work laptop, and raingear, but unwilling to participate in spiritual matters. However, Jim did marvel at the art and architecture of Spain, and I assume this is what he is doing on Shikoku whenever we go our separate ways at each temple. What's important is that he is here. Walking by my side, and that is enough.

Temple 79: Tennoji

At the last temple, and as predicted, Kassy begged for "Just one more." And so, our hired cab whisked us away and dropped us in the handicapped zone of *Tennoji*. Despite the convenience of door-to-door service, we find ourselves staring down a long sidewalk and up a demanding flight of concrete steps.

"You ready?" Jim asks Kassy. She nods and drapes her arms over our shoulders. And off we go.

Like many of the temples along the way, Gyoki founded *Tennoji*, and then a century later, Kukai came along to restore it. Ordinarily, expansion played a part in Kukai's restoration plans, but not at Tennoji. Tennoji, once a massive campus, is now comparatively small.

Kassy is out of incense again – big surprise. She bums a few sticks from me, and we go about our business. Standing before the hall enshrining *Juichimen Kannon*, the bodhisattva with eleven faces, we write out new osamefuda strips.

We both wish for the same thing, a speedy recovery for Kassy's foot and a quick return to the Shikoku. Along with our offering coins, I run the strips up the steps and drop them in the appropriate boxes.

Since this will be our last temple of the day and our last temple together, I forgo the shortcut and lead her through the full *Heart Sutra*. Kassy keeps her arm around my shoulder for support, and I keep mine snuggly around her tiny waist.

When we finish, she looks at me with misty eyes. "I guess this is the end of it."

"Not the end, my friend. The final nine temples will be right here waiting for you. I promise."

Temple 80: Kokobunji

Kassy convalesced in my Okinawan flat. Jim shuttled her to doctor appointments, and as predicted, the diagnosis was indeed a stress-fracture. We had hoped to share the beauty of our island home. However, Kassy wasn't mobile enough to enjoy our favorite places.

Kassy's doctor prescribed crutches and a removable walking cast – a heavy boot-of-a-thing. Kassy purchased the crutches, but she didn't want to pay doctor-office prices for the boot. With a quick search online, we found one for a fraction of the cost. Unfortunately, shipment took two full weeks. For 14 long days, Kassy was either housebound or stuck in the car, but all the while, she never complained. In fact, she was nothing short of grateful.

During her downtime, she reached out and connected with a Japanese woman she met pre-injury. The lady had found Kassy drifting severely off course, picked her up, and chauffeured her for the entire day. This sweet trail-angle offered her services once again. It was a perfect solution.

When Kassy's walking-boot arrived, it was time to say goodbye. I wished to accompany her, but my work schedule wouldn't allow it. I wasn't worried. She had shipped most of the contents of her backpack home, leaving a manageable load – even on crutches. I knew from my own personal experience with the gentle people of Shikoku, Kassy would be in caring hands.

Jim flew back home. Kassy completed her pilgrimage and took off to *Mt. Koyasan* just as I was returning to Shikoku. Traditionally, Mt. Koyasan is the final stop. Henros visit the tomb of Kukai, or Kobo Daishi, to report their deeds and lessons-learned along the way.

Of course, Kassy was gracious enough to invite me to share her temple lodgings in Koyasan, but I declined the rendezvous. I have yet to decide if I'm traditional enough to go beyond closing the loop at the first temple and calling it good. However, if I choose to continue, I want to keep the stages in the prescribed order.

This past week in Okinawa was murder. I counted down the days until it was finally my time to return to Shikoku. Making a pilgrimage in spurts, whenever my schedule lets up, has illuminated how trapped I often feel in my work. Even during these spurts of freedom, I'm still chained to my laptop to keep up with the barrage of emails, grading, and administrative functions.

To make matters worse, my relocation request was denied. Of course, the reasoning was meant to be flattering, "You're needed too much on Okinawa." I get it. I'm an employee. I'm needed, and it's nice to have a job, but I'm not feeling the love right now.

As the plane touches down in Takamatsu, I feel like a giant weight has been lifted from my chest. My shoulders relax, and my breathing deepens. I disembark like a school kid rushing out the door for recess.

On a train bound for *Kokubunji,* I massage my sore jawline. I hadn't realized it before, but I have been smiling for nearly an hour. I am happy – truly happy.

Reveling in my temporary emancipation from the university, my husband, and over-populated Okinawa, Shikoku is brighter and more enchanting than ever. Gone are the snowy cherry-blossoms. In their place blooms roses, peonies, and the vibrant bulb-flowers of May.

Standing before the gate of Kokubunji, I barely pause long enough to execute a bow. I climb the belfry steps, jerk back the rope, and heave it forward, joyously announcing my return.

I calm myself before approaching the hall housing *Juichimen Senju Kannon*, the deity of a thousand arms. I light three sticks of incense, honoring the past, present, and future. The ritual is clarifying.

At the altars of both halls, I continue my wish for Wisdom, Courage, and Grace. These are, perhaps, the greatest gifts I could give myself, and these elements are precisely what I need to move forward with my life.

Temple 81: Shiromineji

Yesterday, my feet barely touched the ground. I was a force to be reckoned with. In fact, I might have given the injury-free Kassy a run for her money! Unfortunately, by the time I arrived at *Shiromineji*, the stamp office was closed. Thankfully, I had assumed this might happen and made reservations beforehand.

When I walk alone, I prefer to fly by the seat of my pants. When all else fails, I sleep in my tent. However, knowing where I was going to crash last night relieved stress and allowed me to focus more on the trail. But best of all, I slept in another temple.

Today is Mother's Day. I'm thinking of my sons, but I'm not missing them. It sounds terrible, but I'm not missing anyone. Of course, I invited my husband to walk this final stretch with me, but he declined. I don't mind. Right now, I am all I need.

I translate a sign next to a large stack of roof tiles. Evidently, some of the temple buildings need re-roofing, and I can support the cause. I purchase five tiles and write each son's name in black *Sharpie* marker on the underside of each tile. It's a perfect way to re-roof a temple and a perfect way to begin my day.

The natural setting of the campus grounds is breathtaking. I press my palms against massive tree trunks, centuries-old, knobby, and split-open by time. I give each one a big hug, trying to absorb a little karmic energy. To an outsider, I'm sure my behavior seems odd. But I've been a tree-hugger for as long as I can remember. Besides, I'm alone, and no one can judge me.

Approaching the main hall, I spy a statue of a large bunny. Recalling my last bout with bunnies, I keep my distance. While it is Mother's Day, I'm not looking to go down that rabbit-hole again.

Temple 82: Negoroji

Walking out the backside of Shiromineji, I leave the menacing rabbit statue behind. The forest trail to *Negoroji* picks up at the far side of temple eighty-one. It's rare not to exit through the main gate before continuing to the next temple. However, this is the case here and at a small handful of temples along the way.

After a short distance, I stop before a tall stone monument protected by three wind-blocking walls and a metal canopy. The statue is comprised of geometric shapes, with a large stone circle as the focal point. I don't know what I'm looking at, but the artifact looks incredibly old and of great importance.

Thankfully, a sign on the far left is printed in English. Apparently, this is *The Manirin Stone Pagoda*, initially erected in 1321. This one before me is a replica, as the original is in storage for preservation. On the backside of the pagoda, my fingers trace the year 1836. It's old, but not as old as I had assumed.

The pagoda signifies sacred ground. *Gejo* is engraved at the base of the structure. Gejo is a command to dismount. All who pass this stone, regardless of station, must dismount their horse or other transportation modes to pass through the sacred ground on foot.

Since I'm already relying on my own two feet, I continue down the trail. In a few moments, I enter the sacred ground, a cemetery. Stone pagodas and leaning monuments, encrusted with lichen and weather-worn, grace the hillside. I'm so tempted to step off-trail to explore, but the grass is tall, and my fear of snakes keeps me steadfast and moving onward.

Emerging from the darkly forested trail and into a clearing of sunshine, my eyes take a while to adjust. Unwittingly, I stumble into a mist of hungry mosquitos. I swat the air, karate-chopping my way down the trail to carve out a bubble of breathing space. But it's no use.

I stop to find my bug net. Big mistake! Like a Humpback whale in a feeding frenzy, I inhale the mist, straining annoying mosquitos through my nostrils and parted lips like baleen. Sacred ground or not, there's nothing to do but run.

Once out of harm's way, I fish out my net and my handkerchief. With a sturdy blow, I dislodge six mosquitos and two gnats – not a bad haul. This is a new record, a personal best, I am sure. I've never been one to snort anything up my nose, not even in the 80s when it was cool.

Despite the unfortunate encounter with bugs, the one-hour hike between temples is truly a blessing. The forest path is soft underfoot. And the foliage is alive with birdsong.

At Negoroji, I size up an enormous statue of *Ushioni*. The hooved-depiction looks part *Krampus* and part man devil-cow. Ushioni has sharp horns, slashing claws, bulging eyes, and gnashing fangs. According to legend, this people-eating beast terrorized locals and wreaked havoc on livestock.

Desperate villagers and farmers hired a master-archer to slay the creature. Before taking off on his hunting excursion, the archer prayed to *Senju Kannon,* the deity enshrined in the main hall of Negoroji. After the archer's prayers were answered, he made an offering of bull-horns to the bodhisattva.

The villagers and farmers gathered to pray for the soul of Ushioni. Despite the beast's reign of terror, the victims thought he deserved to rest in peace. Now, how's that for not holding a grudge?

Temple 83: Ichinomiyaji

Before taking off on my three-hour hike to Ichinomiyaji, I phone ahead to book my night's stay. According to the map, there is a spa hotel within a few blocks. To my relief, the clerk manages enough English to take my reservation. How perfect! I could use a little pampering. After all, it is Mothers' Day!

Back on the trail and back under my bug net, I follow the black velvet wings of a large butterfly up a winding path, watching her flit from lime blossoms to pine boughs and bamboo grasses. The butterfly stops to rest on a picnic table in front of a picture-perfect henro hut. And I join her.

Set on the tabletop is a cooler of ice-water and a treasure chest stuffed with rice crackers and hard candies. I'm starving. So, I help myself. Rice crackers are not the most satisfying, but when paired with three osettai oranges and a mochi cake, I will more than survive.

This henro hut is adorable and complete with a basement bathroom. Inside, osamefuda slips line the walls. These are the calling cards of hundreds of henro who visited before me. There are sturdy pine benches, writing materials, a logbook, and a ladder leading to a loft with space to sleep two or three people. There is even a smoke detector. Part of me wishes to stay here for the night, but a larger part of me has already dipped one toe into the relaxing spa bath only 13 short kilometers away.

For the most part, I've spent the day alone. It's been relaxing. somewhere between temples eighty and eighty-one, I met an elderly but rather energetic henro jogging in the opposite direction. He wore a jingly bell and sang at the top of his lungs. When he passed me, he simply nodded without missing a beat. Now, I hear the jingling and his singing again.

For some reason, I can't tell if the jogging henro is in front of me or behind me. I half expect he is on an alternate trail, somehow adjacent to my position. His song is upbeat and repetitive. At first, I assumed it was some sort of chant. However, the more I listen to Mr. Jingle-man, the more I think he's singing a Japanese version of *99 Bottles of Beer on the Wall.*

The mountain path is steep and dumps me on a narrow roadway below. Each step jars my knees, and I lean back into the hill to slow my pace. Little by little, the jingling stops, and the singing fades.

Dammit. Now I have *99 Bottles of Beer on the Wall* stuck in my head. I try to think of something else, but all I can come up with are Christmas carols and Army cadences – and neither feels appropriate.

Somewhere around the sixtieth bottle of beer, I abandon the chorus to marvel at rows and rows of bonsai-style pines, the kind I've admired gracing the landscaped yards in upscale suburbia. I must be walking through a nursery. After the pines, I'm treated to a peek-a-boo view of the bay and what I think could be the city of *Takamatsu.*

I follow a narrow lane flanking the nursery. Next up – lime blossoms! Now, this is a fragrance I can never get enough of. I'm so tempted to pick a couple of flowers for my hair, but since each flower is a potential lime, I fight the urge. The lime trees are followed by rows of leafy dogwoods with vibrant-green foliage and white blossoms dipped in gentle pink.

My nursery tour ends, dropping me near a matrix of flooded rice paddies. I walk a narrow concrete path dividing one grid from another. Germinating in the silty mud below, I admire the new shoots of spring.

I bow at the gate of Ichinomiyaji and make my way to the fountain. A small statue of Kukai sits above the stone trough. The purifying water trickles from his cupped hands.

At the bell-tower, I gently announce my arrival and then head for the hall enshrining *Sho Kannon*, the bodhisattva holding a lotus flower. The lotus flower represents the *Buddha-mind*, something I am trying hard to improve. Despite my short distraction with childhood road trip songs, I was able to keep my monkey-mind in check today. And I feel so much at peace.

Temple 84: Yashimaji

Last night's spa stay was a delight! The facility was remarkably casual. To alleviate stress, I tried a different approach with my tattoos. Upon check-in, I rolled up my sleeve and showed the young woman my ink. Narrowing her eyebrows, she made a familiar Japanese sound, "Eeeeeh?" I've learned to interpret this as, "Seriously?"

The check-in clerk waved over a colleague, a young man of not more than 20. Together, the two examined an edelweiss, three clovers, a thistle, a compass-rose, and the word *peregrina* – passport stamps to honor my time in Germany, Ireland, Scotland, and Spain. I have two more tattoos, but they are hiding in locations I'm unwilling to share.

Shaking his head, the young man uttered a couple of "hmmphs." In halting English, he asked, "What – is – peregrina?"

"Peregrina means pilgrim in Spanish," I said.

"Hmmph," he shook his head.

I tried again, "Like a Spanish Henro."

"Oh, Henro-san!" His eyes flamed with understanding, and he handed me a towel.

The 400-meter climb to Yashimaji piggybacks on a nearly three-hour hike, mostly on pavement. As I reach the top, my body feels none the worse for it. I credit last night's rejuvenating *me-time*, which included a hot bath and a full-body shiatsu massage.

Yashimaji is a tad touristy, but I don't mind. I'm in the mood for a little shopping. I dump my pack on a bench behind a small kiosk selling henro-related gear. I finger several prayer-bead bracelets. Holding one of them up to the sun, I squint through a window cut in one of the beads. Inside the bead, I see the tiniest image of a ram. It's like magic.

Not only is my zodiac sign an Aries, but I was born in the Chinese year of the ram. I contemplate the bracelet, but I'm watching my pack-weight. Instead, I settle on a rose-scented box of incense, which I need anyway.

I light three pink sticks of incense at the main hall and linger in the hovering smoke, hoping to perfume my hair. It's a girly thing to do, but I carry no cosmetics, no perfumes, and no deodorant. The rose incense is my one luxury.

I'm in full tourist mode, wandering around the temple grounds, photographing statues and flowers, and posting my images online. One figure confuses me. I've seen several depictions along the trail. Standing on his back legs, a happy bear displays the most exaggerated set of testicles I've never imagined. And since I have the emotional maturity of a twelve-year-old boy, I snap a picture and post it on *Facebook* – hoping someone online is brave enough to explain the significance.

As it turns out, this well-endowed bear is not a bear. He is a *Tanuki*, a raccoon-dog that truly exists. But what about the huge gonads? According to folklore, these balls can perform amazing feats.

Mythical Tanukis are shapeshifters and very mischievous. Just as *Yogi Bear* uses *Boo-Boo Bear* to snatch picnic baskets, the Tanuki casts out his man parts like a fishing net to snare his prize.

Real-life tanukis own proportionately-sized jewels, but the sack holding the jewels is another story. Tanuki scrotum is prized by goldsmiths. The uber elastic scrotum can be stretched wide and thin, making it the perfect canvas for creating gold-leaf. Poor Tanuki!

I return to the kiosk where I purchased my incense to retrieve Little Miho. When I pick up my backpack, I'm surprised to see the ram prayer beads clipped to a carabiner I use to hold hair ties. An anonymous osettai! I slide the bracelet on my wrist, feeling blessed beyond words.

With only four temples remaining, I realize I'm a day or two away from closing the loop at the first temple. My pilgrimage will be complete. And I should be thrilled.

A familiar aching perks in my heart. I have felt this sensation before when nearing the end of the Camino. The ache is a precursor to the loneliness I'll face once I'm off the trail and living without the Shikoku 88.

During what should have been a typically stressful time at work, the Shikoku has sustained me. I've spent the past three months either on the trail or planning my next escape. When I'm not on Shikoku, my daydreams are filled with images of the rich culture and lushly forested-trails. Shikoku has become my happy place. What shall I do without it?

Temple 85: Yakuriji

The hike to *Yakuriji* is relatively short, nearly six kilometers. On flat terrain, I can cover this distance in just over an hour, give or take. The way ahead includes a steep 400-meter descent and then a more gradual ascent of nearly 300. Uphill is always harder on my lungs but easier on my hips, knees, and feet. It's the downhill jaunts, the holding myself back, that take so much time and effort.

On the walk down from temple eighty-four, I see multiple warning signs for Tanuki. These raccoon-dogs are known to be aggressive beggars. I don't feed wildlife and cannot be persuaded, but I'd still love to see a real-life Tanuki.

Along with the Tanuki warning signs, several metal placards for wild boar are posted on trees and power poles. With the heart of a farm girl, I do love pigs, especially piglets. However, I absolutely do not want to meet any hogs, wild or domestic, on the trail. I know they are near, not because of the warnings, but because I can smell them.

I listen carefully for snorts and rustlings in the shrubbery lining the narrow path. I'm trying not to allow my imagination to get the best of me. Up ahead, where the sun breaks through the trees, I see a large dark mound resting alongside the road. Could it be a wild boar sunning himself?

I pound my walking sticks against the ground and stomp my feet. Feeling certain no wild boar would care to meet a noisy human, I break out in song. From the deep recesses of my mind, I pull up a campfire song I learned four decades ago. The song warns of meeting a bear in tennis shoes, and it seems appropriate for this scenario.

I holler at the top of my lungs, "The other day, I met a bear, in tennis shoes, a great big bear." But the hump in the road refuses to budge. "I looked at him. He looked at me. I sized up him. He sized up me." Still nothing.

I pause for a moment, wondering what to do next. I see a monk walking up the hill toward me. I wonder if I should warn him, b I don't own the vocabulary to do so. I hold my breath and watch as the monk confidently strides right by the hump of wild boar.

With only a couple of paces between us, I see the monk is biting his lip. As we pass, he averts his eyes. My ears redden. Obviously, he heard my scary bear song and was politely avoiding eye contact and trying not to laugh.

I move toward the bump to get a closer look. Holding out a hiking-pole like a joust, I inch my way nearer. Both quads twitch, ready for flight, like a racehorse itching to leave the gate. And then I see the hump is nothing more than a stump.

Shortly after my run-in with the stump-hog, I come across a monument and a small stone-well house. According to legend, Kukai visited this site and performed a *Kajisui* or a water-incantation to honor Buddha. And now, even during a drought, when neighboring ponds and rivers run dry, this tiny but mighty spring continues to burble.

To my delight, the hike up to *Yakuriji* is cut short by a funicular cable-car. Of course, I could reach my destination without this handy-dandy tourist attraction. But why would I? I can count on one hand how many occasions I've experienced a funicular, and until now, these precious few times were all in Switzerland. I buy my ticket and a package of cookies to enjoy on the way up.

Giddy from the ride, I brush cookie crumbs from my hakui, execute a solemn bow, and pass through the gate of Yakuriji. I stop in front of a large Jizo statue wearing a vermillion bib. Suddenly somber, I watch five colorful pinwheels whirl in the wind – each one an offering for a lost child.

As is often the case when standing before Jizo, my mind drifts to memories of my big brother, Irv, and my little cousin, Holly. How my mother and aunt, or any parent for that matter, manages to endure such profound and ongoing loss, I hope to never know. I linger a few moments, thanking God for my five healthy boys. Once again, I am feeling blessed beyond belief.

Temple 86: Shidoji

To spare my knees, I had hoped to enjoy a funicular ride back down Mt. Goken, but the joint-saving route adds too much extra distance to my already 26-kilometer day. I head back into the woods and back under my bug net.

Instead of gnats and mosquitos, my net protects me from throngs of silk-wrapped caterpillars, suspended like icicles, on long threads of cobweb. These poor fuzzy-wuzzies are hanging-out, waiting for the inevitable. I liberate several of the poor creatures as I crash down the trail, collecting them on my hat, net, and hakui. I'm not afraid of caterpillars, but I do hope I haven't captured a hungry spider mid-supper.

The trail is beautifully perfumed beneath a weighty blanket of lime blossom, bamboo, and pine. I wish I could bottle this scent and uncork it in my car. Indeed, this is the air-freshener of heaven.

Decomposing pinecones crunch beneath my feet, and I love the satisfying noise. In the still of the mountain pass, I am a herd of elephants. Indeed, no wild boar dares sun himself in my path.

I find a whole pinecone and pick up a game of kick-the-can. I kick my pinecone all the way down the mountain and along the city sidewalks. When I arrive at the gate of Shidoji, I pluck it up and tuck the still perfect specimen in the pocket of my hakui. I think it would make a lovely offering to *Juichimen Kannon*, the bodhisattva enshrined in the main hall.

As I enter the gate, I'm greeted by the thick and comforting smoke of a campfire. How lovely. As I move toward the smoke, I must put my net back over my face.

Platoons of blood-lusting mosquitos, like a million tiny dentist drills, swarm in for the kill. The din is shrill and deafening.

I roll down the sleeves of my white sun shirt and button it all the way to the top. Next, I dig through my messenger bag for my gloves. Once every inch of flesh is covered, I move deeper into the forest of ferns toward the main and Daishi halls.

Several burn-barrels belch thick clouds of mosquito-inhibiting smoke, but this platoon is relentless. The nasty blood-suckers sting their way through the fabric of my sun blouse and thin hiking-pants. It's total torture.

Out of nothing more than pure self-preservation, I light three sticks of incense at each temple, utter my gratitude and sincere apologies, and retreat to the safety of the stamp office.

As I exit Shidoji to find my lodging for the night, I hear a crunch in my pocket. In my mosquito-induced haste, I forgot to offer the pinecone to *Juichimen Kannon*. I'll have to try again with *Sho Kannon*, the main deity of temple eighty-seven.

Temple 87: Nagaoji

Last night, after feeding the mosquitos of temple eighty-six, I overnighted outside the gate at *Ryokan Ishiya*. The traditional Japanese inn was charming and overly accommodating. I enjoyed a birds-eye view loft, complete with a sitting area, clothesline, and heaps of futons, blankets, and pillows.

The proprietors, a husband-and-wife team, insisted on making up my sleeping pallet while I was in the shower. But I remade it, *Princess-and-the-pea style*, stacking every available futon and quilt to form a dreamy nest. So dreamy, in fact, I barely heard the phone jangle, calling me down to supper.

Dinner was nothing short of remarkable. In the company of one other henro, I enjoyed a casual affair in front of the television, watching my first ever Sumo match. Evidently, the match was significant. Even the hostess stopped cooking and came out of the kitchen to enjoy the spectacle.

After inhaling the last spoonful of salty miso soup, the husband served two flat, crispy fish with heads still attached. Unsure of how to approach the dish, I watched my dining companion pick one up with his chopsticks and bite off the head. I gawked in amazement as he ate the whole thing – head, eyes, brains, guts, bones, fins, and all. And then, I did the same. Absolutely scrumptious! I devoured the second and dabbed up the crumbs, leaving my plate clean enough to slip back into the cupboard.

In the morning, over breakfast, the couple asked to see my hiking plans for the day. Since we didn't share enough of a common language, I opened my guidebook and traced a finger along the path toward *Nagaoji* and on toward *Okuboji,* the 88th temple. The two shook their heads, making *tsk-tsk-tsk* sounds.

While the entire day fell under 20 kilometers, I hadn't planned on tackling temple eighty-eight today. The monster climb has an elevation gain of 1,000 meters and is said to be quite treacherous. To be honest, I've yet to figure out how to approach it. I assume I'll be sleeping trailside tonight, midway up the mountain.

The couple bantered back and forth, gesticulating more than I've ever seen Japanese people gesticulate. With a resigning "harrumph," my fate was decided. The husband snatched up my pack, tossed it in the trunk of his car, and barked another harrumph, which was my signal to buckle up and shut up. And so, I did.

At the gate of Nagaoji, the hubby hands me a white paper sack stained with spots of oil. "Osettai," he says gruffly. "From wife." I bow and thank him for the gift and incredible hospitality.

The paper sack smells terrible. When the man pulls away, I open the oily bag to look inside. Along with a fat triangle of rice, two greasy flat fish stare up at me. I can hardly wait for lunch!

Hoping to not attract a tribe of ravenous tanukis, I tuck the smelly osettai into the top of my pack and prepare to enter the gate. Unlike most temples, the bell tower is built right into the gate. The rope connecting to the battering ram has been removed. This was probably done to keep the peace with temple neighbors.

I offer *Sho Kannon*, the bodhisattva representing the *Buddha mind*, three rose incense sticks, and my trusty pinecone. After collecting my stamp, I mill about the temple grounds, trying to strategize my next move.

To be honest, I've been so *in-the-now* lately that I haven't come to terms with nailing the last temple. I certainly didn't plan on doing it today. Now, only a 13-kilometer hike stands between me and my final goal, and the feeling is surreal.

Eighty-seven temples and nearly 1,200 kilometers have passed beneath my feet. I've walked, hitchhiked, gracefully endured osettai rides, jumped on busses, hopped trains, sored high above the treetops in a cable car, and inched up a steep mountain in a funicular railcar. It's been an incredible adventure, to say the least.

As I head toward the gate, I stop mid-stride to watch an unbelievably tall woman prepare to enter the gate. Clad in *Raggedy-Ann-style* blue and black striped tights, her legs look impossibly long. Moving like a ballet dancer stretching before a performance, she reaches up a slender arm, grabs the butt of the battering log, pulls it way back, and releases. The log smashes into the side of the bell with an earthshaking bong. She has arrived. Nodding with approval, she executes an elegant bow and glides into the campus.

What a force! Like a magnet, I gravitate toward her energy. I haven't seen another westerner in an awfully long time, and it's been quite a while since I've seen a walking-henro, especially another woman. With her fair hair and stature, my guess is she is Dutch or maybe a Dane. Either way, I'm praying she speaks English. It would be so lovely to chat and possibly compare notes about the way ahead - and by *compare notes*, I mean to find out exactly what she is doing and then do the same. I have so little of my own ideas to offer.

As it turns out, my new friend is from Denmark, and her name is *Tiff*. I follow her back towards the main hall, half pretending it's still on my to-do list. We chant together, and our mutually clumsy Japanese breaks the ice, and it isn't long before we are seated side-by-side, outside the stamp office hashing out options.

Like me, Tiff enjoys her solo-time. So, we hug good-bye and promise to wait for one another at the top. She lingers awhile at temple eighty-seven, catching up with her journal entries. And I hurry on my way, feeling energized in my newfound friendship and ready to tackle the obstacles ahead.

Temple 88: Okuboji

I'm lucky to have met Tiff. Before we parted ways, she told me of a bus leaving *Okuboji* at four o'clock this afternoon. It's the only chance to catch a ride back down the mountain. Tiff is confident in her abilities to make the deadline. In fact, she's ditched her backpack. She carries only a modest bottle of water and a satchel containing one avocado and one cucumber.

Tiff left her backpack with her innkeeper. Her plans are to return via the bus and spend another night at the same lodge. In the morning, she will hop a train back to the first temple and close the loop. So gutsy.

Tiff eyed the size of my pack, stunned to learn I carry a tent, pad, and sleeping bag. "You are making this too hard on yourself," she urged. "Leave your pack here at the temple. I'm sure they'll keep it for you."

I thanked her for the suggestion, but I'm not at all confident enough to climb a mountain with a mere liter of water, two pieces of produce, and no survival gear.

"We carry the weight of our fears," I offered.
"Your only fears are that you'll get hungry or thirsty."

Tiff narrowed her eyebrows and leaned in closer. Just above a whisper, she politely inquired, "What are you so afraid of, my friend."

Of course, I could have offered a laundry list including wild boars, rabid monkeys, trickster tanukis, rapists, murders, hillbillies… But I kept it simple. "I'm afraid I will fall or get lost. And I'm afraid of migraine headaches and running out of daylight."

Tiff wrapped me up in two long arms and delivered a heartfelt embrace. She pulled back and held me at arm's length. "You are smart," she said. "And you are brave. And you are powerful."

I fought back the tears. "I know. Thanks for the pep talk." I managed a half-smile, "I'll see you up at the top, and we'll celebrate with a cold beer." With one more hug, I was on my way.

The first few kilometers cut through *Sanuki City* and, on a different day, would feel uninspiring. However, I'm still jacked-up by my pep-talk from Tiff. She's correct. I am brave and smart and powerful, but that doesn't mean I shouldn't prepare for worst-case scenarios.

I find a convenience store to restock my cash supply and load up on emergency provisions. While last night's lovely innkeepers supplied me with more than enough sustenance for lunch, I need reserves to carry me through dinner and even maybe breakfast – just in case.

After a couple of hours walking roadside in the morning sun, I feel frazzled by the aggressive tempo of traffic. A tour bus, chugging up the hill, presses me against a guardrail. I lower my head as it passes by, peppering me with dust and grit. My glasses are speckled in road grime and badly in need of hot soapy water.

Ahead on the left, I see a rest stop or visitor center. Slogging my way up the steep grade, I slowly bridge the distance between me and a clean pair of glasses. As I approach the parking lot, a queue of passengers reboards the offending motorcoach. I glare at the driver, but once again, he fails to notice me.

As dumb luck would have it, I'm not in just any ordinary tourist center. I'm standing in the middle of *Maeyama Ohenro Koryu Salon*, a Shikoku pilgrimage center. I blink back the confusion as my eyes adjust to the indoor lighting.

A kind woman behind the reception desk points down a hallway toward the bathrooms without me even having to ask. I'm sure my need is one commonly held by henros and tourists alike. As I emerge, shaking the water droplets from my lenses, a gentleman stretches out his arm, offering me an ice-cold bottle of water. I accept with a grateful bow.

Before I realize the routine, I'm swept away to a table and seated before a large bowl of cookies. Have I died and gone to heaven? I'm confused, but I'm not about to fight a soft chair, a cool drink, and pink and white frosted animal crackers with sprinkles. Who would ever be so foolish?

The cookie man wants to see my stamp book as well as my passport. I'm still confused, but there are cookies. It seems like a fair trade.

When the man returns with a certificate, my dim-bulb finally lights up. Oh, I get it! This is where walking-henros receive a certificate of completion, like the *Compostela* documents I have received for each of my successful Caminos.

I read about the *Henro Ambassador* certificate in an online forum. However, I didn't expect to find this facility until after nailing all the temples and returning to close the loop at temple one. I assumed the center would be somewhere in *Bando* – at the journey's end. Since I haven't walked every step of the way, I never planned to seek such an honor.

A flush of guilt rises to my cheeks as I read the part written in English: *This is to certify that you have successfully completed the 1200km of Shikoku 88 Temples Pilgrimage on foot and that you are named as a Henro Ambassador. We wish that the interaction with the people, the culture and the nature of Shikoku enriches your life and that you will spread the Henro Culture worldwide.*

The Shikoku has enriched my life. I know I will treasure the interactions, no matter how brief or temporal, with the people, the culture, and the nature of this beautiful island for the rest of my life. And I certainly plan to spread the light of *henro-culture*, just as I've done as a peregrina. No matter how much I'd love to be a *Henro Ambassador*, nothing can change the fact I didn't walk the entire route on my own two feet.

Thankfully, the cookie man speaks a little English. I push the document across the table toward him and shake my head. Speaking slowly, I try to explain, "No, I didn't walk the whole way."

He nods and pushes the document back toward me. I elaborate, "Sometimes, I get a ride." I pop out a thumb to indicate I am a hitchhiker. But he only smiles. "And sometimes, I take the bus or train." At this last statement, he picks up the document and disappears.

Suddenly guiltfree, I pop another cookie into my mouth. Holding it on my tongue like a communion wafer, I wait until all the creamy frosting melts away before chewing it up and swallowing it down. And then, I repeat.

As I'm preparing to leave, the man returns with the certificate slipped into a plastic document protector. In halting English, he says, "You walk far enough." He executes a bow and says, "Congratulations, Ohenro ambassador."

Out of nowhere, a warm spring rain washes across my heart and streams down my cheeks. Cookie-man smiles and fetches a tissue. I dab away at my silliness, but once composed, I slip another animal cracker into the pocket of my hakui, a little pink elephant to eat in celebration after collecting my 88th stamp.

I have received two gifts of osettai candy today. The first was a bitter ball of boiled molasses given to me by the stamp-office lady of temple eighty-seven. I tucked the sickly lump in my cheek until the cloying sweetness got the best of me. I chucked it into the shrubbery for a lucky army of ants and swished out my mouth with water. When I was certain no one was watching, I spat a long string of gooey saliva the color of squashed grasshopper guts.

I received the second gift of candy shortly after entering the forest. I stumbled upon a crooked old lady perched streamside on a rotting stump. In the dim forest, she sat so still I almost walked right on by. And when she croaked, "Osettai, osettai," I nearly jumped out of my socks.

Once my heart returned to its rightful place, I thanked the frog-grandmother, tucked the two candies in my pocket, and headed up the trail. I know it's probably my imagination, but I swear I can still hear her cackling through the trees. Perhaps it is only the babbling brook, slapping against the rocks below.

The odor of fresh pig poop and ammonia makes the hairs on my arms prickle. I know the pungent combo well. While it's been over three decades since I mucked out a pigsty, an old farmgirl never forgets that lingering stench.

I crash up the trail as loud as I can, but I cannot muster the courage to sing. I startle at every snapping twig and brandish a hiking-stick each time the wind knocks through the slender poles of bamboo. My state of *fight or flight* is robbing my stores of precious energy.

In a clearing, at one of many false summits, I devour my rice triangle and start in on the fried fish. I don't have the gusto, nor the level of beer consumption, to bite off the head and eat the wee fishy, eyeballs and all. Instead, I nibble my way down from gills to tail and wrap what is left back up in the oily sack. The top-pocket of my pack reeks of fish, but it will have to stay this way until I find a proper trash bin. The last thing I want to do is leave the bones trailside and cause some fish-craving critter to cross paths with a jumpy henro like me.

Well-hydrated and with food in my belly, I continue the quest. It's early in the afternoon, and I haven't much further to go. I'm moving out at a faster-than-normal pace. This is the advantage of managed fear. If I can prevent the bloom of stupefying panic, I can leverage fear, allowing it to tap the valves of my adrenal glands and release a sense of urgency into my step.

I hear a thud-thudding coming up the draw below. Something or someone is kicking rocks and crushing branches like a wildebeest or perhaps, a sasquatch. Calmly, I turn around and study the wood line below. My eyes are drawn directly to the source. I breathe easily and watch the striped-leggings hop over a log and scramble up a hillside of sliding rocks.

Tiff offers me a one-armed, sweaty, half-hug, and I don't flinch. Mid-hike, she's not one for small talk, so I holler after her to save me a beer. Her long Danish legs make it look so easy. Green with envy, I watch the blue and black stripes disappear around one of the never-ending switchbacks.

The trail becomes more daunting as I near the summit. A rock scramble of basketball-sized boulders forces me down on all fours. Up until now, I've had little trouble managing my gear, but now I'm weighted-down like an old tortoise, carrying my home upon my back.

After recovering from the scramble, I press my body against a craggy cliff, holding on for dear life to a cable stretched across the rocky face. Crumbling beneath my feet, the trail is barely wide enough for my shoes. I imagine Tiff scaling this section with the grace and speed of a jackrabbit. And the old tortoise feels sorry for herself once again.

Sitting in the sun, enjoying the panoramic view from the summit, I bite off the wrapper from one of the frog-grandmother's lollies and pop it into my mouth. I hadn't looked at the candy to see its shape, but it feels oddly familiar. I jostle it from cheek to cheek, exploring the ridges with my tongue. It's mint and toffee, a strange combination. Even more intriguing is the shape. It's not round or square or even a triangle. Curiosity gets the best of me, and I spit it into my palm.

I stare down at a light brown scalloped shell and smile. The scallop is the waymarking symbol used all over Europe for the *Way of Saint James*, or the Camino de Santiago. The hinge represents the trail's end at the cathedral in *Santiago de Compostela*. And the ridges represent the infinite paths of pilgrimage.

And so, here I am, on a mountaintop in Japan. And my Camino awaits – right in the palm of my hand. No matter how far I roam, my pilgrim-heart continues to grow.

Drunk on sunshine and happiness, I long for a nap. But it's already after two. I have a challenging descent and a final temple to nail. I heft myself upright, feeling surprisingly light, and ease on down the trail.

At a henro hut, I step off the path in search of chocolate. I've learned to rely on treasure chests and tins of treats left in shelters along the way. I've shared my chocolate and oranges and snack bars when I had some to spare, and I've eaten my share of chocolates and cookies when I had nothing to offer in exchange.

As expected, I find a rectangular tin on a rotting bench beneath the shed roof. I open the box, sign the logbook, and claim my prize. Score! There's a fat bar of chocolate. It's one of those triple-sized blocks found in proper supermarkets. The wrapper is torn open. Several squares are missing, but there is plenty left for me. With great restraint, I snap off a small and darkly satisfying chunk.

I sit on the bench, savoring the chocolate, allowing the square to dissolve slowly on my tongue. Off to the left and away from what I thought was the main trail down, I notice a rotting old signpost.

I read the Japanese characters aloud, sounding out the word, "O – Ku – Bo. Okubo!" Wait a minute. I am going to *Okubo-ji,* and the *ji* means temple. This sign must point the way to Okubo-Ji – the 88th and final temple, but the arrow is in the opposite direction. If not for chocolate, I would have gotten lost!

Inside the gate of Okuboji, I linger at the purification fountain and scan the campus for Tiff. I've had my fill of me-time today and hoped to close out the last temple chanting side-by-side with my new pal, but Tiff is nowhere in sight. Perhaps, she is already enjoying a cold beer and waiting on me and the bus.

With over an hour to spare, I take my time at each station, carefully moving through the rituals and performing tasks with as much precision as my tired mind and body will allow.

The temple grounds are disconcertingly quiet. I didn't expect a parade, but I didn't expect a ghost town either. Where are all the other henros?

This should be a place of celebration, but it is not. A grim-faced monk with a dry calligraphy brush scribbles something across the 88th page of my stamp book. The ink lacks luster, and the three vermilion stamps are faint. Without a congratulatory word or nod, he scoops up my coins and turns away. Evidently, my efforts today are not even worth a dip of fresh ink.

Unceremoniously, I pop the celebratory pink elephant cookie into my mouth and lick away the melted frosting from my fingertips. With an hour to kill, I stroll by the closed souvenir shops until I find a café shutting down for the day. I buy two cans of cold beer and a banana and head off to find the bus stop. Hopefully, Tiff is waiting for me.

With less than five minutes to spare, Tiff finally emerges. Gone is her effortless gait and confident demeanor. Apparently, she did not turn off at the henro shelter. Instead, she continued down the wrong trail for nearly an hour until it came to a dead end.

"I totally panicked!" She looks at me with wide eyes. "I thought, where is that crazy American woman with her tent and sleeping bag?"

I pop open a cold beer and hand it over. Tiff drinks half of it down in one go.

"And then," Tiff continues. "I had to literally run back up the mountain to make it her on time."

"Did you get your stamp?" I ask.

"Yes," she nods. "Rather anticlimactic, don't you think?"

Yes. I suppose I expected a little more hoopla after nailing the final temple. But there is beer. I also have a banana. What more could I possibly desire?

Closing the Loop

Temple 1: Ryozenji

Doubling back to *Ryozenji* is oddly satisfying. I remember my first night on Shikoku, accidentally jumping the turnstile at the train station, getting busted by the conductor for freeloading, and then fighting back the loneliness and brewing panic as I exited the train at the abandoned station in *Bando*. The darkness nearly swallowed me whole.

I was lost and alone. And then I met two kind souls out on an evening stroll. The ladies delivered me to the doorstep of the henro house and into the care of my mentor, *Takahara-san*.

I am not the same woman I once was. What I didn't know back then is that these three ladies of Bando were preparing me for all the love, grace, and gentle compassion I would receive the whole pilgrimage through. Gone is the panic and the need to be rescued. Now, the student must become the teacher.

While I haven't totally mastered the Japanese transportation system, I can confidently make my way through the countryside. As the single railcar screeches to a stop, I move toward the door and tap the shoulder of a western henro with his face buried in his guidebook. He looks up, and I nod my head.

Flustered, the young man springs from his seat and wrestles an oversized backpack. He's so new that I can still smell the fabric softener on his clothes. I can also smell the leather of his brand-new hiking boots. I lead him through the narrow streets of Bando and deposit him on Takahara-san's doorstep.

Before I depart, I give him a small bag of juicy oranges – a gift I received this morning. "Osettai," I say with a departing bow.

The new henro knocks on Takahara-san's door just as I disappear around the corner. Part of me wants to hang back, to say hello, and reminisce, but Takahara-san is a busy woman. I know the first thing she will do is escort the green-henro to the post office to ship home some of his belongings.

I take my time at the purification station. I feel my ears redden as the ghost of embarrassment reminds me of how Kassy and I contaminated the fountain during the birthing hours of becoming Ohenros. I was the first offender, allowing the water cupped in my hand to spill back into the fountain. Kassy, not one to be outdone, put the ladle to her lips, took a big swig, swished it around, and spat right back into the pool below. My goodness, how far we both have come.

I perform each element of my temple ritual with careful consideration. After the first 50 temples or so, it was easy to shift into autopilot, going through the motions like a zombie, and checking all the boxes and collecting stamps. But not today.

At the main hall, I offer a mantra of repentance, translated in my own tongue.

"All my past deeds originating from greed, hatred, and ignorance are products of my own physical, verbal and mental misdeeds. I repent all wrongdoings committed by my body, mouth, and mind."

Before completing my rounds, I light a candle and three sticks of incense for *Fudo Myoo*, thanking the fierce guardian for keeping me safe along the way.

As I make my way to the stamp office, I spy the striped pair of leggings seated on a blue bench inside the gate. Tiff is here! She looks up from her journal and waves me over.

"Look at these!" Tiff says, pulling a produce bag from her backpack. "I was just at the post office, and this guy gave me a whole bag of oranges!"

Tiff offers me two. I accept, keeping the history of the boomerang fruit a secret, but I can't help but grin. My goodness, that young henro is a quick-study!

After several inky brush strokes and three brilliant stamps, an elderly gentleman behind the counter rises to his feet. He leans over the counter and slips a bracelet of knobby prayer beads around my wrist. The brown beads are misshapen, like trod-upon rabbit droppings – seed pods, I am sure.

The man and I exchange bows. With much reverence, the old gentleman says, "Congratulations. You did it, Ohenro-san!"

Part Five
Reporting to Kobo Daishi

Part Five:
Reporting to Kobo Daishi

Over dinner last night, Tiff filled me in on the details of her next adventure. She's off to *Kyoto* to take part in a week-long silent retreat. We laughed about the concept because outside of our recent conversations, the final days on Shikoku *have* felt like a silent retreat.

My original plans were to return to Okinawa this afternoon. However, this morning finds me unprepared to reenter the hustle of Okinawa City and business-as-usual with my university. I need more time, and I need space to sort out the meaning of my pilgrimage.

For me, the process of meaning-making proves more fruitful when conducted on the fly. I lace up my trail-runners, strap into my backpack, and head off on foot to fin-d the *Nankai Ferry* leaving Tokushima's port for the Kii peninsula.

Following a 13-hour journey by foot, ferry, bus, train, and even another funicular, I'm dumped curbside in the center of *Mt. Koya town*. It's well after ten, and all the shops are dark. A smattering of dim streetlights hum above me, but the lumens are no match for the depth of blackness saturating the mountain sky.

A block away, I see a man hopping up and down and waving. He must be Tommy – from no other than the *Guesthouse Tommy*. I'm so relieved.

Tommy insists on taking my backpack before leading me through a maze of alleys until we reach his family-inn. As it turns out, Tommy is as charming as his guesthouse. Over a cup of tea, Tommy practices his English, which is quite good. He points out all the must-see and "Ahh-may-zing" places to visit in the morning. He even jots down a suggested schedule – starting at 0600! His hospitality and genuine enthusiasm are wonderful – truly. But right now, all I really want is a tour of my eyelids.

In the morning, I wake early, slide into my grubby hiking-pants, pop on a clean shirt, and pull my down jacket from the depths of Little Miho. I love this jacket, red and puffy – a featherweight *Patagonia* wonder. Fearing the trail would be far too warm, I nearly left the coat home. I hadn't needed it the entire time on Shikoku, but I caught a chill on the train last night, and it was even colder on the funicular-car inching up the mountain.

Following Tommy's direction, I head straight for the cemetery to watch the sun as it rises through the trees. "The huge trees are ahh-may-zing!" Tommy exclaimed, "but you must see them in the morning to appreciate!"

As I cross over the first footbridge, leaving the town behind. I enter the forest of Tommy's trees. Holy smokes. Amazing or even *Ah-may-zing* are gross understatements.

Long branches of thousand-year-old cedars, majestic and towering like California Redwoods, stretch out in the crisp morning light. Rays of sunshine break through the dense canopy of evergreen, splashing the tree trunks with a flood of deep-marigold light.

The granddaddy cedars cast long inky shadows across endless monuments and gravestones, creating a splendor that is as equally haunting as it is beautiful.

With my neck craned skyward, I feel my stomach drop. The forest sways back and forth, and the hallowed ground rocks beneath my feet. But I'm not afraid. This is no earthquake. It's only the wrecking-ball of vertigo dropping in to crush my equilibrium. This is my price for looking up.

I lower myself down and sit on a smooth boulder. Once out of harm's way, I realize that not only had I craned my neck too hard, but I also had forgotten to breathe. I sit for a moment, listening to birdsong and focusing on my breath. My gut stops lurching, equilibrium stabilizes, and the stillness of the morning returns.

A ray of sunshine inches its way across the forest floor, illuminating each twig and stone and lowly weed. The morning dew sparkles, making even the humblest pebbles glitter like precious diamonds.

I close my eyes and wait for the beam of light to wash over me. Within a few moments, the hair on my head prickles to life. The tingling sensation spreads across my brow, down my neck, and deep into my chest. Out of pure pleasure, a low hum vibrates up through my core and rests against my closed lips. *Mmmmmm. So happy.*

The bright sun saturates through my closed eyelids, painting a watercolor slideshow – a study in yellow. A blurry field of sunflowers. Spring daffodils. A sunset bathing a gray-sand beach with light. *Home. I am ready to go home.*

Standing before the tomb of Kukai, posthumously known as Kobo Daishi, I feel humbled and suddenly emotional. I'm not sure what I had expected to feel, but whatever it was, it was *less* than this. For the last time, I recite the *Gohogo* for Kukai. "Na-mu dai-shi Hen-jo Kon-go. Na-mu dai-shi Hen-jo Kon-go..."

I have passed through the pilgrimage dojos of *Awakening, Ascetic Training, Enlightenment,* and *Nirvana.* I nailed all 88 temples, closed the loop, and traveled to Mt. Koyasan to report my deeds to Kukai. But what have I learned? And where am I in terms of spiritual growth?

Despite wearing the proper henro-garb, stumbling through the sutras, and collecting stamps, I am still more tourist than henro. However, I am taking away an elevated sense of *Awakening.* I immersed myself and swam in an unknown philosophy. My love and kindness for others have deepened. Who could ever ask for more?

When I began this journey, I questioned if there might be enough room to house Christian underpinnings with the *Buddha-Nature.* For this, I heed the Dalai Lama's sound advice: *Don't try to use what you learn from Buddhism to be a Buddhist; use it to be a better whatever-you-already-are.*

Instead of asking myself, "What did I learn?" perhaps better questions are, "How have I changed?" and "Who am I now?"

I am as I was born to be – a seeker of light, a henro, a peregrina – the relentless pilgrim. I still carry the weight of my fears, but the burden of fear lessens with each cycle of peregrination. I am lighter, braver, wiser.

Like bookends, my first Camino pushed me off the sofa and out into the world. Now, Shikoku grants me permission to return *home.* Home to my husband. Home to my sons. And home to my five grandchildren.

I have discovered my own gentle *Buddha-Nature,* and I'll use it as fodder to nurture my pilgrim-heart. I leave Shikoku and Mt. Koyasan to embrace the next phase of my life. Instead of a backpack full of fear, I carry an awakened sense of W*isdom, Courage,* and *Grace.*

In Loving Memory of a Faithful Friend

Jasper
2010 – 2019

About the Author

C.W. Lockhart is a professor, an emerging potter, and a long-distance wanderer. Following two decades of military service, she pursues lifelong passions for education, art, and travel. An award-winning travel-writer, Lockhart teaches English, writing, literature, and art history courses in the United States, England, Germany, Ireland, Scotland, Italy, and Japan. She wanders the world with her husband, *Jim*, and *Seamus*, their chocolate Labrador puppy. Lockhart makes her permanent home along the rugged-coastline of the Pacific-Northwest.

9 780578 864266